THE

# THE SPANISH ECONOMY:
## AN INTRODUCTION

# THE
# SPANISH ECONOMY

*An Introduction*

## RAMÓN TAMAMES

C.HURST & COMPANY, LONDON

The Spanish version of this work,
*Estructura Economica de España,*
is published by Alianza Editorial, Madrid
(16th edition, 1985).

English adapted edition first published in 1986 by
C. Hurst & Co. (Publishers) Ltd.,
38 King Street, London WC2E 8JT
© Ramón Tamames, 1986
ISBN 1-85065-014-4
Printed in Great Britain

1514215

# PREFACE TO THE ENGLISH EDITION

I am pleased that this book is finally available to English-speaking people all over the world, since English, as everyone knows very well, is the real *lingua franca*, particularly in the field of economics. The book had its origin 25 years ago, when I was a very young economist trying to synthesise the main features reflecting Spain's economy and society. Since that time, many things have changed in Spain, and the book, in its turn, has changed with the times.

This English edition is in fact a translation of the sixteenth updated Spanish edition, to which quite a few further passages, specially designed to clarify subjects requiring an additional explanation for readers not living in Spain, have been added. It also includes a new final chapter, dealing with the different aspects surrounding Spain's accession, as a full member, to the European Communities under the Treaty signed at the Royal Palace in Madrid on 12 June 1985 between Spain and the other eleven countries of the Communities (including the other new Iberian partner, Portugal).

I would like to express my appreciation to the people who made possible the publication of this book in Spanish during the last quarter of a century. As for the English edition, I should like to thank Darlene Marie Cervantes — a native of San Francisco, California — who did her best to make an accurate translation. The old Italian aphorism *traduttori, traditori* cannot be applied in this case. I am also indebted to Mr Christopher Hurst, the English publisher, for our long exchange of letters regarding this book. I have borne in mind many useful suggestions he has made concerning changes necessary to achieve a better level of understanding.

It is my hope that this book will enhance the English-speaking world's knowlege of Spain. Spanish literature, paintings, wars and legends have been frequently addressed in the past. It is now time to direct attention towards the economy of this southern European country, with its contrasts and potential to meet the future.

*Madrid, October 1985*                                    RAMÓN TAMAMES

# CONTENTS

vii

# FIGURES

# TABLES

# PART ONE
# INTRODUCTION

## I. THE ECONOMIC HABITAT

### 1. *The general framework*

Physical and human resources are the foundation of the Spanish economy, as with all national economies. Available natural resources provide nature's framework or 'habitat'. Taking a more comprehensive look, we find that a national economy is a human creation, in which production and trading activities are developed by a population working with physical resources.

Together with its two archipelagos (the Balearic Islands and the Canary Islands), Spain — part of the Iberian peninsula — occupies 503,478 square km. (some 194,236 square miles) or approximately four-thousandths of the world's land surface. The country is located between 35° 39′ and 43° 47′ north latitude and between 3° 19′ east latitude and 19° 18′ west latitude.

Given its favourable *latitude*, one might say that Spain is situated on a parallel of civilisations. Nevertheless, the country does not benefit from many of the advantages enjoyed by the rest of Europe; for whereas most of Europe falls within the borders of a temperate zone, Spain, located further south, suffers from African summers, while high regional altitudes produce cold winters in most of the country. More important, rainfall is scarce and irregular almost everywhere. While the general profile of other European coastlines lends itself to maritime influences and traffic, with the exception of the Galician *rias* (small fiords), the Spanish coastline has very few natural ports.

### 2. *Physical geography*

Physical geography has always played a key role in Spain's history and economy. It is commonly said that the country ranks second among European countries in average altitude (Switzerland ranking first). Approximately 20% of Spanish territory is 1,000 metres or more above sea level; 40% is between 500 and 1,000 metres; and only 40% is under 500 metres. The basic feature of Spain's rugged physical geography is the *meseta*, 210,000 square km. (81,015 square

1

miles) in extent and comprising little less than half the area of Spain, bordered by the Cantabrian mountains in the north, the Sierra Morena in the south and the Iberian system in the east. Sliced in half by the central cordillera, the average altitude of the northern *meseta* is some 700 metres while that of the southern half is 650 metres. Three tertiary depressions, backed up against the periphery of the *meseta*, can be distinguished: the Ebro Valley, the Guadalquivir Valley and the Portuguese Mesozoic Basin, the latter being the only even outlet of the *meseta* to the sea, cut across by the political barrier of the Spanish-Portuguese border. Other primary geographical features are the Cantabrian Corniche, the Levante coastal strip and the Catalonian coastal chain.

Spain's geographical complexity has influenced historical and economic development. National isolation (being cut off from the rest of Europe by the Pyrenees) and the mutual isolation of the regions were formidable problems until modern means of transport were finally introduced.

Spain's mineral wealth has been proverbial since ancient times, and the actual deposits have been well-known for centuries. Mining activities carried out in Roman times in Spain could only be compared to those of Spaniards in Mexico and Central and South America from the fifteenth to the nineteenth century. This mineral wealth also attracted foreign capital investments to Spain in the nineteenth and twentieth centuries when the best iron, copper, zinc, lead, potash and other deposits were being thoroughly worked by enterprises from abroad. To believe that Spain's golden age of mining is past is not pessimistic. The best iron, copper and lead deposits are now exhausted, and many others are being used up. Nevertheless, zinc, pyrites, mercury and potash mining still offer bright prospects; and the prospects for radioactive mining, still something of an unknown, are highly promising. Although Spain has no bauxite, chromium or nickel reserves, the mineral shortage most detrimental to the country's industrial development has always been that of energy in its various forms (oil, coal etc.).

## 3. *Soil*

Soil, climate and technical advances in agronomy are the foundations of agricultural development. In agronomic terms, Spain's soil is generally of poor or mediocre quality: 10% of the land is bare rock; 35% is virtually unproductive due to excessive altitudes, drought or poor composition; 45% is moderately productive land, but water is scarce and topographical conditions are less than favourable; and only 10% of Spain's soil is of exceptionally good quality.

A better idea of agricultural possibilities in Spain can be achieved by comparison with other countries with a standard climate. Such a comparison has been made with France:

|  | *Real surface area (km²)* | *Equivalent surface area with a standard climate (km²)* |
|---|---|---|
| France | 551,000 | 511,000 |
| Spain | 503,000 | 265,000 |

In other words, although the surface area of both countries is almost identical, Spain's agricultural production is only a little more than half that of France. Similar considerations on productivity led the Spanish geographer Del Villar to take note of what he called the low 'production potential' of Spain compared with that of other countries.

## 4. *Climate*

Climate can be defined as the set of atmospheric conditions that characterise a region: solar radiation, temperature, relative humidity, precipitation (snow or rain), air pressure and wind. Spain has three different climates — Atlantic, Continental and Mediterranean — making diversified agricultural production possible (see Fig. 1).

The Atlantic climate of the northern provinces (from the French border to the north-west), Galicia and the northern half of Portugal represents 'wet Iberia', where annual rainfall exceeds 800 mm. The Continental and Mediterranean climates of the rest of the country (with the exception of the higher areas) represent 'dry Iberia', where annual rainfall rarely exceeds 700 mm. In some areas (Monegros in Aragón, the Manchego steppes of the interior and Murcia and Almería in the south-east) it barely reaches 300 mm.

The periods of heavy rainfall (the spring and autumn) in 'dry Iberia' do not coincide with high temperatures. Consequently, the use and redistribution of scarce water resources is one of the country's most pressing problems. As Macías Picavea said in 1899, 'Spain's most vital issue is to find and secure the means to redistribute the country's highly irregular average rainfall, to contain huge annual losses, to use all available deposits and to supply each and every region, area and province of Spain with a moderately adequate amount of water.'

## Fig. 1. CLIMATE

The climates of the Iberian peninsula are presented here, * with the typical Spanish 'crop limits' for Mediterranean-type harvests (grapes, olives and citrus) or sub-tropical-type harvests (sugar cane and bananas). These limits mark new climatological subdivisions: those of olive and grape cultivation within the continental cold zone; and those of citrus, sugar cane and banana cultivation within the transitional warm and coastal climate.

Cold and warm poles, based on long-term meteorological observations published by the Instituto Nacional de Estadisticas (INE — National Statistics Institute), have also been recorded. The *'Sartén Andaluza'* (Andalusian frying-pan) to the south and locations around the Iberian System and on both *mesetas* register the country's maximum and minimum temperatures, ranging from 45.6° to −24.0° C., making 69.6° C., the national thermal gradient.

The peninsula's different climates are influenced by its physical geography. The mountain barrier formed by the Cantabrian Cordillera and the Pyrenees make it difficult for rain clouds to reach the extensive interior *meseta*. (Fig. 2 presents the border between dry Iberia and wet Iberia.) The relationship between precipitation and temperature is also important. The most common combination of these variables is shown in the graph. In dry Iberia, rainfall usually occurs when temperatures are low, making summer irrigation the only way to improve crop yields.

Microclimates also exist. Small areas of land may differ greatly from the general picture indicated.

* *Source:* Köppen, modified by A. Lopez García, *Atlas Geográfico de España*, Madrid: Aguilar, 1962.

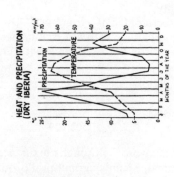

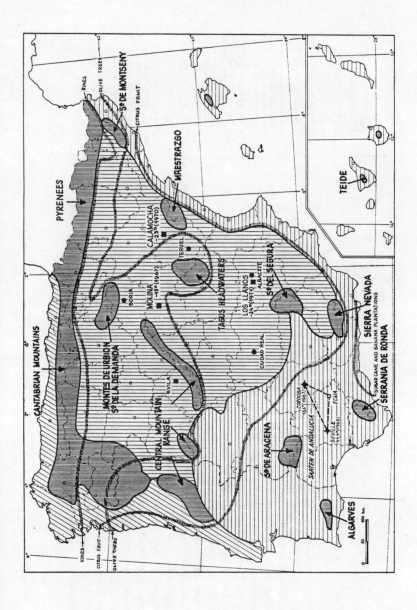

## Fig. 2. AVERAGE ANNUAL RAINFALL

This map shows average annual precipitation levels for all of Spain. The 800 mm. isohyetal line, equal to 800 litres of water annually per m.², marks the border between dry Iberia and wet Iberia. Within dry Iberia, mountain ranges experience heavier rainfall. Pluviometric poles, taken from the INE's meteorological records, have also been included.

The Tierra de Campos in the northern *meseta*, the Monegros, the Calanda Desert in the Ebro Valley, the Segura Basin and the coast of Almeria in the south-east (an ideal area for filming Western exteriors) are all arid regions where rainfall is low and evapotranspiration levels are high.

Based on estimates in the *Western European Economic Atlas* (Oxford University Press), we have drawn up the two graphs that appear in the bottom left-hand corner of the figure. The evapotranspiration isolines in the first graph vary between 700 and 1,300 mm. of rainfall per year. The rainfall isolines in the second graph mark extensive arid zones and indicate the level of additional precipitation (up to 750 mm. per year) needed for an area to be qualified as wet. Changes in vegetal landscape, from the evergreen *umbrias* of Galicia and the Cantabrian region to the hard, dry land of the south-east in summer, are technically reflected in the graph.

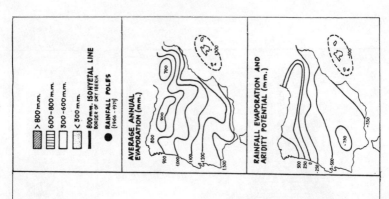

> 800 m.m.

600 - 800 m.m.

300 - 600 m.m.

< 300 m.m.

800 mm. ISOHYETAL LINE
BORDER OF DRY IBERIA

● RAINFALL POLES
(1966 - 1975)

AVERAGE ANNUAL
EVAPORATION (mm.)

RAINFALL EVAPORATION AND
ARIDITY POTENTIAL (mm.)

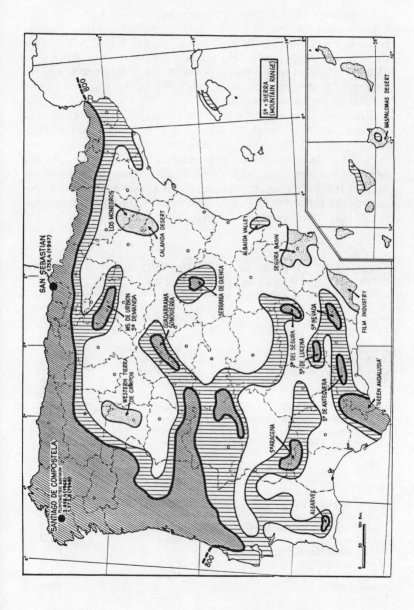

Irregularity and decomposition are the main features of Spain's *hydrographic system*. While in normal years the Mediterranean basin receives only 20,900 million cu. m. (17,500 of which flow through the Ebro river), the Atlantic region receives more than 31,000 million cu. m. Rivers are poorer throughout Levante and the southern Mediterranean coast, the very areas where intensive cultivation should be developed.

Moreover, the use of rivers for irrigation and hydroelectric purposes is costly, since the irregularity of flows requires large-capacity, and in many cases hyperannual, reservoirs.

In recent decades the great importance of Spain's *geographically generated income* has been pointed out. Many advantages are derived from the country's proximity to highly prosperous areas, such as the European Economic Community (EEC) and European Free Trade Association (EFTA) member-countries.

Table 1.1. OFFICIALLY PROTECTED NATIONAL AND NATURAL PARKS

|  | Province | Area (ha.) |
|---|---|---|
| NATIONAL PARKS |  |  |
| Doñana | Huelva, Seville | 75,765 |
| Teide | Tenerife | 13,571 |
| Caldera de Taburiente | La Palma | 4,690 |
| Timanfaya | Lanzarote | 5,107 |
| Garajonay | Gomera | 3,974 |
| Montaña de Covadonga | Oviedo and León | 16,925 |
| Aigües Tortes y Lago de San Mauricio | Lérida | 22,396 |
| Valle de Ordesa | Huesca | 15,709 |
| Las Tablas de Daimiel | Ciudad Real | 1,812 |
| *Total* |  | 159,949 |
| NATURAL PARKS |  |  |
| Dehesa del Moncayo | Zaragoza | 1,389 |
| Torcal de Antequera | Málaga | 1,200 |
| Lago de Sanabria y alrededores | Zamora | 1,200 |
| Sierra Espuña | Murcia | 9,961 |
| Hoyado de la Tejera Negra | Guadalajara | 1,391 |
| Monte Alhoya | Pontevedra | 746 |
| Cuenca Alta del Manzanares | Madrid | 4,304 |
| Monte el Valle | Murcia | 1,900 |
| Monfragüe | Cáceres | 17,852 |
| *Total* |  | 43,770 |

*Source:* Ministry of Agriculture.

## 5. *Environment*

When economic 'habitat' is taken in its widest context, *environmental problems* (air, soil, water and noise pollution and overcrowding) take on increasing importance. Unfortunately, not enough attention has been given to these problems, and comparatively few natural conservation areas have been set aside (see Table 1.1 and Fig. 15). Involved in this field are the Comisión Interministerial del Medio Ambiente (CIMA—Interministerial Environmental Commission), the Instituto de Conservación de la Naturaleza (ICONA—the Natural Conservation Institute), and ecological associations.

To conclude at this point that Spain is without the natural resources to reach the economic levels of other European countries would be incorrect. Many of the difficulties found in such an adverse habitat can be overcome, as the Spanish population has overcome them to a great extent already. Spain must simply pay a higher price than other European countries in order to move ahead. The habitat is therefore the foundation on which a population (being more important to economic development than natural resources), through the capital accumulation of labour, can raise an economic structure that steadily increases a country's standard of living.

# II. POPULATION

## 1. *Evolution and distribution*

In strictly economic terms, a population carries out two basic functions: it satisfies the demand for goods and services (through consumption) and it contributes to the obtaining of the same (through production). In terms of consumption, a population is the divider of National Income, which explains why in the early days of economics the term 'National Dividend' was given to this indicator. At the same time, a population represents the very basis of production and the primary asset of a national economy.

An official census has been conducted in Spain since 1857, one year after the state organised statistical services. From 1877 to 1900 censuses were carried out every ten years, and then from 1900 the census computed population figures as at 31 December of all years ending in zero. Nevertheless, to avoid the complications of heavy holiday migration, the census date was changed in 1981 to 31 March.

Spain's steady population growth, reflected in Table 2.1, has affected the economy in a series of ways. To maintain the country's living standard, the rate of economic growth should be equal to or greater than the rate at which the population is growing. Since this has not occurred during certain periods (e.g. 1939–50), Spain's living standard has dropped. While economic problems are bad enough in times of demographic expansion, they sharpen when the population, instead of growing, falls off.

The population density of Spain, according to data taken from the 1981 census, is 74.66 inhabitants/km.$^2$ a figure far below that of Portugal (107), France (97), Italy (189), the United Kingdom (230) and the Netherlands (341). However, neither absolute population (39 million inhabitants in 1984) nor population density (77.3 inhabitants/km.$^2$) tells us anything about the distribution of the population throughout the country. Based on 1981 figures, we find that only 33.1% of the total population reside in the Spanish interior (representing 66.9% of peninsular territory); whereas 66.9% of the peninsular population lives on the Spanish periphery (representing only 33.1% of the country's surface area). The interior has an average density of 52.34 inhabitants/km.$^2$, characteristic of a weak consumer market, while the periphery has 140 inhabitants/km.$^2$, a density much closer to the average European-type consumer market (Figs 3 and 4).

Another way to establish the population/space ratio is by means of a population distribution study on rural, intermediate and urban

Table 2.1. EVOLUTION OF THE TOTAL POPULATION
(CENSUSES SINCE 1857)

|  | Thousands of inhabitants | Annual increase during inter-census period (%) | Population index |
|---|---|---|---|
| 1857 | 15,454 | 0.41 | 100.0 |
| 1860 | 15,645 | 0.37 | 101.2 |
| 1877 | 16,622 | 0.56 | 107.6 |
| 1887 | 17,549 | 0.32 | 113.6 |
| 1897 | 18,108 | 0.89 | 117.2 |
| 1900 | 18,618 | 0.72 | 120.5 |
| 1910 | 19,992 | 0.71 | 129.4 |
| 1920 | 21,508 | 0.73 | 139.2 |
| 1930 | 23,845 | 1.04 | 154.3 |
| 1940 | 26,188 | 0.94 | 169.4 |
| 1950 | 28,172 | 0.80 | 182.2 |
| 1960 | 30,776 | 0.88 | 199.1 |
| 1970 | 34,041 | 1.01 | 220.3 |
| 1981[1] | 37,682 | 1.00 | 243.8 |
| 1981[2] | 37,963 | — | 245.6 |
| 1982[2] | 38,351 | — | 248.1 |
| 1983[2] | 38,750 | — | 250.7 |
| 1984[3] | 39,021 | — | 252.5 |
| 1985 | 39,294 |  |  |

*Notes*
1. Population Census of March 1984.
2. Estimated population (as of December 1981) based on working population survey.
3. Estimated population based on a 0.7% growth-rate.

*Source:* National Statistics Institute.

zones. The main problem arising in this case is that of selecting one of the many available conventions to separate these different zones. According to the 1981 census, of Spain's 8,022 municipalities, 4,771 (58.2%) have fewer than 1,000 inhabitants, accounting for less than 5% of the population. This means that almost half the country's territory contains a minimum percentage of the population. In contrast to these marked 'municipal minifundia', the largest municipalities with over 50,000 inhabitants represent more than 18 million inhabitants, or 50% of the total population.

This population imbalance, due to many small and few really large cities, is one of the more important issues facing the Spanish economy at present. On the one hand, a large number of municipalities have such a limited volume of resources and possibilities that basic services do not even meet minimum quality levels. On the other hand, large cities, receiving huge migratory flows in recent years, are unable to find the means to handle this influx properly.

*Introduction*

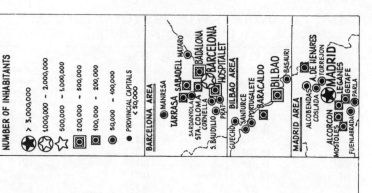

Fig. 3. POPULATION CENTRES ACCORDING TO THE 1981 CENSUS

Information taken from the 1981 census was used to prepare this map on population centres with more than 50,000 inhabitants. Apart from its usefulness as a point of reference, two immediate observations can be made.

(1) Madrid, Barcelona and Bilbao constitute the country's demographic poles. Densely populated and highly urbanised, these areas have had a fundamental influence on the centre of demographic gravity in recent times. During years of accelerated growth in the 1960s and early 1970s, the centre quickly moved in a north-easterly and easterly direction. From 1973, however, the economic crisis curbed this movement, along with urban expansion and rural depopulation. Most of the country's economic activities are concentrated in Madrid, Barcelona, Bilbao and Valencia, which represent the four peaks of the north-eastern quadrant. The capitals of these areas are nerve-centres, for they generate the prime force behind the economic and social system.

(2) The coast, having a far greater number of population centres with more than 50,000 inhabitants, gives the outer edges of the country a much denser and more urbanised population than the interior. This map can be compared to Fig. 4 on density by province.

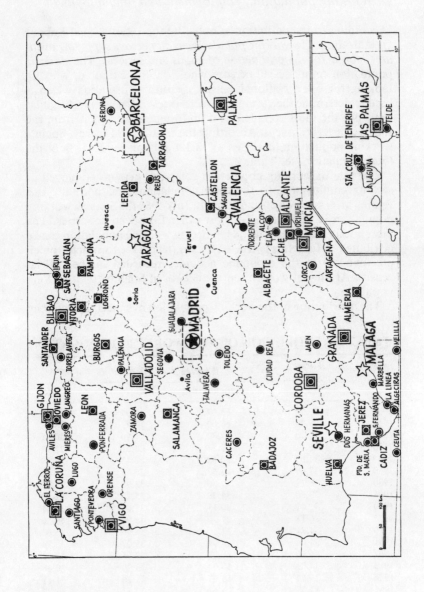

## 2. *Working population, employment and unemployment*

'According to the definition adopted by the International Labour Organization, the *working population is all persons supplying available labour for the production of goods and services.* The working population comprises all persons who either have a job or who are looking for one.' National censuses gather information which is used to determine the various characteristics of the working population, but the most complete and up-to-date data comes from the INE's quarterly surveys. According to the July 1984 survey, Spain's working population had risen to 13.196 million, or 33.58% of the total population (see Table 2.2).

The rate of working population compares persons employed or seeking employment to the total population, and normally this figure varies between 30 and 55%. In July 1984 the Spanish working population is below that of most other European countries. The most notable international differences in working population can be attributed to (and this is true of Spain) the degree to which women are involved in the economic activities recorded in the official census. At present women represent 29% of Spain's total working population.

The distribution of the working population by percentages among

Table 2.2.   EVOLUTION OF THE WORKING POPULATION

| | *Working population as % of total* | *Working population distribution (%)* | | |
|---|---|---|---|---|
| | | *Agriculture* | *Industries* | *Services* |
| 1900 | 35.31 | 63.64 | 15.99 | 17.77 |
| 1910 | 35.37 | 66.00 | 15.82 | 18.18 |
| 1920 | 35.10 | 57.30 | 21.90 | 20.81 |
| 1930 | 35.51 | 45.51 | 26.51 | 27.98 |
| 1940 | 34.61 | 50.52 | 22.13 | 27.35 |
| 1950 | 37.09 | 47.57 | 26.55 | 25.88 |
| 1960 | 38.11 | 39.70 | 32.98 | 27.32 |
| 1965 | 38.50 | 34.30 | 35.20 | 31.20 |
| 1970 | 37.41 | 29.11 | 37.28 | 33.61 |
| 1975 | 36.11 | 21.70 | 38.00 | 40.30 |
| 1980 | 34.21 | 17.36 | 36.06 | 45.66 |
| 1981 | 34.04 | 15.94 | 35.27 | 48.79 |
| 1982 | 34.16 | 16.03 | 33.95 | 50.02 |
| 1983 | 34.09 | 15.64 | 33.70 | 50.66 |
| 1984 | 33.64[1] | 15.63 | 33.26 | 51.11 |
| 1985 | 33.58 | 15.62 | 32.11 | 52.27 |

*Note:* 1. Forecast.
*Source:* National Statistics Institute.

different economic sectors provides one of the best indicators of a country's stage of development. Table 2.2 shows the progress made in Spain since 1900. In 1940, as a result of the civil war, a regression was observed and the agricultural working population had increased from 45.5 to 50.5%.

During the 1940s and early 1950s, Spain's unemployed were scattered among a growing agricultural population, and later emigration kept domestic unemployment down. Since 1974, however, unemployment levels have steadily risen. According to the INE working population survey, which is far more reliable than the 'registered unemployment' estimates of the Instituto Nacional de Empleo (INEM — National Employment Institute), the unemployment rate for the second quarter of 1984 was 2.7 million, which means that in mid-1984, 20.15% of the working population was unemployed. This figure, the highest in Western Europe, reflects the seriousness of the crisis and the ineffectiveness of the economic policies being followed (see Chapter XVI). The fact that the situation is mitigated by illegal employment in the informal economy (see Chapter XI) is an entirely different matter. All things considered, unemployment is the country's most pressing problem today, mirroring job destruction (due to bankruptcies, suspensions of payments and lay-offs) and the lack of new job creation for those entering the labour market for the first time.

## 3. *Natural population movements and migration*

The evolution of natural movements (birth, death and marriage rates) since 1900 is summarised in Table 2.3. The figures speak for themselves: a constant drop in birth and death rates, and fluctuations in a marriage rate which is extraordinarily sensitive to economic cycles.

The difference between the birth and death rates is measured by the Burdofer index (births minus deaths). This index shows that the Spanish population declined by 7 per thousand during the last inter-census period. But the rate of real growth takes into account the migratory balance. With this adjustment, the real population growth rate in Spain is a little less than 10 per thousand annually (20 per thousand being the world average).

Migratory movements are produced by differences in competition for available economic resources. The performance of this mechanism can be clearly appreciated through internal migratory flows. The highest vegetative growth rate in peninsular Spain is traditionally found in Castile-León, Galicia, La Mancha,

## Fig. 4. POPULATION DENSITY BY PROVINCE, 1981

Population density by province shows that the interior of Spain is sparsely populated. Most of the coast and the Ebro axis have density levels above the national average. By using the national average (index = 100), an isoline (density = 100) can be drawn to separate the two Spains, the less (two-thirds) from the more (one-third) densely populated.

This map can be compared to that of Fig. 5 on internal migration. Rural activity is clearly predominant in sparsely populated areas, where (particularly in the south) the vegetative growth-rate has been high. Differences in income (see Fig. 22) have prompted people to move from these areas to the more industrialised, densely peopled areas. Both this map and Fig. 5 show how the political decision to establish the nation's capital in the geographic centre of the peninsula created a dense island in the middle of a demographic semi-desert. This semi-barren land, together with the 'border effect' (high tariffs), explains why the area surrounding the Spanish-Portuguese border has generated little economic activity.

Figs 4 and 5 support the well-known law that populations tend to move from mountainous zones to valleys and from the interior to the coast. This is the spontaneous trend, albeit not always the most desirable or sensible one.

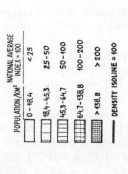

POPULATION/KM$^2$    NATIONAL AVERAGE INDEX = 100

| | |
|---|---|
| 0–18,4 | < 25 |
| 18,4–45,3 | 25–50 |
| 45,3–64,7 | 50–100 |
| 64,7–138,8 | 100–200 |
| >138,8 | > 200 |

— DENSITY ISOLINE = 100

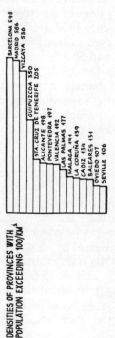

**DENSITIES OF PROVINCES WITH POPULATION EXCEEDING 100/KM$^2$**

BARCELONA 598
MADRID 586
VIZCAYA 536
GUIPUZCOA 350
STA. CRUZ DE TENERIFE 205
ALICANTE 198
PONTEVEDRA 197
VALENCIA 192
LAS PALMAS 177
MALAGA 164
LA CORUÑA 159
CADIZ 154
BALEARES 134
OVIEDO 107
SEVILLA 106

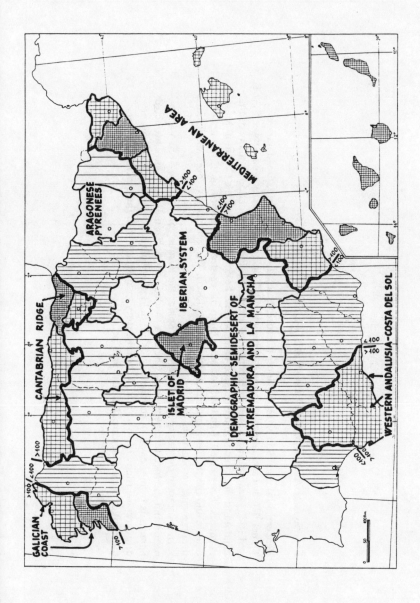

## Fig. 5. AREAS OF MIGRATION AND DEPOPULATION

Between 1941 and 1950 eight provinces (Orense, Huesca, Gerona, Soria, Guadalajara, Teruel, Huelva and Almeria), between 1951 and 1960 eighteen provinces, and between 1961 and 1970 twenty-three provinces experienced a large decline in population as many of their inhabitants migrated to industrialised areas within the country and to the Common Market countries. Between 1971 and 1981 another loss was registered in 19 provinces (running from Galicia and the Iberian System to northern Andalusia). These areas have been shaded in on the map with vertical lines.

In contrast to the depopulated interior of Spain, the Basque country, the Ebro Valley region and the Mediterranean coast (the area shaded with horizontal lines) have attracted Spaniards from the rest of the country. We should underline both the singularity of the demographic island of Madrid and the migratory magnetism (with the development of tourism) of the Canary and Balearic archipelagos.

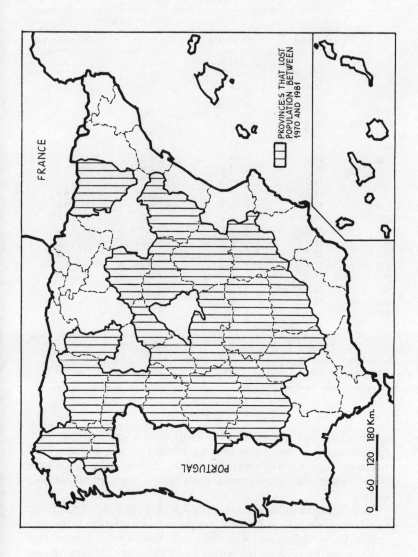

PROVINCES THAT LOST
POPULATION BETWEEN
1970 AND 1981

FRANCE

PORTUGAL

0   60  120  180 Km.

Table 2.3.  POPULATION, BIRTH, DEATH AND
MARRIAGE RATES

| | Population (millions) | × 1,000 inhabitants | | |
|---|---|---|---|---|
| | | Birth rate | Death rate | Marriage rate |
| 1900 | 18.6 | 33.8 | 28.3 | 8.8 |
| 1910 | 19.9 | 32.6 | 23.0 | 7.0 |
| 1920 | 21.4 | 29.3 | 23.2 | 7.2 |
| 1930 | 23.7 | 28.5 | 17.8 | 7.6 |
| 1940 | 25.9 | 24.3 | 16.5 | 8.4 |
| 1950 | 28.1 | 20.0 | 10.8 | 7.5 |
| 1960 | 30.4 | 21.6 | 8.6 | 7.7 |
| 1965 | 31.6 | 21.1 | 8.5 | 7.2 |
| 1970 | 34.0 | 19.7 | 8.5 | 7.4 |
| 1971 | 34.3 | 19.4 | 8.9 | 7.4 |
| 1972 | 34.7 | 19.2 | 8.1 | 7.7 |
| 1973 | 35.0 | 19.1 | 8.5 | 9.7 |
| 1974 | 35.4 | 19.3 | 8.3 | 7.5 |
| 1975 | 35.8 | 18.7 | 8.3 | 7.6 |
| 1976 | 36.2 | 18.8 | 8.3 | 7.2 |
| 1977 | 36.7 | 18.0 | 8.1 | 7.2 |
| 1978 | 37.1 | 17.3 | 8.1 | 7.0 |
| 1979 | 37.6 | 16.1 | 7.8 | 6.6 |
| 1981[1] | 37.7 | 15.1 | 7.7 | 5.7 |
| 1981[2] | 38.0 | — | — | — |
| 1982[2] | 38.3 | — | — | — |
| 1983[2] | 38.7 | — | — | — |
| 1984[2] | 39.0 | — | — | — |

*Notes*
1. Take from the Population Census of 1 March 1981.
2. Taken from table 2.1
*Source:* National Statistics Institute.

Extremadura and Andalusia. Spaniards have migrated from these regions of lower *per capita* income levels towards industrialised areas with lower rates of vegetative growth. Provincial capitals have also attracted immigrants from areas within their administrative borders.

The heightened industrialisation of the 1961–70 period prompted, in real terms, more than 3 million people to migrate from the *meseta*, Galicia, Extremadura and Andalusia to the outskirts of Madrid and of the industrial cities of the North and Catalonia. This vast movement sharpened intolerably the problem of housing, at the same time depopulating provinces in the interior (see Fig. 5 and Table 2.4). Little was achieved with the official growth centres of the 1964–73 Development Plan (see chapter XVI).

The provinces of the Ebro Valley axis experienced marked

Table 2.4.  EVOLUTION OF THE SPANISH POPULATION
BY PROVINCE, BETWEEN 1970 AND 1981

| | Census 1970 | Census 1981 x1,000 inhabitants | Growth | % growth |
|---|---|---|---|---|
| Madrid | 3,761 | 4,687 | 926 | 12.44 |
| Barcelona | 3,915 | 4,623 | 708 | 12.27 |
| Valencia | 1,770 | 2,066 | 296 | 5.48 |
| Sevilla | 1,337 | 1,478 | 141 | 3.92 |
| Vizcaya | 1,041 | 1,189 | 148 | 3.16 |
| Alicante | 922 | 1,149 | 227 | 3.05 |
| Asturias | 1,052 | 1,130 | 78 | 3.00 |
| Coruña | 1,031 | 1,093 | 62 | 2.90 |
| Málaga | 854 | 1,026 | 172 | 2.72 |
| Cádiz | 879 | 988 | 109 | 2.62 |
| Murcia | 832 | 955 | 123 | 2.54 |
| Pontevedra | 781 | 883 | 102 | 2.34 |
| Zaragoza | 757 | 829 | 72 | 2.20 |
| Granada | 742 | 759 | 17 | 2.01 |
| Córdoba | 731 | 721 | − 10 | 1.92 |
| Las Palmas | 513 | 475 | − 38 | 1.26 |
| Guipúzcoa | 549 | 709 | 160 | 1.88 |
| Sta Cruz | 626 | 695 | 69 | 1.84 |
| Baleares | 576 | 659 | 83 | 1.75 |
| Badajoz | 533 | 656 | 123 | 1.74 |
| Jaén | 702 | 644 | − 58 | 1.71 |
| León | 668 | 640 | − 28 | 1.69 |
| Cantabria | 563 | 525 | − 39 | 1.39 |
| Tarragona | 469 | 513 | 44 | 1.37 |
| Navarra | 433 | 513 | 80 | 1.36 |
| Valladolid | 467 | 509 | 42 | 1.35 |
| Ciudad Real | 413 | 482 | 69 | 1.28 |
| Toledo | 478 | 475 | − 3 | 1.26 |
| Gerona | 412 | 467 | 55 | 1.24 |
| Castellón | 387 | 432 | 45 | 1.14 |
| Orense | 441 | 430 | − 11 | 1.14 |
| Cáceres | 468 | 421 | − 47 | 1.12 |
| Huelva | 403 | 419 | 16 | 1.11 |
| Almería | 378 | 411 | 33 | 1.09 |
| Lugo | 423 | 405 | − 18 | 1.08 |
| Salamanca | 380 | 364 | − 16 | 0.97 |
| Burgos | 361 | 364 | 3 | 0.96 |
| Lérida | 347 | 353 | 6 | 0.94 |
| Albacete | 341 | 339 | − 2 | 0.90 |
| Alava | 200 | 258 | 58 | 0.68 |
| La Rioja | 235 | 254 | 19 | 0.68 |
| Zamora | 259 | 228 | − 31 | 0.60 |
| Cuenca | 252 | 216 | − 36 | 0.58 |
| Huesca | 222 | 215 | − 7 | 0.57 |
| Palencia | 202 | 188 | − 14 | 0.50 |
| Avila | 212 | 184 | − 28 | 0.48 |
| Teruel | 174 | 153 | − 21 | 0.41 |
| Segovia | 162 | 149 | − 13 | 0.40 |
| Guadalajara | 150 | 143 | − 7 | 0.38 |
| Soria | 117 | 101 | − 16 | 0.26 |
| Ceuta | 63 | 65 | 2 | 0.18 |
| Melilla | 61 | 54 | − 7 | 0.14 |
| *Total* | 34,041 | 37,682 | 3,641 | 100.00 |

*Source:* National Statistics Institute.

immigration during the years when migration was at its peak: the Basque country and Navarra being at the north-western end of the axis; the province of Aragoza at the centre; and the length of the Mediterranean coast, from Gerona to Alicante, at the lower end. Interior migration is not expected to regain its 1960s and 1970s levels because the population of the former areas of emigration is ageing and birth rates are falling.

Foreign migration from 1959 onwards was stimulated by the first effects of the Stabilisation Plan (in response to the 1959–61 recession) and by the large wave of prosperity that hit Europe in 1958 (the year of the signing of the Treaty of Rome and the creation of the EEC). It is interesting to note that workforce migration was a leading factor behind the short-term success of the Stabilisation Plan. Migratory movements abroad peaked during the 1961–70 decade. In 1969 3.4 million Spaniards were working outside the country. Re-immigration began from 1973 onwards.

Spaniards also migrate on a seasonal basis, spurred by job offers in France during the grape harvesting season. In early September many Spanish farm labourers make their way up to France where they work for as much as three months. According to the Dirección General de Empleo (the General Employment Office), seasonal emigration is estimated at around 100,000 workers.

# PART TWO
# THE SYSTEM OF PRODUCTION

## III. FOOD AND AGRICULTURE

### 1. *Introduction to the system of production*

Man produces by making use of and transforming natural resources. When society as a whole produces, the different activities of production become interdependent. The best macroeconomic synthesis of the system of production is provided by an *input-output* scheme (drawn up for 1954, 1958, 1962 and 1970) where different activities are grouped into economic sectors, and transactions are registered on a double-entry table.

When we consider conventional sectors from the input side of the table, we find that they are productive sectors and final sectors. Productive sectors contribute goods, the real components of production, while final sectors are involved in the rendering of services and compensation (fees, social security payments, profits, indirect taxes and savings). Spain can be grouped into three super-sectors: the FAO sector, the industrial sector and the services sector. Like the specialised UN agency of the same name, the first sector includes agriculture, livestock, forestry and fisheries. The second, also called the secondary sector, deals with the manufacture of raw materials into intermediate and finished goods. The tertiary sector encompasses activities such as transport, commerce, communications and entertainment. This sector, a mechanism for physically distributing goods obtained by means of production (transport and commerce) and for redistributing the earnings generated by production (public administration and entertainment), is not strictly part of the system of production.

### 2. *Background on the agrarian sector*

The country's agrarian structure has been shaped by natural resources and economic policies. To understand this structure, we must take a look at the history of land distribution and tenure systems. This introduction would not be complete without any mention of Spain's eighteenth-century agrarians. Campomanes, Olavide and Jovellanos were the first who severely criticised feudal institutions for their adverse effect on agriculture: the abuse of the 'Mesta' (a sheep breeders' association); the concentration of the best lands (through entail and mortmain) in the hands of the Church, religious orders and the nobility, as was brought out in the Cadastre of Ensenada (mid-18th century); the restrictions placed on free domestic trade etc. While all these obstacles were removed in the course of the nineteenth century, special attention should be given to the way in which disentailment occurred, this being the root of the present-day problem with the latifundia (large holdings run by landlords).

2.1. *Disentailment.* Apart from the trade-protectionism controversy and the constitutional problem of religious freedom, disentailment was one of the key issues in Spain during the nineteenth century, a period of almost chronic civil and social conflict. Disentailment was not promoted as an agrarian policy, for it was an operation closely tied to the problems of Spanish finances. It was first promoted because the Church did not pay taxes on the majority of its mortmain property. The confiscation and sale of this property at public auction meant immediate receipts for the Treasury and the collection of future rural taxes from new owners. Moreover, during the first third of the nineteenth century, the belief was widespread that the public debt, heavily abused in the last part of the previous century (with the issuing of royal bonds) and the early decades of the nineteenth century, could only be repaid by having the State conduct extraordinary sales of mortmain property. The Carlist wars (1833-9, 1847-9 and 1872-6), fought by those in favour of the New Liberal Order and the supporters of the *Ancien Régime*, also fuelled disentailment. Desperately needed resources and the support of the bourgeoisie could only be secured with mortmain property sales.

Following a series of frustrated and then renewed attempts, during the progressive decade of 1834-43, disentailment was finally seriously undertaken. Mendizabal, its chief promoter during the first stage, viewed the disentailing mechanism as the quickest and surest method to win the civil war declared by the Carlists when Ferdinand VII died in 1833, and was succeeded as monarch by his daughter Isabel. Disentailment was carried out on two fronts. Land was taken away, first, from the landed class, the municipalities and the state (civil disentailment), and secondly from the Church (ecclesiastical disentailment). In the case of the latter, ecclesiastical property was declared a national asset and sold at public auction under the Act of 29 July 1837. Much land was engulfed by this first wave of disentailment. After a moderate interval from 1843 till 1854, the General Disentailment Act of 1 May 1855, advanced by Pascual

Madoz, made possible the alienation of most of the remaining national property. By 1876 the goals of disentailment had practically been reached. Only very few communal, state and Church properties were able to escape the long, complex and disorderly disentailing process.

Almost a century after the process was concluded, it is still difficult to pass final judgement on disentailment. It was, of course, a necessary step in the bourgeois revolution. Its political aspect was the vast extensions of under-used land being brought into the mainstream of the country's economy. Nevertheless, the process did not become a panacea for agriculture, as economists and public finance experts had hoped. The main achievement of disentailment was the substitution of a capitalist structure of the land, with vestiges of feudalism, for a feudal structure. Latifundia replaced large family estates and Church property, feeding off communal property and driving municipalities to ruin. Disentailment undoubtedly encouraged population growth once the formerly uncultivated lands were broken up. The social scene, however, did not greatly change. Extensive areas of the country remained in the hands of a few hundred families (see Fig. 8); plough men were deprived of most of their communal rights; and emancipated serfs became day workers. A vast agricultural proletariat emerged, with an ardent desire for land redistribution.

2.2. *Water policy.* Between the Restoration (1874) and the proclamation of the Second Republic (1931), the agrarian issue did not make much of a political stir. Concern to improve agriculture was channelled towards water policy.

According to Joaquín Costa (its main propagator) and Macías Picavea, water policy was 'a sublimated expression of the economic policy of the nation'. Costa's programme was far-reaching. In his opinion, a 'water ministry', which was necessary to combat dry soil, would act as an 'agent for individual activities, as a regulator of social life and as an agency involved and interested in population growth, the regeneration of the race and greater public wealth, as a source of taxation . . .' The government's duty consisted in 'helping this work along by providing the benefits of irrigation to the largest possible extent of land, with the means within its reach, not private means.'

The enthusiasm of Costa and Macías Picavea and their followers was officially reflected for the first time in the '1902 Water Works Plan', prepared by a team of civil engineers, headed by Rafael Gasset. However, political instability between 1902 and 1923 temporarily negated the water policy. The few reservoirs constructed

Fig. 6. HOLDINGS LARGER THAN 500 ha.

This figure is based on the INE's 1969–70 'Survey on Private Holdings of 500 or more hectares.' The fact that the map only considers private holdings (some 10 million ha.) make it all the more significant, for it excludes communal, municipal and other public land.

Approximately 5,722 private holdings have more than 500 ha., totalling 5,726,944 ha., or 12.83% of all tillable agricultural land (according to the last agrarian census on 43,890,967 ha.). The average size of these holdings was 1,001 ha. These large holdings — latifundia — are distributed differently, depending on the region, as can be seen by the isoquantum lines drawn on the map.

The latifundia in the north, for example, represent less than four percent of the land taken up in the census. In the Meseta del Duero, Old Catalonia and most of Levante, latifundia are found on 4–10% of the land, with minifundia clearly remaining predominant. In New Castile, Extremadura and Andalusia, however, the intensity of latifundia varies between 10–40%. Caceres (36.8%) and Ciudad Real (33.5%) show the highest concentration of these holdings.

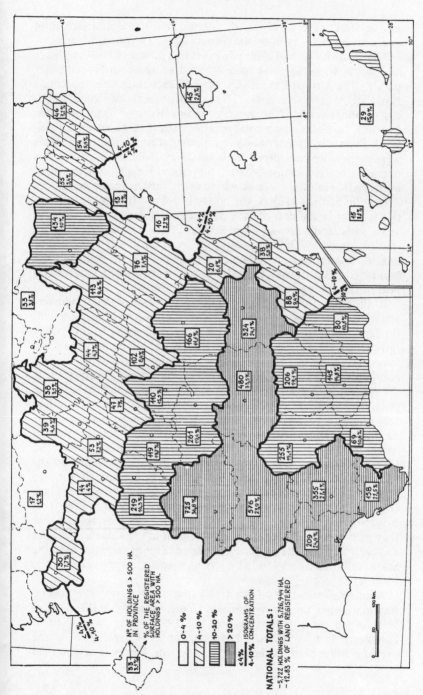

NATIONAL TOTALS:

– 5,722 HOLDINGS WITH 5,726,944 HA.
– 12.83 % OF LAND REGISTERED

by the state were barely used, for planned canal and irrigation ditches were never built by the owners of the surrounding lands.

The dictator General Primo de Rivera, in power 1923–30, technically addressed the agrarian issue by conducting a coordinated water policy. The Decree-Law of 28 May 1926 was enacted to create National Water Councils. The establishment of these councils — one for each of the country's major rivers — was a great step forward, for following a comprehensive study of an area's agricultural, livestock, forestry and even industrial problems, river basins were eventually considered units of development. To ensure this overall view, syndication became compulsory for all the farmers and industrialists of each basin, to whom public authority was delegated.

In spite of their efforts, the councils did not live up to expectations. After losing part of their authority and democratic nature in 1939, some areas proved more active than others, despite the fact that (as stated by Gómez Ayáu) they were constantly subjected to unsettling administrative changes. Unfortunately, the councils were hampered by centralism, the mistrust of the Treasury and the selfishness of certain regions.

In the years following the dictatorship, water policy supporters sought a more effective policy, adopting a position in keeping with the land reclamation policy of that time. According to this policy (given the willing apathy of owners), the state built dams, canals and irrigation ditches, providing all necessary irrigation system components. The *Ley de Obras de Puesta en Riego* (OPER — Irrigation Works Act) of 13 April 1939 was undoubtedly the point of departure for the land reclamation policy of that period. It recognised that water works alone were not enough to bring about necessary changes. Apart from basic works, the country needed irrigation and drainage systems, roads and housing units. The OPER Act provided for the building of irrigation systems by the Ministry of Public Works or by owners or unions, if they so requested within three years following the approval of a given plan. Once the works were completed, owners were allowed to keep their irrigated land, provided that they agreed to use it sensibly and that they paid the State the unearned increment in the value of the land and their share of the project. If these conditions were not met, the State could take over lands by paying owners the net value of the property.

Another illustration of the trend that arose during the Second Republic, when the land reclamation issue was raised at the national level in all its complexity, was the 1933 Water Works Plan, hammered out by Manuel Lorenzo Pardo. After criticising the previous water plan for lacking a real system, Pardo based the 1933

Plan on balancing out the river flows of the Atlantic and Mediterranean basins and on increasing yields in both areas. Pardo said that the rivers of the Atlantic slope carried more water but that crop production in the west was smaller than in the east, where rivers were poorer. This basic idea spawned the need to transfer water from the Atlantic to the Mediterranean slope by means of a canal that would collect Tagus River waters from the Bolarque and Alarcón reservoirs at an altitude of 1,000 metres and carry them along the Júcar river-bed and through the newly-built canal in Albacete to the lands of Murcia and Alicante. But protesting irrigators in Júcar, fearful that water would be taken from them, held up the execution of the plan, which fell into oblivion, until it was eventually revived by Minister Silva Muñoz for the Second Development Plan in 1968–71.

2.3. *The agrarian reform of the Second Republic.* With the pro-clamation of the Second Republic, the agrarian issue came out into the open. Concern for agricultural and farmers' problems was shown in article 47 of the Constitution of December 1932 and in the promise that agrarian reform would be rapidly effected. After a long parliamentary debate, an agrarian reform bill was enacted in September 1932. This act, comprising 23 sections, contained a reform mechanism designed to redistribute land and to settle landless '*campesinos*'. The Instituto de Reforma Agraria (IRA Agrarian Reform Institute) was created to enforce this law, with provincial councils and *campesino* communities under its authority. The institute was granted a low annual 50 million pesetas credit and authorised to issue special bonds.

The fifth principle of this act (excluding communal land, forests and pastureland) listed expropriable land. Reform activities, primarily the expropriation of land for redistribution among *campesinos*, were based on an expropriable land inventory. No form of compensation had to be paid for land expropriated from family estates and Spanish grandees, except in cases of unamortised improvements and of mandatory food allowances for those in need. Remaining eligible land was expropriated according to a rate of capitalisation which rose with the value of the land in question.

Payments were made partly in cash and partly in special government bonds that gave an annual interest rate of 5% to be redeemed in fifty years. The percentage of the payment made in cash gradually fell as the value of the expropriated area increased. This expropria-tion and payment system was harshly criticised, particularly because no payment was made to Spanish grandees for their expropriated lands. It is interesting to note the vast extent of the land held by these

Table 3.1.    LAND OWNED BY PRINCIPAL SPANISH
ARISTOCRATS, 14 APRIL 1931

| Owner | Ha. |
| --- | --- |
| Duke of Medinaceli | 79,146 |
| Duke of Peñaranda | 51,015 |
| Duke of Vistahermosa | 47,203 |
| Duke of Alba | 34,455 |
| Marquis of La Romana | 29,096 |
| Marquis of Comillas | 23,719 |
| Duke of Fernán Nuñez | 17,732 |
| Duke of Arión | 17,666 |
| Duke of Infantado | 17,171 |
| Count of Romanones | 15,171 |
| 89 other landowners | 249,985 |
| Total | 577,539 |

Source: Agrarian Reform Institute.

aristocrats. In 1931, 99 Spanish grandees owned 577,359 ha., or an average of 5,831 ha. per owner. Many grandees possessed much more land, as can be seen in Table 3.1.

Land expropriated as described above passed from the hands of the IRA to those of provincial councils and finally to tenant farmer communities. These communities would decide whether the land would be worked collectively or individually. The act contained other regulations regarding unharvested crops at the time of expropriation and standards for *campesino* settlements, farm development, land loans, municipal property, the rights of landowners, long-term land leasing and education.

The end-result, however, was a far cry from the hopes in the act placed by *campesinos*. A minimum of 60,000 tenant farmers had been forecast for settlement each year, but less than 12,500 were established at the end of the first two years. There were many reasons for this disproportion between forecasts and reality. First, the act was too complex, involving too many official procedures and lacking basic direction. Proof of this was that *campesino* settlements had been allowed to decide how the land was to be worked. Secondly, the poor organisation of the IRA slowed down the implementation of the act even further. The Minister of Agriculture, Marcelino Domingo, who defended the bill before Parliament, was unprepared — as were many of his IRA colleagues. Moreover, the reform was quickly brought to a standstill after the rightists, through the Lerroux/CEDA (Coalición Española de Derechos Autónomas: Spanish Federation of Autonomous Rights), won the 1933 elections.

Following the revolution of October 1934, reform was left in *de facto* abeyance, and in 1935 the scope of the act was limited.

Objectively, as far as the expropriation system was concerned, the Act of 1932 was replete with technical weaknesses, and indeed was not very advanced for its time compared with the other European agrarian acts of the 1920s. Inventory preparations were not feasible given the number of holdings involved; no reference was made to minimum crop units; nothing could be done with the expropriated surfeit of certain oversize holdings; and the exclusion of pasture lands from reform broke the marriage bond between agriculture and livestock raising.

The victory of the leftist Popular Front coalition in the February 1936 elections spelled out another change of direction. In March of 1936 agrarian reform was stepped up faster than ever before with the application of the principle of social utility, the repeal of the Act of 1935 and the reinstatement of the Act of 15 September 1932. Between February and June, 232,199 ha. were occupied and 71,919 landless agricultural workers were settled; more was accomplished in these four months than in the previous five years. The reorganisation of the IRA and bureaucratic streamlining made it possible to carry out the reform much more quickly.

The outbreak of civil war in July 1936 sped up land distribution even further. On 4 September, under President Largo Caballero, the Communist Luis Vicente Uribe was appointed Minister of Agriculture and a decree in October gave legal force to the existing measure to expropriate land owned by supporters of the Nationalist upheaval. In May 1938, the IRA announced that it had settled farmers on 2,434,202 ha. expropriated from political defectors; on 2,008,000 ha. by declaration of social utility; and on 1,252,000 ha. on a provisional basis.

## 3. *Agrarian policy as of 1936*

From the beginning of the war, the Nationalists' agrarian policy moved in a very different direction. One of the first provisions of the new regime clearly rejected the republican agrarian policy. The Decree of 28 August 1936 suspended unexecuted agrarian reform plans, giving rise to a new current blocking the 1907 Settlement Act and the water policy envisaged in the 1932 OPER Act. Legal-social reform was shelved as technical reform, designed to develop land irrigation and parcelling, moved to the foreground.

The Servicio Nacional de Reforma Economico-Social de la Tierra (National Socio-Economic Land Reform Service) was set up in 1938

## Fig. 7. MAIN IRRIGATION ZONES

This figure is based on the map drawn by the Ministry of Public Works and Urban Development of irrigation zones created through State Water Works investments. Also included are other irrigable zones not directly managed by the state shown in the National Geographic Institute's *National Atlas of Spain*. This map represents the peninsula's 56 most important irrigation zones, the largest zones in the two archipelagos, and extensive projects under discussion or under way.

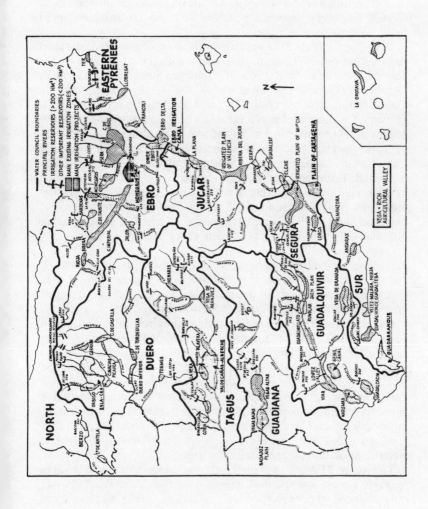

to dissolve agrarian reform and to implement the new policy. The first assignment of this service was to study the effects of agrarian reform, particularly as of July 1936. These studies showed that the land tenure system had undergone profound changes during the months of the war, especially in Andalusia, Extremadura and New Castile. For many months the service was busy returning occupied farms to their former owners.

Once the dissolution of agrarian reform was completed, the land reclamation policy began to take shape with the suspension of the Servicio Nacional de Reforma Económico-Social de la Tierra in October 1939 and the creation of the Instituto Nacional de Colonización (INC — National Land Reclamation Institute) 'to carry out far-reaching land reclamation plans in accordance with the programmes provided by the Ministry of Agriculture'. Twelve years later, the Servicio Nacional de Concentración Parcelaria (National Land Consolidation Service), the other main tool of this policy, was organised. Both these agencies developed an agrarian policy in two basic directions: land reclamation and land consolidation. In the remainder of this section we will discuss these two lines of policy, maintained up to 1975, as a background to examining the agrarian bills enacted since the advent of democracy in 1977 (section 4).

3.1. *Land reclamation policy.*   With the land reclamation acts of 1939, State participation in irrigation works grew until it was involved in a wide range of activities, including the construction of large works and the building of irrigation ditches.

Each of the first three main land reclamation bills, enacted in 1939, 1946 and 1959, was unique. The Act of 26 December 1939 'for land reclamation of large zones', a so-called appeal to capital and private initiative, did little in fact to promote private enterprise. The Act of 27 April 1946 'for small land reclamation projects', less ambitious than previous legislation, was more effective in that it supported medium-sized agricultural improvements (by individuals, municipalities and land reclamation groups) through the creation of small irrigated areas and the construction of livestock shelters, electrification and agricultural industries.

The Act of 21 April 1949 on 'land reclamation and distribution in irrigable zones' was the most effective of the three. The 1939 Act only delayed the expansion of irrigation, while water-starved harvests in 1945 and 1947 made more visible the need to bring irrigation to vast areas. To this end the state assumed full responsibility for the irrigation operations in large areas (see Fig. 9). Pursuant to the Act of 1949, certain irrigable zones were declared of 'great national interest', and the INC designed a general land reclamation project which set maximum and minimum cash payments to be made at the time of expropriation, standard crop units, and a maximum area of land reserved for landed farmers. Existing irrigated land was never expropriated, and remaining land was termed 'surplus land.' This land was parcelled out, first, to tenants and sharecroppers in the zone; secondly, to farmers from other regions; and thirdly, to previous landowners when they so requested.

Tenants had access to land under an administrative leasing programme. To become owners they had first to pay for the initial value of the land and taxes by INC-set deadlines. The property then belonged to the tenant, but special laws prohibited parcel divisions, and the INC continued to oversee farms. Minimum crop and production intensity levels had to be met both for land reserved for owners and for parcels assigned to settlers. While the INC reserved the right to expropriate land when the required intensity indexes were not reached, this measure was never enforced.

The conservative Irrigable Zones Act of 1949 was technically out-of-date because of the preference it gave to small 3–7 ha. family lots. Since a large part of the INC's resources were tied up in land expropriations and purchases, implementation of the act was slow. With a compensation mechanism of this nature, not only did the policy to increase agricultural productivity and total production suffer delay, but the redistribution of wealth and income did not take effect; this was because landowners were paid for their lands in cash, most of which was drawn from indirect taxes.

A summary of the work completed by the INC and by the Instituto de Reforma y Desarrollo Agrarios (IRYDA) since 1971 is broken down into three different periods in Table 3.2. For the first period (1939–62) we have employed data provided by the INC to the World Bank for its study on the Spanish economy. Information on the other two periods comes from statistical data compiled by the Ministries of Agriculture and Public Works and Urban Development. The number of tenants installed between 1939 and 1962 grew to 45,299. Huge investments in irrigation (no exact total can be offered due to a lack of data) benefitted a small few: the 45,299 tenants; landowners who, after irrigation systems were installed, held on to 72% of their land; and large purchasing companies (dealing in cotton, rice and sugar) set up on new irrigated lands. These companies virtually monopolised the purchasing rights to entire irrigation zones developed through public expenditure.

The INC and land reclamation policy in general should be criticised for tackling an excessive number of projects at the same time. In 1962, 71 projects at either the design or construction stage were envisaged for a total of 1 million ha. (with irrigation systems to

Table 3.2.   NEWLY IRRIGATED LANDS (*ha.*)

|  | *Annual averages* | *Accumulated surface area* |  | *Newly irrigated lands* | *Accumulated surface area* |
|---|---|---|---|---|---|
| 1939–52 | 9,707 | 9,707 | 1971 | 83,734 | 675,734 |
| 1953–6 | 18,097 | 82,096 | 1972 | 41,294 | 717,028 |
| 1957–60 | 21,987 | 170,043 | 1973 | 32,826 | 749,854 |
| 1961 | 17,004 | 204,860 | 1974 | 50,983 | 800,837 |
| 1962 | 19,345 | 224,205 | 1975 | 54,544 | 855,381 |
| 1963 | 23,153 | 247,358 | 1976 | 33,600 | 888,981 |
| 1964 | 31,099 | 278,457 | 1977 | 45,195 | 934,176 |
| 1965 | 43,434 | 321,891 | 1978 | 68,526 | 1,002,702 |
| 1966 | 46,288 | 368,179 | 1979 | 87,127 | 1,089,829 |
| 1967 | 34,242 | 402,421 | 1980 | 67,135 | 1,156,964 |
| 1968 | 74,209 | 476,630 | 1981 | 52,261 | 1,209,225 |
| 1969 | 47,165 | 523,795 | 1982 | 68,202 | 1,277,427 |
| 1970 | 68,205 | 592,000 |  |  |  |

|  |  |
|---|---|
| *Total irrigated land in 1982* | 2,914,000 |
| *Area theoretically irrigated in 1939* | 1,636,573 |

*Source:* Ministry of Agriculture.

be started up on 33,005 ha. that same year). The magnitude of the project unavoidably prevented deadlines being met, given available resources. Consequently, irrigation system start-ups were unnecessarily drawn out, tying up huge amounts of capital that produced nothing whatever for years. In 1971 all land reclamation acts published hitherto were codified in Act 118/1973 on *Agrarian Reform and Development*.

3.2.   *Land consolidation.*   Land consolidation is aimed at remedying the problems of excessive parcelling. The main drawback of excessive parcelling is the time employed in moving from one parcel of a farm to another. This economic waste was brought forward in a 1953 estimate in which the value of 'unproductive time' was calculated at 4,312 million ptas for the whole of Spain (some 73,000 million translated into 1983 values). Moreover, the loss of fertile farmland to boundaries grows as parcel sizes decrease. Thus parcelling cut into large areas of crop land. The minifundia also makes the use of modern machinery, irrigation and the war against pests and soil erosion difficult, if not impossible. Parcel division, a serious matter in the northern half of Spain, takes on alarming dimensions in the provinces of Castile, Leon, Galicia and Asturias.

Jovellanos, one of the Spanish *ilustrados* of the seventeenth century, who showed his concern over the latifundia in his *Report on Agrarian Law*, bemoaned the subdivision of land to the point of making it useless in one of his letters on Asturias: 'I would like to see one law to stop the disastrous subdivision of land in Asturias and another to encourage the division of vast estates in Andalusia.' Other Spanish writers also underlined the problem and its importance, and discussed possible solutions: Fermín Caballero, in a work published in 1863; Diego Pazos in 1900; various writers in the *Bulletin of the Agrarian Reform Institute* (1932–6); others at the El Duero Regional Congress in 1946 and the National Agronomical Engineering Congress in 1950; and so on.

Some legal provisions fostered the consolidation of parcels, such as the Acts of 11 July 1866 (on groups of neighbouring landholdings belonging to one owner) and of 3 June 1868 (on the right to own indivisible holdings), and the second part of article 1056 of the Civil Code. None of these provisions had any effect. In 1907, a year when undeniable concern, promoted by González-Besada, the Minister of Public Works and the Economy, took root in Spain for agrarian legislation, a commission was appointed to study the 'subdivision of land and its legal, social and agronomical causes, conditions and effects, and to propose solutions to the problems posed for farmers, rural stability and agricultural progress by excessive subdivision.' The report prepared by this commission and the bill it proposed contained all the groundwork for an effective land consolidation policy. Nevertheless, the bill was not enacted at that time, although similar laws had already been in force in Europe (basically Germany and Switzerland) since the 1870s.

It was not until forty-five years later, on 20 October 1952, that the first experimental law on land consolidation was finally promulgated in Spain. A subsequent act, that of 20 July 1955, was revised in 1962 and 1968 in respect of rural planning (Act 54/68 of 27 July), and the entire process was encapsulated in the Act 118/1973 on Agrarian Reform and Development, which we have already mentioned.

The objective of land consolidation operations is to apportion to each owner one consolidated holding or a much smaller number of parcels equal in size, kind of terrain and crop variety to what he formerly owned, and to provide new parcels with access to roads. These operations are entrusted to the Servicio Nacional de Concentración Parcelaria y Ordenación Rural (SNCPOR — the National Land Consolidation and Rural Planning Service), today part of the IRYDA, and carried out in municipalities where 60% or more of the landowners, or landowners representing 60% or more of

Fig. 8. ONE CASE OF LAND CONSOLIDATION IN THE NORTHERN *MESETA* (La Mudarra, Valladolid)

This figure offers a typical case of land consolidation in La Mudarra, Valladolid. Note the difference between the tattered 'before' diagram (typical of minifundiary areas) and the more rational 'after' diagram.

The 'general consolidation summary' (see table on left) shows the overall change in the town. The table on the right presents the 'owner standing before and after'; vertical and horizontal lines are used to distinguish between the two stages. In both cases, the owners have very little land by present-day farming standards.

Solutions to the problems of agricultural development in minifundiary zones, the subject of section 3.2, can only be found in comprehensive actions, not simply in the IRYDA's modest rural planning methods. Cooperatives should be developed at all levels, particularly in the area of land development.

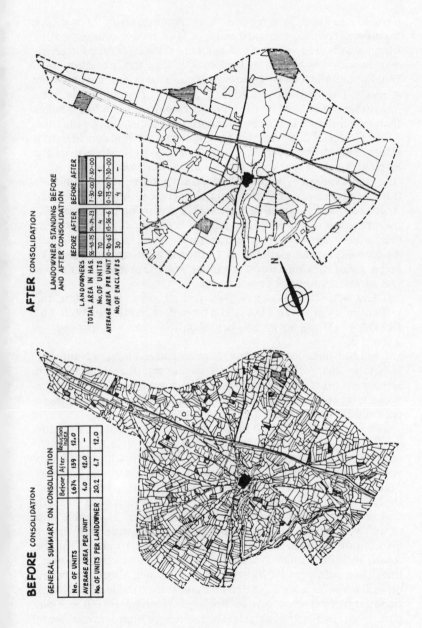

**BEFORE** CONSOLIDATION

GENERAL SUMMARY ON CONSOLIDATION

|  | Before | After | Reduction Index |
|---|---|---|---|
| No. OF UNITS | 1,674 | 159 | 12.0 |
| AVERAGE AREA PER UNIT | 12.0 | 12.0 | – |
| No. OF UNITS PER LANDOWNER | 20.2 | 1.7 | 12.0 |

**AFTER** CONSOLIDATION

LANDOWNER STANDING BEFORE AND AFTER CONSOLIDATION

| LANDOWNERS | BEFORE | AFTER | BEFORE | AFTER | BEFORE | AFTER | BEFORE | AFTER |
|---|---|---|---|---|---|---|---|---|
| TOTAL AREA IN HAS. | 36-45-75 | 54-24-23 | | | 7-30-00 | 7-30-00 | | |
| No.OF UNITS | 70 | 4 | 10 | 1 | | | | |
| AVERAGE AREA PER UNIT | 0-40-65 | 13-56-6 | | | 0-73-00 | 7-30-00 | | |
| No.OF ENCLAVES | 30 | | | | 4 | – | | |

N

the land (see Fig. 10), so request. A 'minimum crop unit' sets a limit for new parcels; a 'standard unit' of land is also established for farming with modern means. When land consolidation got started, owners with a total area of land smaller than the 'minimum unit' could obtain the loans necessary to acquire the additional land they needed. The parcels resulting from the regrouping become indivisible when their division produces one or more lots smaller than the minimum unit or the standard unit, depending on the case.

The Decree of 2 January 1964 strengthened the land consolidation effort with 'rural planning', an agrarian political instrument inspired by the French (*aménagement du territoire*), designed to 'raise the standard of living of the agrarian population by completely transforming areas and providing incentives to improve agrarian structures'. Rural planning includes the following operations: the redistribution of property to establish economically viable farms; the promotion of group agriculture; the fostering of farm modernisation; the planning of territorial improvements to make better use of existing natural resources; and the preparation of crop and agrarian industrial programmes.

These activities, along with irrigation projects, became the responsibility of the IRYDA at the time of its creation in 1971. The IRYDA's efforts towards consolidation are summarised in Table 3.3.

Land consolidation has many technical and economic advantages. It permits the use of agricultural machinery; the application of fertilisers; more successful war against pests; easier irrigation projects where water is available; and less workers being employed per hectare/year/yield.

The Spanish land consolidation effort has improved the situation of all landowners and therefore deserves praise. Nevertheless, if we consider the degree to which landowners have been helped and farms sufficiently upgraded, land consolidation stopped at the half-way point. In minifundiary zones where consolidation has been effected, the land is poorly distributed. Land consolidation dispelled the myth that 'land ownership is well distributed in Castile.' The arable land of the vast Castilian region has been fragmented into parcels, but the distribution of ownership, on a scale different from that of the south, is quite similar. Normally, 10% of landowners own more than half a municipality; consequently, all municipalities have ended up with a few large consolidated holdings at the local level and many small, irrational consolidated holdings. Turning fifteen 0.2 ha. parcels into two 1.5 ha. parcels is absolutely no improvement, when studies conducted in 1963 indicated that mechanised dry farming in the northern *meseta* required a minimum of 175 hectares.

Table 3.3.     EVOLUTION OF LAND CONSOLIDATION

|  | Requested consolidation (1,000s of Ha.) (A) | Consolidated areas (1,000s of Ha.) (B) |
|---|---|---|
| 1953 | 80.2 | — |
| 1954 | 27.5 | 7.8 |
| 1955 | 158.6 | 10.1 |
| 1956 | 176.5 | 10.8 |
| 1957 | 366.3 | 21.4 |
| 1958 | 242.7 | 51.4 |
| 1959 | 108.6 | 68.9 |
| 1960 | 180.0 | 72.7 |
| 1961 | 54.0 | 89.6 |
| 1962 | 415.5 | 101.1 |
| 1963 | 676.1 | 145.1 |
| 1964 | 440.0 | 206.2 |
| 1965 | 932.8 | 301.9 |
| 1966 | 489.8 | 351.1 |
| 1967 | 550.1 | 407.1 |
| 1968 | 264.0 | 382.1 |
| 1969 | 296.7 | 350.2 |
| 1970 | 319.6 | 356.6 |
| 1971 | 280.7 | 365.0 |
| 1972 | 371.2 | 303.1 |
| 1973 | 386.9 | 254.4 |
| 1974 | 301.6 | 257.0 |
| 1975 | 301.5 | 227.8 |
| 1976 | 216.1 | 171.5 |
| 1977 | 181.6 | 187.2 |
| 1978 | 168.0 | 97.1 |
| 1979 | 143.9 | 175.9 |
| 1980 | 261.7 | 208.6 |
| 1981 | — | 38.4 |
| 1982 | — | 90.7 |
| 1983 | — | 110.6 |
| *Total* |  | 5,431.5 |

*Source:* Ministry of Agriculture.

More than simple land consolidation, the country needed a *comprehensive programme* aimed at creating larger individually or collectively run farms that would make it possible to obtain substantial advantages of economies of scale. Up to a certain point, this is the present aim of the IRYDA in its areas of action. We have said 'up to a certain point' because the end-result of cutting down parcels and farms to minifundiary agricultural size is still a long way off.

3.3. *Legislation regarding large holdings. The IRYDA.* Part of the problem of *latifundia* was tackled with the Act of 3 December

## Fig. 9. GRAIN MARKETING AND FINANCING CHAIN

Here we have drawn the marketing and financing chain for Spanish grains (primarily wheat). Farmers sell their wheat to the Servicio Nacional de Productos Agrícolas (SENPA — National Agricultural Commodities Service), formerly the Servicio Nacional de Cereales (SNC — National Grain Service), a grain clearing house, and are paid in promissory notes discounted at private banking institutions. Banks, in turn, rediscount the notes at the Bank of Spain, where repayment is made through cash transfers sent by the SENPA as grain is sold to flour industries, livestock owners and mixed feed manufacturers.

Eventual surpluses that are amassed when harvests exceed domestic consumption are handled in two ways: through exports and through adulterated grain sales to livestock owners and mixed feed manufacturers. In both cases, SENPA's selling price is naturally much lower than that originally paid to farmers; the deficit resulting from these two operations (A + B) is covered by the Fondo de Orientación y Regulación de Productos y Precios Agrícolas (FORPPA — Commodities and Commodity Price Regulatory Fund), an agency that also supplies the SENPA with funds for *production subsidies*. The resources required by the FORPPA for subsidies and deficit coverings are provided by the Ministry of Finance, which draws from customs duties and regulatory tariffs levied against grains in which the country is deficient either regularly (corn) or sporadically (all other grains when harvests are poor).

The country's grain marketing chain is typical for non-perishable commodities, and therefore includes storage, both in SENPA silos and in farmers' granaries. Farmers receive premiums on base purchasing prices when they delay grain deliveries. A price maintenance chain for perishables would be much more complex than that analysed in this figure.

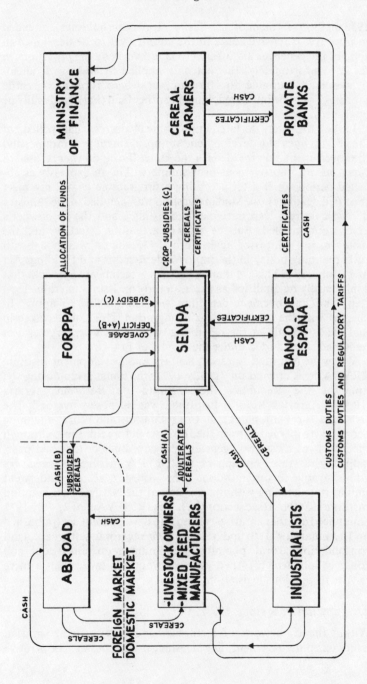

1953 on the 'treatment of manifestly improvable holdings', intended to improve 'extensive zones in the country yet to be developed in spite of the generous aid offered to landowners by the provisions in force'. Unfortunately, this act only applied to areas with uncultivated lands suitable for farming, or where forestry or cattle breeding could be improved, ignoring other land that could really be upgraded.

Large farms were declared improvable by decrees that spelled out the general lines of a development or improvement programme, and the government aid provided for the same. If a landowner refused to carry out an improvement programme within an expressly established period, or if after accepting a programme he did not meet specified deadlines, the land in question was included in the Ministry of Agriculture's 'expropriable land listing', and the landowner's taxes were doubled. But the act was actually ineffective, and the issue was not addressed again until 1971, when it was mixed with rural planning policy in the Improvable Regions and Holdings Act of 21 July 1971. This act manifested a new technical approach, that could hardly be qualified as agrarian reform. Its innumerable legal steps and improvement deadlines were impossible to apply. In keeping with the movement against agrarian reform undertaken in 'nationalist' Spain at the beginning of the civil war, large estates remained safeguarded under the regime of Franco.

When the National Agrarian Reform and Development Institute (IRYDA) was created on 21 July 1971, the name given during the time of the Republic, the Instituto de Reforma Agraria (IRA — Agrarian Reform Institute), was purposely avoided. The INC and the National Land Consolidation and Rural Planning Service were merged to form the IRYDA. Before this time, although the efforts of these two agencies were coordinated, they had overlapped; thus the founding of the IRYDA involved a necessary administrative reorganisation. The forestry sector underwent similar restructuring with the creation of the Natural Conservation Institute (ICONA) (see section 7.7). The IRYDA Act of 21 July 1971 announced another agrarian reform and development act (published on 12 January 1973) to update provisions regarding settlement, land consolidation, rural planning, minimum crop units and soil conservation, which turned out to be nothing more than a mere rewrite of previous legislation.

## 4. *Agrarian acts since 1977*

Within the framework of restored democracy, general agrarian issues (crop management, land leasing, pricing policy, cooperative enterprises, agrarian reform and development, farm insurance, farm council elections and land savings banks) were first discussed during the *Pactos de la Moncloa* (Moncloa Agreements — see Chapter 16), endorsed by the government and all parliamentary political parties on 27 October 1977. The agrarian programme envisaged in the Moncloa Agreements was developed unevenly, and genuine reform efforts were thwarted. There follows a summary of the main texts:

(*a*) *Crop Insurance*. Act 87/1978 of 28 December set out to make crop insurance common and inexpensive.

(*b*) *Manifestly Improvable Holdings*. Act 34/1979 of 16 November was to be applied to the following classes of estate:

(i) those that have not been worked for a minimum of two years;

(ii) those that have not put to use the means or resources made available by government-funded projects;

(iii) those comprising more than 50 ha. of irrigated land or 500 ha. of dry land or timberland suitable for intensive crop production.

Manifestly improvable holdings may also be included in the listing, in which case landowners are required to submit an improvement plan within two months. Should a landowner not react in time, the IRYDA may force-lease the land for up to twelve years or sublet it through competitive bidding.

(*c*) *Community Woodlands*. Act 55/1980 of 11 December is designed to return the woodlands to communities that have been dispossessed of them by municipalities, provincial assemblies or the state. To this effect community woodlands are considered as property that is indivisible, inalienable, imprescriptible and which cannot under any circumstances be seized.

(*d*) *Land Leasing*. Act 83/1980 of 31 December limits leasing rights to 500 ha. for dry land and 50 ha. for irrigated land. With extensions, a tenant can hold on to land for up to twenty years, at the end of which he is paid for improvements made and has the right to purchase the land should it be put up for sale.

(*e*) *Farm Prices*. In March 1981, following much lengthy negotiation, landowner representatives joined the General Council of the FORPPA, the public agency through which agricultural prices are set, to study regulatory prices and submit proposals to the government. This issue was later rounded out with Act 19/1982 of 26 May on commodity trading.

(*f*) *Pending matters.* Areas contemplated in the Moncloa Agreements but still to be dealt with are the management of crops, co-operatives and farm associations, the preparation of a new agrarian reform and development act, and the true democratisation of land savings banks as co-operative credit institutions. Projects are also planned for idle land, land left by emigrants, ways to give young farmers access to property, by-laws on family farming, soil and livestock hygiene, and the acceleration of land consolidation. The protection of mountain agriculture is regulated under Act 25/1982 of 30 June.

## 5. *Agricultural pricing policy*

In 1936 various institutions involved in agricultural commodity markets sprouted up: the Servicio Nacional de Trigo (SNT — National Wheat Service), which first became the Servicio Nacional de Cereales (SNC — National Grain Service), and is today called the Servicio Nacional de Productos Agrarios (SEN-PA — National Agricultural Commodities Service); the Comisión de Compras de Excedentes de Vinos (Wine Surplus Purchasing Commission), now phased out; and the Comisaría General de Abastecimientos y Transportes (a state agency for foodstuff trading activities, today consolidated in the FORPPA). A certain consistency was given to this sporadic process in 1968 with the creation of the Fondo de Orientación y Regulación de Productos y Precios Agrícolas (FORPPA — Commodities and Commodity-Price Regulatory Fund). This agency was clearly inspired by the French Commodity Market Regulation Fund, which was also used as a model for the European Agricultural Regulation and Guarantee Fund (FEOGA). Each year the FORPPA establishes the seasonal prices of regulated commodities: grain, beets, wine, meat, milk etc. It later acts either directly or indirectly in the marketplace to prevent real prices from diving under or soaring above regulated prices. Each year the FORPPA draws up a financial plan summarising its estimates for all its activities (subsidies, purchases etc.).

A strong relationship exists between different agricultural price levels. Table 3.4 shows the evolution of the *general index* for prices received by farmers for regulated and non-regulated commodities since 1964. In the same table we can also see the index for *prices paid* by farmers for input purchases (seeds, machinery, fertilisers, fuel etc.). The ratio for prices paid and received, given in the last column, is the parity index, which measures price improvements (> 100) or deteriorations (< 100).

Table 3.4.   INDEX OF PRICES RECEIVED AND PAID BY
FARMERS

|  | *Prices received* | *Prices paid* | *Parity prices* |
|---|---|---|---|
| 1964 (*base year*) | 100.0 | 100.0 | 100.0 |
| 1965 | 116.5 | 103.3 | 112.7 |
| 1966 | 120.8 | 106.4 | 113.5 |
| 1967 | 117.2 | 108.9 | 107.6 |
| 1968 | 124.8 | 110.0 | 113.4 |
| 1969 | 131.1 | 111.7 | 117.3 |
| 1970 | 128.5 | 114.6 | 112.1 |
| 1971 | 136.5 | 119.9 | 113.8 |
| 1972 | 151.0 | 121.6 | 124.1 |
| 1973 | 169.7 | 135.1 | 111.1 |
| 1974 | 184.5 | 175.9 | 104.8 |
| 1975 | 215.5 | 190.0 | 113.4 |
| 1976 | 237.8 | 207.8 | 114.3 |
|  |  |  |  |
| 1976 (*base year*) | 100.0 | 100.0 | 100.0 |
| 1977 | 126.3 | 114.0 | 108.4 |
| 1978 | 142.8 | 128.5 | 110.8 |
| 1979 | 152.1 | 146.6 | 106.8 |
| 1980 | 156.8 | 173.6 | 89.6 |
| 1981 | 176.8 | 206.1 | 85.8 |
| 1982 | 204.9 | 228.1 | 90.2 |
| 1983 | 223.8 | 264.0 | 84.8 |
| 1984 | 245.4 | 318.2 | 77.1 |

*Source:* Ministry of Agriculture.

## 6. *Agrarian structure today*

Having covered the role of agrarian policy within agricultural
development, we now have enough background information to look
at the present-day structure of agriculture and its three main factors:
land, labour and capital. Land, the first factor of production, is
divided up by kinds of crops, kinds of farming (dry and irrigation),
farming systems, and forms of land ownership. As for labour, since
we have already addressed the working population in general in an
earlier chapter, this section will focus on the contribution of the
agricultural working population. Agricultural capital, the stock of
goods which are used in production and which have themselves been
produced, are all the components involved in production except for
land and labour; they include machinery and fertilisers. However,
irrigation and other projects, although genuine agricultural capital,
will be referred to under the section on land, since they have become
part of it.

6.1. *Land and its distribution.*   Of Spain's 50 million ha., 8% is unproductive, 51% is woodland and pastureland, and the remaining 41% (20.7 million hectares) is arable land. Therefore, 92% of Spain, more than 45 million hectares, is made up of usable land. This percentage is similar to that of other European countries, even though Spain's yields are much lower, given the climate of the country.

Two characteristics clearly mark Spanish agriculture when one considers land distribution by crop. First, more than 60% of all arable land is left fallow, and secondly, a huge area of land is covered by tree and bush crops, particularly olive trees and grapevines. Grain, olive oil and wine are the three key products of dry farming in Spain.

Spain has approximately 3 million ha. of irrigated farmlands, which represent 14.4% of cultivated lands. The main irrigated areas include the Ebro basin (La Rioja and La Ribera, the Aragon Canal, the Imperial Canal, the Lower Ebro and Upper Aragon irrigated lands), Levante (the irrigated lands of Valencia and Murcia), Andalusia (the irrigated lands of Almanzora, Motril, Las Marismas, Vega de Granada and the Jaén Plain) and Extremadura (La Vera de Plasencia and the irrigated lands of the Badajoz Plain). The *meseta* (the irrigated lands of Talavera, Aranjuez and Arganda in New Castile and the Castile Canal and other systems in the northern *meseta*) has been less developed (see Fig. 7).

Studies completed by the Ministry of Agriculture conclude that there are 1,750,000 ha. of unclaimed irrigable lands: 1,350,000 ha. could be irrigated by surface waters; and 400,000 ha. could be supplied by groundwaters. This gives Spain a maximum irrigation area of 4.75 million ha. Investment in irrigation systems is, without a doubt, one of the most profitable forms of investment in Spain given the high returns. Nevertheless, Spain has to maximise existing irrigation systems before any new projects should really be embarked on.

Another basic issue regarding land distribution is the parcelling of land and the number and size of farms, Spain being heavily parcelled and the number of farms very great. Many farms comprise small operations on scattered plots. This poor design has been somewhat mitigated by farmers who, apart from working their own land, develop other land under a tenancy or share-cropping system. According to the latest agrarian census, the average size of farms is 19.9 ha. Table 3.5 summarises the parcelling situation based on the 1962, 1972 and 1982 agrarian censuses.

At the other end of the scale lurks the problem of latifundia or large holdings. A 1969 survey showed that 5,722 private holdings had more than 500 ha. For obvious reasons, this figure was less than that given for farms larger than 500 ha. (10,200 in 1972).

Table 3.5. PARCELLING IN 1962 AND 1972

| Size of parcel | Thousands of parcels | | |
|---|---|---|---|
| | *1962* | *1972* | *1982* |
| Less than 0.5 ha. | 34,879 { | 18,392 ⎫ | |
| 0.5–0.99 ha. | { | 4,152 | 20.496 |
| 1–4.99 ha. | 3,460 | 3,682 | |
| 5 or more ha. | 653 | 830 ⎭ | |
| Total number of holding (in thousands) | 38,992 | 27,056 | 20,496 |
| Census surface area in thousands of ha. | 44,649 | 45,634 | 44,312 |
| Average surface area per parcel (ha.) | 1.1450 | 1.6866 | 2.1619 |

*Source:* Agrarian Censuses, 1962, 1972 and 1982.

Latifundism abounds in Andalusia, Extremadura, La Mancha and Salamanca. It is characterised by low yields, absenteeism, disproportionate income distribution and capital flight to cities; landowners are generally unwilling to set up irrigation systems and undertake intensive crop farming. The sociological and political consequences of latifundism are still strongly felt. In latifundiary Spain, there are vast numbers of seasonal workers who go long periods unemployed. These are areas of serious cultural backwardness, where intense social and political grievances are felt. Till recently the most ardent desire of most landless farm labourers in latifundiary areas was that the large estates should be shared out, but this attitude is now undergoing profound changes. Farm labourers who cling to their work in the field want higher wages, better housing, social security and schools, and a future for their children. Many of them no longer see their salvation in the mere distribution of land into individual plots, for they realise that, in an era of mechanisation and improved agricultural technology, minimum family dry farming units do not offer desirable standards of living. Although they may not always clearly say so, farm labourers are looking for new jobs in enterprising companies to raise their living standards.

Also important is the way cultivated land is distributed by farm tenancy systems. In 1972 tenants and share croppers worked 26.5% of all farmland (12.1 million ha.), of which more than 50% suffered from the structural problem of absenteeism. Recently this problem has been eased since in effect most of the small absentee landowners (emigrants and their relatives) no longer act as landowners; farm operators now make most of the important decisions in the absence of proprietors who are concerned less and less with their land, and who no longer even return to work it directly.

Despite their legal safeguards, tenancy and share-cropping systems are not without their disadvantages. The principal one is that not enough incentives are built into the system to encourage farm workers to improve land that is not theirs. Land distribution among owners and the relative importance of tenancy or farming systems are reflected in Table 3.6.

Although considerable changes have been seen since 1972, there are many areas where extremes still govern farm distribution: there are a great number of small farms (92.9% of the total, on only 28.5% of the land), few average-type farms (3.7% on a little more than 18% of the land) and a waning number of large estates (less than 2%) on almost the majority of the land (50.9%).

Small farms generally lack the economic resources to make the best use of their land. The use of machinery can be uneconomic, posing overwhelming financial difficulties. Technical assessments are almost always disappointing: routine ploughing, dim prospects due to a lack of training, unacceptable accounting systems, and often a defeatist if not a fatalistic attitude. The economic and technical situation of large farms is appreciably better, but it is still far from satisfactory. It is strange that, despite all the social and political changes introduced, there continue to be many large and medium-sized estate owners who are not real farmers, spending most of their time away from their land (semi-absenteeism).

6.2. *Fixed and working capital.* Capital, the third factor of agriculture, includes fertilisers and fungicides, machinery and farm animals (the last of these components is falling into disuse). The comparatively low yields per hectare and per labourer obtained in the different sectors of Spanish agriculture can only be raised through greater spending, irrigation systems and better use of these components.

Spain's insufficient and irregular rainfall makes fertiliser use difficult; Table 3.7 offers some figures on fertiliser consumption in recent years. Although dry farming in Spain will never reach the levels of fertilisation of, say, the Netherlands, the greater use of irrigation and modern methods for dry farming certain crops has increased fertiliser consumption considerably. The scarcity of fertilisers was the main reason for the slow recovery of Spanish agriculture after the civil war. Not until mineral fertiliser supplies returned to normal in the 1950s did production levels per hectare begin to regain their pre-war levels. The same happened with fungicides and insecticides.

Table 3.6. DISTRIBUTION OF FARMS BY SIZE, 1962, 1972 AND 1982

| Kind and size | No. of farms | | | | | | Surface area | | | | | |
|---|---|---|---|---|---|---|---|---|---|---|---|---|
| | 1962 | | 1972 | | 1982 | | 1962 | | 1972 | | 1982 | |
| | ×1000 | % | ×1000 | % | ×1000 | % | 10³ ha. | % | 10³ ha. | % | 10³ ha. | % |
| Without land | 151 | 5.0 | 4 | 1.7 | 31 | 1.3 | — | — | — | — | — | — |
| With land | 2,856 | 94.9 | 2,515 | 98.3 | 2,344 | 98.6 | 44,649 | 100.0 | 45,634 | 100.0 | 44,312 | 100.0 |
| Small | 2,751 | 91.5 | 2,396 | 93.6 | 2,220 | 92.9 | 17,120 | 38.3 | 15,475 | 33.9 | 13,183 | 28.5 |
| 0.0–0.9 | 806 | 26.8 | 582 | 22.7 | 595 | 24.9 | 351 | 0.8 | 291 | 0.6 | 265 | 0.5 |
| 1–4.9 | 1,031 | 34.3 | 979 | 38.2 | 881 | 36.9 | 2,667 | 6.0 | 2,529 | 5.6 | 2,127 | 4.7 |
| 5–49.9 | 914 | 30.4 | 835 | 32.7 | 744 | 31.1 | 14,102 | 31.5 | 12,655 | 27.7 | 10,791 | 24.0 |
| Medium | 76 | 2.5 | 88 | 3.4 | 93 | 3.7 | 7,045 | 15.8 | 8,265 | 18.1 | 8,489 | 18.9 |
| 50–99.9 | 52 | 1.7 | 59 | 2.3 | 62 | 2.5 | 3,645 | 8.2 | 4,140 | 9.1 | 4,234 | 9.4 |
| 100–199.9 | 24 | 0.8 | 29 | 1.1 | 31 | 1.2 | 3,400 | 7.6 | 4,125 | 9.0 | 4,255 | 9.5 |
| Large | 29 | 1.0 | 31 | 1.2 | 31 | 1.1 | 20,484 | 45.9 | 21,894 | 48.0 | 26,650 | 50.9 |
| 200–499.9 | 17 | 0.6 | 19 | 0.7 | 19 | 0.7 | 5,450 | 12.2 | 6,100 | 13.4 | 5,887 | 13.2 |
| 500–999.9 | 7 | 0.2 | 7 | 0.3 | 7 | 0.2 | 5,250 | 11.8 | 5,250 | 11.5 | 4,777 | 10.7 |
| 1000 or more | 5 | 0.2 | 5 | 0.2 | 5 | 0.2 | 9,784 | 21.9 | 10,544 | 23.1 | 11,974 | 27.0 |
| | 3,007 | 100.0 | 2,559 | 100.0 | 2,375 | 100.0 | 44,649 | 100.0 | 45,634 | 100.0 | 44,312 | 100.0 |

*Sources:* Agrarian Censuses, 1962 and 1972.

Table 3.7. FERTILISER CONSUMPTION

| | Fertilisable surface area (1,000 ha.) | Nitrogen | | Phosphorus | | Potash | |
|---|---|---|---|---|---|---|---|
| | | Total (1,000 tonnes) | Kg./ha. | Total (1,000 tonnes) | Kg./ha. | Total (1,000 tonnes) | Kg./ha. |
| 1970 | 16,978 | 615 | 36.2 | 399 | 23.5 | 211 | 12.4 |
| 1975 | 17,156 | 749 | 43.7 | 488 | 28.4 | 263 | 15.3 |
| 1976 | 17,007 | 748 | 44.0 | 470 | 27.6 | 279 | 16.4 |
| 1977 | 16,734 | 850 | 50.8 | 478 | 28.6 | 288 | 17.2 |
| 1978 | 16,955 | 793 | 46.8 | 434 | 25.6 | 273 | 16.1 |
| 1979 | 16,794 | 903 | 53.8 | 456 | 27.2 | 282 | 16.8 |
| 1980 | 17,057 | 985 | 57.7 | 473 | 27.8 | 295 | 17.2 |
| 1981 | 16,965 | 806 | 47.5 | 420 | 24.8 | 254 | 15.0 |
| 1982 | 17,222 | 884 | 50.5 | 405 | 23.1 | 255 | 14.6 |
| 1983 | 17,514 | 686 | 39.2 | 366 | 20.9 | 225 | 12.8 |

AGRICULTURAL MACHINERY

| | Tractors (M) | Walking tractors (WT) | | Harvesters (H) | | HP/100 ha. | |
|---|---|---|---|---|---|---|---|
| | Units | 1,000 HP | Units | 1,000 HP | 1,000 units | Only T+WT | T+WT+H |
| 1970 | 260 | 11,642 | 72 | 619 | 31.5 | 59.8 | 75.8 |
| 1975 | 379 | 13,719 | 148 | 1,736 | 39.7 | 98.2 | 120.5 |
| 1976 | 401 | 20,260 | 164 | 2,019 | 41.2 | 107.8 | 132.1 |
| 1977 | 421 | 21,738 | 181 | 2,324 | 42.0 | 116.8 | 132.1 |
| 1978 | 456 | 23,654 | 194 | 2,497 | 43.4 | 125.5 | 150.7 |
| 1979 | 492 | 25,711 | 206 | 2,664 | 44.6 | 136.2 | 162.4 |
| 1980 | 524 | 27,731 | 221 | 2,834 | 41.6 | 149.1 | 176.6 |
| 1981 | 548 | 29,117 | 231 | 2,989 | 42.4 | 156.7 | 184.7 |
| 1982 | 569 | 30,018 | 231 | 3,133 | 42.7 | 155.3 | 187.5 |
| 1983 | 593 | 31,785 | 247 | 3,207 | 44.0 | 168.0 | 195.6 |

*Source:* Ministry of Agriculture.

The growing number and total capacity of tractors employed in agriculture provides the clearest idea of the country's degree of farm mechanisation (see Table 3.7). The main problem presented by machinery is the high cost of its purchase and maintenance and its uncertain economic advantages on smallholdings. One increasingly popular formula is that of renting farm machinery, such as fully equipped combines and threshing machines.

## 7. *Final agricultural output and net returns*

Land, labour and capital are, in accounting terms, the three factors of production in agriculture. Actually the amount of labour and capital put into 1 hectare of land gives us yields per hectare. As more and more labour and capital are invested, yields steadily increase until they reach a point of diminishing returns. Most Spanish farmland is still at a stage of increasing returns, and therefore larger doses of labour, capital and improved technology can still boost production. This means that in the coming years agricultural production could take off, provided that the necessary investments and structural changes are made and that Spain's accession to the EEC proves helpful.

To this effect, the development of forced cultivation (through the use of hothouses, plastic, layers of sand, hydroponics (cultivation with water and nutrients only, without soil), drip irrigation, sprinklers, etc.) makes it possible to obtain high early yields and delicate crops. There is also a great potential for growth through agrogenetics by employing select seeds and hybrids and through biological warfare to control pests. Unfortunately, Spain's advances in agriculture have not been very brilliant on any of these fronts. Notable exceptions, however, are Almería, the Costa del Sol of Granada, Huelva and the Canary islands, where new agricultural technology is most widely used.

The economic importance of Spain's agricultural sector is best expressed by net agricultural returns or yield indicators. Since 1954 the accuracy of the Ministry of Agriculture's estimates on net agricultural returns has steadily increased. The preparation of these estimates is based on the method recommended by the Economic Commission for Europe, which has been slightly modified so that it can be properly applied to statistical data available in Spain. According to Table 3.8, summarising the 1981 study completed by the Ministry of Agriculture, final agricultural output is equal to the difference between total agricultural output and the output put back into the system (re-employment). Consequently, final agricultural

Table 3.8.  AGRARIAN MACRO-ECONOMIC INDICATORS
( × *1,000 million ptas*)

| | 1980 | 1981 | 1982 | 1983 |
|---|---|---|---|---|
| Total agrarian production | 1,842.7 | 1,950.2 | 2,252.8 | 2,580.6 |
| Re-employment | 351.6 | 385.0 | 425.3 | 468.8 |
| Final agrarian production (A–B) | 1,491.1 | 1,565.2 | 1,827.5 | 2,111.8 |
| Agriculture | 834.8 | 807.2 | 959.1 | 1,134.7 |
| Cattle raising | 571.3 | 663.9 | 770.3 | 870.3 |
| Forestry | 45.8 | 51.5 | 53.6 | 56.5 |
| Improvements | 39.2 | 42.6 | 44.6 | 50.3 |
| Expenses in non-agrarian sector | 543.6 | 665.1 | 758.2 | 899.8 |
| Gross Added Value at market prices (C–D) | 947.5 | 900.1 | 1,069.3 | 1,212.0 |
| Subsidies | 32.6 | 43.4 | 46.8 | 64.0 |
| Gross Added Value at factor cost (E + F) | 980.2 | 943.5 | 1,161.1 | 1,276.1 |
| Depreciation | 58.4 | 68.0 | 79.3 | 89.8 |
| Net product (G–H) | 921.8 | 875.5 | 1,081.8 | 1,186.2 |

*Source:* Ministry of Agriculture.

output does not include intermediate production (seeds, natural fertilisers, milk used on the farm etc.) or sales made between farms for the purpose of final agricultural production. Net agricultural returns and the agricultural sector's share of national income (today estimated to be 8%) can be determined from final agricultural output.

Turning quickly to the subject of Spain's agricultural balance of trade, the country's rural sector has always been a key part of foreign relations, generally showing a highly favourable export balance. Nevertheless a higher standard of living (with which goes a greater demand for meat and, in turn, for maize and soybeans), a growing timber deficit, and traditional coffee, cocoa, cotton and tobacco imports have been giving Spain a trade deficit since the early 1970s.

In Table 3.9 the breakdown of *main product groups* within final agricultural production indicates the relative importance of each group. The surface area and production levels of these groups can be seen in Table 3.10.

7.1. *Grains.*  Grain-cultivated farmland, totalling more than 12 million ha., (including fallow land) represents 10% of all cultivated farmland in Spain. Final grain production levels are normally less than 10% of total agricultural output. In other words, land devoted to grain cultivation is generally low-yielding. Most grains are grown

Table 3.9. FINAL AGRARIAN PRODUCTION
*(at current prices)*

| | 1979 | | 1980 | |
|---|---|---|---|---|
| | *(×1 million ptas)* | % | *(×1 million ptas)* | % |
| Meat and poultry | 376,100.6 | 25.3 | 374,410 | 27.2 |
| Vegetables | 173,545.7 | 11.9 | 247,081 | 11.7 |
| Grains | 182,556.1 | 12.2 | 185,838 | 8.8 |
| Milk | 133,178.0 | 8.9 | 196,397 | 9.3 |
| Fruit (except citrus) | 110,817.0 | 7.4 | 181,615 | 8.6 |
| Industrial crops | 71,012.0 | 4.7 | 107,702 | 5.1 |
| Potatoes | 51,559.2 | 3.4 | 63,354 | 3.0 |
| Eggs | 53,225.9 | 3.5 | 126,708 | 6.0 |
| Wine | 86,274.6 | 3.8 | 71,801 | 3.4 |
| Vegetable oil | 53,733.0 | 3.6 | 101,366 | 4.8 |
| Citrus fruit | 48,758.2 | 3.2 | 69,689 | 3.3 |
| Wood products | 27,950.0 | 1.8 | 2,112 | 0.1 |
| Legumes | 11,506.5 | 0.7 | 10,559 | 0.5 |
| Hunting and fishing | 12,600.0 | 0.8 | 21,118 | 1.0 |
| Other products | 92,183.2 | 6.5 | 152,050 | 7.2 |
| *Total* | 1,485,000.0 | 100.0 | 2,111,800 | 100.0 |

*Source*: Ministry of Agriculture.

in the interior of the country, and the characteristics of those areas set grain cultivation in Spain apart from that in the rest of Europe. In the battle against meagre rainfall and poor, shallow soil, Spaniards have for centuries been using farming techniques that, although frequently criticised in a simplistic manner, are not very different from American dry farming procedures. The most important of these techniques are crop rotation and fallow land practices; more than 5 million ha. are usually left idle for one or more years to recover humidity and the organic inputs of natural grasses and fertilisers.

The amount of land used for wheat cultivation has been rising since the turn of the century. Up to 1936 this growth was basically due to heightened protectionism. Between 1939 and 1947 the total of wheat-cultivated areas shrank due to problems such as shortages of farm animals and fertilisers. After 1948, however, wheat-cultivated farmlands surpassed the 1931–5 average, and kept on growing. This trend was decisively influenced by the policy initiated in 1937 by the Servicio Nacional de Trigo (SNT — the National Wheat Service), which thereafter set prices so as to guarantee national supplies.

The 'wheat' policy began to undergo modifications in 1967, when feedgrain prices rose in a move to encourage more feedgrain

Table 3.10.   SURFACE AREA (× 1,000 ha.) AND
AGRICULTURAL PRODUCTION (× 1,000 tonnes)

|  | Surface area | | | Production | | |
|---|---|---|---|---|---|---|
|  | 1983 | 1984 | 1985 | 1983 | 1984 | 1985 |
| *Grains* | | | | | | |
| Wheat | 2,603 | 2,267 | 2,025 | 4,268 | 6,044 | 5,326 |
| Barley | 3,735 | 3,944 | 4,550 | 6,662 | 10,695 | 10,680 |
| Oats | 454 | 473 | 465 | 454 | 473 | 719 |
| Rye | 217 | 233 | 222 | 217 | 233 | 295 |
| Maize | 354 | 435 | 516 | 1,803 | 2,505 | 3,328 |
| Sorghum | 20 | 22 | 20 | 79 | 102 | 92 |
| Rice | 41 | 73 | 74 | 224 | 452 | 457 |
| *Legumes* | | | | | | |
| Lentils | 65 | 64 | 64 | 37 | 44 | 51 |
| Chickpeas | 91 | 88 | 88 | 49 | 60 | 58 |
| Beans | 110 | 113 | 106 | 77 | 75 | 80 |
| *Fruit and Vegetables* | | | | | | |
| Oranges | 139 | 139 | — | 2,067 | 1,889 | 1,852 |
| Mandarins | 51 | 51 | — | 1,234 | 1,009 | 993 |
| Lemons | 47 | 47 | — | 544 | 499 | 457 |
| Apples | 68 | 68 | — | 1,075 | 1,019 | 1,057 |
| Pears | 39 | 39 | — | 551 | 489 | 576 |
| Table grapes | 83 | 83 | — | 500 | 556 | 568 |
| Bananas | 12 | 12 | — | 455 | 457 | 416 |
| Potatoes | 340 | 343 | 327 | 5,163 | 5,950 | 5,770 |
| Tomatoes | 60 | 65 | 62 | 2,349 | 2,553 | 2,418 |
| Onions | 32 | 34 | 37 | 959 | 1,114 | 1,258 |
| *Wine production ($10^6$ hl.)* | 1,618 | 1,618 | — | 30,913 | 35,537 | 32,770 |
| *Olive production* | | | | | | |
| Olives used in oil production | 1,935 | 1,930 | — | 1,252 | 3,078 | 1,642 |
| Olive oil | — | — | — | 266 | 658 | 355 |
| *Industrial crop production* | | | | | | |
| Sugar beet | 241 | 209 | 178 | — | — | |
| Raw cotton | 40 | 60 | 60 | 121 | 159 | |
| Sugar | — | — | — | 1,178 | — | |
| Tobacco | 23 | — | — | 45 | — | |

*Source:* Ministry of Agriculture.

cultivation so as to meet the growing livestock demand. For this reason, wheat production figures fell, stabilising at 4–5 million tonnes, while feed grain production, particularly that of barley and corn, began its ascent. This process is quite logical bearing in mind Engel's Law as it applies to the case of wheat: i.e. *per capita* consumption diminishes as incomes increase, which is a statistically proven fact; the *per capita* consumption of 110 kg. of bread grains in recent years is lower than the *per capita* consumption levels of the 1920s (fluctuating around 150 kg.) and of the 1945–55 period (estimated at 130 kg.).

Before the civil war, the national wheat exchange, free of state intervention, experienced sharp price fluctuations, affecting the incomes of farmers. To put an end to this problem, shortly after the outbreak of the civil war, the Junta Técnica del Estado de Burgos (the Technical State Junta of Burgos), the first Franco government, decided to set up the SNT by virtue of the so-called Wheat Management Decree of 23 August 1937, — which, as we have seen, was subsequently transformed into the SNC in 1964 and the SENPA in 1971. The service was originally established to manage the production and distribution of wheat and its main by-products and to regulate purchasing, mobilisation and prices. Today these activities are still the responsibility of the SENPA (Fig. 9). Traditionally, the SENPA had sole wheat purchasing rights at the official price set each year. Moreover, this service was the only flour supplier for the industry and the only surplus exporter. From 1970 onwards, more flexible formulas were adopted, and in 1984, in accordance with EEC policy, wheat trading was decontrolled, ending the SENPA's monopoly, although prices continued to be regulated.

For the purpose of purchase financing, the SENPA had the necessary economic means at its disposal, since the banking system had agreed to provide sufficient credit. The service pays farmers with certificates that can be discounted at banks and rediscounted at the Banco de España. When the service began taking over harvests, it tried to overcome the storage problem by establishing a system of progressively higher prices for delayed deliveries. The main body of the deliveries, however, came immediately after the harvest, forcing the service to build its own silos — which today form part of Spain's rural landscape.

Remaining grains are called *secondary grains*, or feed grains, and include barley, maize, oats and, to a less degree, rye. These grains are behind high cattle raising yields. Until the 1967–8 crop year secondary grain production, with the exception of maize, followed a regressive trend, stemming from the 'wheat' policy mentioned earlier. In 1939 a marked preference was shown for wheat cultivation in dry regions, since the SNT assured healthy wheat prices. The cultivation of maize, the only grain advanced, expanded because most maize croplands are unsuitable for wheat, and because excellent maize yields can be obtained through the use of hybrids. From its creation the SNT, in theory, acted as a secondary grain purchaser which bought at state regulated prices that were actually lower than market prices, and therefore never stimulated an expansion in production. This imbalance harmed Spain's cattle raising and, over the long-term, forced the country to place heavy reliance on imports of grain and particularly meat, spending more in foreign currency purchases than was saved by being partly self-sufficient in wheat supplies. This situation changed during the 1967–8 crop year, when state intervention held wheat prices constant while raising feed grain prices and production levels.

*Rice* production in Spain has some special characteristics. Levante is the country's main rice growing area. While the most prosperous districts are in the irrigated plain of Valencia, especially the area around the lake of Albufera, abundant harvests are also reaped in the marshes of the Guadalquivir delta and the new irrigated lands of the Badajoz Plain. Large rice surpluses emerged in the 1960s, and by 1978 quotas were imposed. The SENPA buys rice offered by farmers at interventionist prices and sets up regulatory stocks. Rice, the only Spanish grain with a certain export tradition, can only be exported at low prices if it is to compete with the great rice-exporting countries that have either an enormous cheap labour force (e.g. Burma and Thailand) or government-subsidised prices (e.g. the United States).

7.2. *Fruit production.*   Fruit is one of the country's most important agricultural commodities. Groves of fruit trees cover 700,000 ha., or a little more than 3% of all the cultivated land in Spain; and final fruit production represents 10% of final agricultural output. These two figures — cultivated area and final output — show that in purely physical terms fruit growing is highly productive.

Fruit production is marked by two main characteristics. First, all varieties of fruit production are on the rise, since fruit consumption increases as incomes grow. In recent years the demand for fruit has climbed throughout the whole of Europe. This leads us to the second characteristic: the importance of fruit exports for Spanish foreign trade.

Citrus fruits are the most heavily exported, *oranges* being the most popular. Until the twentieth century, the market for Spanish oranges was a local one only but by the middle of this century the effects of the industrial revolution (which turned Western European countries into great fruit consumers) and steam navigation fostered the expanded production and export of oranges. After 1849, when the first crate of oranges was exported to England, the amount of oranges consumed domestically fell in relative terms, until the Spanish market represented a very small percentage of total production; Spain's domestic consumption later began to creep upwards as incomes rose. Not until the Second World War interrupted exports was greater attention given to the domestic market, a market which today can absorb more than 700,000 tons of average to high-quality oranges a year.

Orange exports became one of the main pillars of Spanish foreign trade and the driving force of development in Valencia and Murcia, which contain the main production areas. In recent crop years exports have reached almost 2,000,000 tons, 80% of which goes to the Common Market and EFTA countries. However, between 1950 and 1970 Spain's relative share in the European market, the destination of all Mediterranean products, fell while the market for Italian, Israeli and Algerian oranges steadily increased. Moreover, having had virtually no market share before the Second World War, Morocco did a spectacular turn-around and (accommodating many Spanish fruit growers and dealers) became the second largest Mediterranean exporter. In the 1970s the Spanish export sector reacted by upgrading quality, reducing the number of varieties and consolidating packing and export companies. Most Spanish citrus fruit exports are transported by land, giving Spain an advantage over Israel and North Africa. A *Comité de Gestión de la Exportación de Frutos Cítricos* (Administrative Committee on Citrus Fruit Exports) was set up in 1978 to co-ordinate the entire sector, especially exports destined for the EEC.

Apart from citrus fruit, we should mention the *remaining fresh fruits*, namely fruit that is usually consumed directly, without any prior preparation, and almost immediately after harvesting. Fresh fruit can be divided into three groups: pitted, seeded and other. Pitted fruit (peaches, apricots and plums), which is usually grown in irrigated or humid unirrigated land, is a leading export commodity, particularly in its pulp and canned forms. Seeded fruit (apples, pears and quinces) is cultivated in humid unirrigated land and, with the exception of the Lérida pear (in Catalonia), is exported very little. Other fruit includes bananas and table grapes, which will be discussed in some detail. We should also mention dried fruits and nuts, for Spain is one of the world's largest exporters of almonds and hazel nuts.

Regular banana production is only possible in the Canary islands where bananas from Cochinchina were brought in by Sabino Berthelot in the last quarter of the nineteenth century. For many years Canary banana exports to all European countries encountered no difficulties, and hence the banana plantations expanded. It was not until maritime transport and refrigeration techniques were improved, following the First World War, that the Canary islands began to feel competition from Brazil, Jamaica, Colombia, Ecuador and Central America, all of which have plentiful water, cheap labour and rich soil, and hence lower costs. Banana trading is controlled by the Comisión Regional del Plátano (CREP — Regional Banana Commission), an official agency founded in 1937 and transformed by Decree Law 1773/1978. The CREP regulates exports by setting weekly shipment quotas to maintain prices in peninsular Spain. In 1930, before the world depression and the 1933 banana crisis, more than 80% of exports from the Canaries (168,000 tonnes) were shipped abroad and a little less than 20% (39,000 tonnes) to the peninsula. Today these figures have been turned around: 95% of production is absorbed between the Canary islands themselves and the peninsula (which is a closed market) and only 5% is exported.

Although many of the varieties of grapes used in wine production can be eaten fresh, good table grapes are a genuine specialty. Adequate storage facilities are always a decisive factor behind prices, especially when exports are involved. One high-quality grape that exports well is the 'Almería grape', also known as the 'white grape of Ohanes', which is harvested in autumn and winter. This thick, waxy-skinned grape, which grows on large, cone-shaped branches, is cultivated in Murcia and throughout the irrigated lands of Almería, particularly in Ohanes (hence its name). Aromatic and sweet, muscat grapes are produced in the region of Levante in summer, but their thin, delicate skin rules out exports. 'Aledo' grapes, also grown in Levante, are an autumn fruit that is quite popular in Germany, France and Switzerland. Spain's strongest competitors for the early or late fruit export markets are Italy, Greece and Turkey, while autumn competitors are Hungary, Bulgaria and France.

Quickly turning to the rest of Spain's fresh fruit and vegetable production, potatoes are cultivated in fifty provinces, which explains both the wide variety available and staggered harvests, which occur almost all the year round. The country's four different potato crop areas are the humid unirrigated lands of the north, the irrigated lands of the interior and the coast, the Canary islands and the Balearic islands. The early potatoes of the Canary and Balearic islands are exported to the rest of Europe, primarily Britain, when they are not invaded by the potato beetle.

Spain also produces various varieties, both early and late, of tomatoes. Although the Canary islands and Valencia are the main provincial producers, tomatoes are also harvested throughout

Andalusia, Extremadura, Levante and Catalonia and in the irrigated lands of central Spain. Tomatoes have a considerable influence on Spain's foreign trade, given the value of exports and the extraordinary regularity of production. Canary island tomatoes are particularly well-liked in the British market and are available earlier than those grown by other European countries, such as the Channel islands and the Netherlands. The archipelago exports tomatoes from November to May when cold temperatures only make it possible to harvest expensive, hot-house-grown tomatoes in the rest of Europe. The development of tomato exports from Levante is the outgrowth of the new autumn varieties cultivated in the provinces of Alicante and Almería. Since the 1970s an export co-ordination agency has been working between the Canary islands and the province of Levante.

The rest of Spain's vegetables are all grown in irrigated lands, with production at its most intense in areas surrounding large centres of consumption. Vegetable production is increasing with the steady rise in demand both for direct consumption and from the canned foods industry. Spain's already considerable vegetable exports will certainly continue to grow, particularly those of earlier-harvested crops, since the income elasticity of demand is great. Fruit and vegetable production forms the base of the country's strong *canned vegetable* industry, which has its main centres in Valencia, Murcia and Rioja-Navarra, and its smaller centres in the Ebro basin, Vera de Plasencia and the Montijo (in Extremadura), and El Bierzo and Bajo Segre (in Catalonia).

7.3. *The wine economy.* Wine growing is tremendously important to Spain, bearing in mind the surface area involved, the value of final production and the volume of exports. In this section we will study the characteristics of each region of production, for regional difference strongly influences the quality and strength of wine (Fig. 10).

The region of Castile-La Mancha devotes the most land to wine production. La Mancha employs a single-crop farming system, especially in Valdepeñas, Manzanares, Tomelloso, Daimiel and, to a less degree, Campo de Calatrava. White table, red table and rosé wines of 13–15% alcohol content are provided by this region. A large number of large capacity co-operative wine cellars have sprouted up since 1953; the wine crisis of that year showed that the best way for wine producers to protect themselves was through co-operation.

In the Valencia area, wineyards are found on the unirrigated non-coastal lands and on coastal terraces, the latter being unsuitable for obtaining the highest possible yields. Requena and Utiel are the most productive districts in Valencia; unfortunately the altitude of this area does nothing to enhance the grapes, which become an average-quality wine, light in colour and having an alcohol content of 10–12%.

Catalonia, more than any other region, saw the size of its wine growing areas cut down as a result of a devastating phylloxera epidemic and an export crisis. Nevertheless, regional urban centres offer a wide market for the development of more profitable crops. The provinces of Barcelona and Tarragona are the most important producers in this region. In the Barcelona area the Penedés district produces white, rosé, claret and red wines of an average 12–12.5% alcohol content. Good sparkling wines are made around San Sadurní, and sweet muscat and malmsey wines of up to a 16.2% alcohol content are produced in Sitges. Tarragona is known for having some of the best natural wines of Catalonia; Conca de Barberá and Camp de Tarragona have good wines such as the Vilaseca white wine. But Priorato produces the top wine of Tarragona; this red wine, with a 15–17% alcohol content before ageing and up to 18% after ageing, is a giant export item, especially for the German market.

Andalusia has four major wine-growing areas: Jerez, el Condado de Niebla, Montilla and Málaga. The area of Jerez is in the shape of a triangle formed by Jerez itself, Sanlúcar de Barrameda and Puerto de Santa María. In this marshy area, rich in limestone, the cultivation and ageing processes have reached near-perfection. By using the *solera* system,* aged wines generally have an alcohol content of 18%. The wines of Jerez the famous 'sherry', exported to England since the early Middle Ages, generate far more foreign currency than any other Spanish wine.

La Rioja produces the best Spanish table wines. Viticultural centres are located in the Baja Rioja (Alfaro and Calhorra), the Alta Rioja (Haro) and the Basque Rioja. These fresh, acidic wines have an alcohol content of 10–13% and are delicately coloured and aromatic. In spite of these qualities, for a number of reasons (limited production, wide acceptance in the domestic market, and little promotion abroad) the amount of Rioja wines exported, although increasing, continues to be modest. The quality of the wines of Navarra tends to be lower than those of la Rioja.

The cloudy, semi-acidic white wines of the Ribeiro and Valdeorras districts in Galicia enjoy wide local acceptance; in Aragon the regional Cariñera is quite strong; and in the Balearic islands there is Binisalem. As a rule, the common Spanish wines of small vineyards and of some co-operatives are very good. We should not forget to

---

* Each year a portion of old wine is withdrawn and a portion of new wine added.

mention the *garnacho* of Cebreros (Avila) and the *chacoli* of Guetaria in Guipúzcoa, two wines that have been marketed very little, and for that very reason are occasionally excellent.

As soon as production levels during a good year exceed 35 million hectolitres and exports slow down, the problem of surpluses becomes dramatic because an excess in supply of 5–10% above the forecast demand can provoke a sharp fall in prices of origin if the state does not intervene in time. This is precisely what occurred in 1953, the year in which the Comisión de Compras de Excedentes de Vino (Wine Surplus Purchasing Commission) was established to prevent vineyard prices from collapsing. This commission set out to buy stocks of wine 'considered to be in excess and underpriced' (functions that are carried out today by the SENPA). Instead of aiding the sector, the wine surplus purchasing policy did the reverse. By trying to solve short-term problems, it abandoned more basic ones that needed to be corrected before the Spanish wine producing economy could improve. These problems are:

(*a*) *Statistical.* There is not enough information on which to base a rational wine policy. The organization of the wine cadastre and the annual balance sheet on supplies and demand have improved matters.

(*b*) *Wine statute.* This statute is not fully observed; more precise definitions must be established for wine classification, the basis of technical quality standards and the jurisdiction of the different economic authorities in the sector.

(*c*) *Appellation d'Origine.* The international trading of wines bottled for immediate consumption will become increasingly difficult for wines which do not have a controlled *appellation d'origine.* For this reason, Spain needs to have its Appellation d'Origine regulatory authorities (of Jerez, Rioja, Tarragona, Moriles, Montilla etc.) reorganised with a view to a more vigorous and dependable international performance.

The 1970 Wine Statute tackled some of these problems. Apart from introducing greater strictness over the authorisation of new crop plantations, these new regulations established the Instituto de Denominaciones de Origen (INDO — Appellation d'Origine Institute), which has the specialised task of overseeing the quality wine Appellation d'Origine Authorities.

7.4. *Olive production.* Classic olive cultivation areas are the coastal and sub-coastal zones of the Mediterranean basin, located between 30 and 45° north latitude. This area includes the whole of Spain with the exception of the Galician provinces and the

## Fig. 10. WINE PRODUCTION

The importance of location for industrial goods and most agricultural commodities is insignificant when compared with its effect on wine production. Ecological factors (soil, water, temperature etc.) have a decisive impact on the characteristics of wines of different vineyards, thus giving rise to great variety within all wine-producing countries. Spain has a wide range, from the 'generous' wines of Andalusia to the table wines of Rioja and Navarra; from the robust wines of Valencia and Tarragona to the mild wines of Galicia and the Basque country, as well as the strong, somewhat sour wine of Aragon. Based on two graphs prepared by agriculturist Luis Garcia Yravedra, this figure records a total of 78 different kinds of wine according to their areas of production.

Enological techniques also determine the quality of wines. Here, apart from the degree of care given by the wine growers of different regions, the 23 Spanish *Appellation d'Origine* regulatory boards play a key role. Their areas of authority are marked with a thick black line. The boards, in turn, are responsible to the Instituto de Denominación de Origen (INDO — Appellation d'Origine Institute) and operate in different ways. Some, like the Jerez and Rioja boards, have had long experience; others, less demanding, do not comply with the standards established for wines eligible for the seal of the regulatory boards.

Besides the 23 controlled areas, the map also shows the other 55 traditional zones for regional wines — *vins du pays*. These wines are generally known by their place of origin, even though they have no organisation responsible for guaranteeing their quality and typical characteristics. In 1981, the regulatory boards of Tierra de Barros and Ribera del Duero were created.

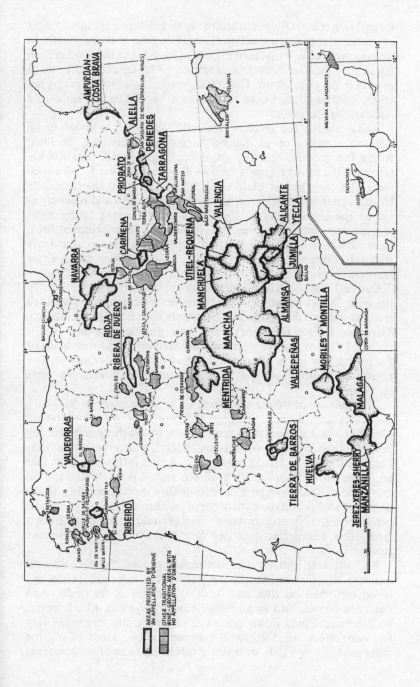

Cantabrian coast. Olive cultivation expanded during the last decades of the nineteenth century and the first six decades of the twentieth. In seventy years olive crop-lands expanded from 1.1 million to 2 million ha., a 90% increase at an annual rate of 1.3%, far above the rate of growth in the population. This trend, spurred by ever-increasing *per capita* consumption, began to change in the 1950s and came to a standstill in the 1970s.

Andalusia has the greatest production capacity, although its oil does not measure up to that of Aragon and Catalonia. In Jaen, where the greatest quantity of olives is produced, 360,000 ha. (almost 28% of the region's total 13,492 km.$^2$) are used for cultivation. The olive groves of Martos, which extend to the 'Loma de Ubeda', passing through the region of Villacarrillo and reaching as far as the Segura Sierra, form a block of olive-growing areas unequalled in any other country. Throughout the province of Jaén, olive growing is a single-crop farming operation. It is no coincidence that this farming system is used in a latifundiary area, where seasonal unemployment is sharp and the rate of emigration high.

Castile-La Mancha is second to Andalusia in olive production. To the west, in Extremadura, where climatic conditions are similar to those of western Andalusia, olive trees are abundant, particularly in Tierra de Barros (Badajoz). Catalonia produces quality oil for export. In Levante olive trees are cultivated on the poorest lands of the region, and lower Aragon too has its share of olive groves. The remaining regions of Spain have a minimal interest in olive cultivation.

Olive oils are commercially classified as either 'pure' or 'refined', the difference in price being great. *Pure olive oil* is natural oil obtained directly at ambient temperature by crushing and pressing healthy olives. Many 'pure' oils are 'fruity', which means that they keep the flavour or aroma of the fruit. And it is this fragrance that sets pure olive oil apart from all the rest. Up till 1920 most oil marketed in Spain was pure, and its quality varied according to the degree of acidity and the state of the olive when crushed. Under these conditions, the olive oil consumer market could clearly distinguish it from other oils, preferring it precisely because of its characteristic flavour.

Refining was initially a revolutionary process for the olive oil industry. Besides obtaining higher yields per olive weight, processing could turn bad oil that was inedible because of its acidity and unpleasant taste, into an all-purpose neutral-quality oil. However, widespread refining slowly put an end to 'pure' oil, and today very few consumers can distinguish between the two kinds of oil, the 'pure' and the 'refined', or between oils made from olives and from oilseed. Oils extracted from oilseed (soybeans, peanuts, cottonseed, sunflowers, sesame and rape seed) are much cheaper than olive oil, mainly because oilseed harvesting is entirely mechanised, whereas the manual harvesting of olives makes olive oil much more expensive. Consequently, when refined olive and oilseed oils began to take on the same characteristics (namely, of having no flavour or aroma), olive oil consumption tended to drop off, a decline that was intensified when oilseed oil imports were authorised.

Price intervention, and more specifically rationing from 1939, also left its mark on the Spanish fats market. Up till the introduction of rationing, olive oil was rarely used for culinary purposes in the north-west and most of the north, where consumption of animal fat was the rule. Rationing allocated the same amount of olive oil to every Spaniard indiscriminately, and thus almost the whole population grew accustomed to it. Potential domestic demand climbed so high that in 1951, when olive oil rationing ended and the exceptional harvest of that year was consumed, a definite shortage problem arose. Spain, a traditional olive oil exporter, became a country deficient in vegetable oil, and the deficit was made good with imported oilseed oils.

Spain is the world's leading olive oil producer and exporter, turning out an average of 400,000 tonnes in a normal crop year, 650,000 tonnes in a good year but not much more than 150,000 tonnes in a bad year; production levels usually represent 40% of the world total. Following the regression set off by the spurt in domestic consumption, olive oil exports experienced a recovery because the domestic market built part of its oil stocks back up with cheaper imported oilseed oils. Spain's largest customers outside Europe are the United States, Canada, Cuba and Brazil; in Europe they are Italy, Britain and France. One notable feature of Spanish olive exports is the method of shipping. Almost half of exported oil and olives is transported in barrels or drums and bottled once it reaches its destination. Thus foreign buyers benefit from this system, selling the merchandise under their own labels and rarely mentioning that the product is Spanish. If the same real volume of exports was better packaged and distributed, reaching consumers or retailers in the form in which it is shipped, the value of exports would be significantly greater.

7.5. *Industrial crop production.* The main common characteristic of industrial crop production (including sugar beet and cane, cotton and tobacco) is that no crops are produced for immediate consumption, as occurs to varying degrees with most other agricultural commodities; on the contrary, these crops go straight from where they are grown to the factory for processing. Given the close relationship between sugar beet and sugarcane, cotton and tobacco and the processing industries, the organisation and capital formation of these three groups of crops eclipse those of other agricultural areas. The industrial organisations themselves generally provide selected seeds, give farmers instructions as to how to secure the best qualities, and on occasion supervise farming directly. Fertilisers (as well as irrigation systems) are more vigorously employed with these crops than with any others. Industrial crop production has two other notable common characteristics: first, that the sector is monopolised by a small number of concerns, and secondly that these crops are amply protected from foreign competition.

Historically, Spanish sugar production is a recent development. The first sugar beet extraction factory was founded in Granada in 1884, but neither sugar crops nor the sugar industry really took off till 1898, when Spain lost Cuba, Puerto Rico and the Philippines. The amount of cropland devoted to sugar beet production is quite elastic. An annually-harvested, irrigated crop, sugar beet is sensitive to official prices; if prices are not maintained after a surplus crop year, cropland — and therefore production — will be reduced. For this reason production levels have swung up and down over the last few decades as a result of price adjustments. But, notwithstanding these fluctuations, a longstanding upward trend towards self-sufficiency has been observed. With it traditional imports (primarily Cuban) have been reduced, and the need to export markedly subsidised surpluses has arisen. As with rice, a beet crop quota system was introduced in 1972–3 by establishing maximum production quotas by territory.

Sugar beet is farmed mainly in the Ebro valley, the Duero basin and Andalusia. Sugarcane can only be grown on the Mediterranean coast around Almeria, south of Granada and Málaga and in the Canary islands. Cane-sugar production normally represents 10% of the country's total sugar production. Irrigation is used on more than 90% and 95%, respectively, of all sugar beet and sugarcane croplands.

The state has a hand in sugar beet and cane production. Annual harvests are regulated by decrees that set minimum production levels, the base price for a ton of beets or cane in zones of average wealth, and the maximum selling price to the public for different kinds of sugar. On the other hand, the sugar industry is characterised by economic concentration and by monopolistic activities that make such concentration and legal market management possible. A high percentage of the total production is in the hands of a small number of companies. Moreover, sugar companies, forming a tightly-knit group interconnected by common directorships, belong to the 'Asociación Nacional de Fabricantes de Azucar' (National Association of Sugar Producers), an employers' association aimed at jointly managing and protecting sugar interests with the Government, and pushing sugar prices as high as possible and beet prices as low as possible without completely discouraging production.

Cotton has been farmed in Spain since the late Middle Ages. It was introduced by the Arabs and developed on the coastal plains of Granada, the irrigated lands of Motril and the island of Ibiza. Little is known about Spanish cotton production between the Middle Ages and the end of the eighteenth century, but in the eighteenth and, particularly, the early nineteenth centuries, some Spanish cotton was exported to France and Britain; however, shipments ceased when the cotton gin was invented and came into use, slashing United States and Brazilian prices. The competition of these great American producers made Spanish cotton production untenable, even in the domestic market, and in 1869 the Figuerola Tariff was published: with its application cotton cultivation virtually disappeared.

After a series of initial promotional measures during the Dictatorship and the Second Republic, cotton farming made an important advance after the Civil War. In the face of serious foreign supply difficulties, natural and artificial textile fibre production was developed, with special attention being given to expanding the cotton sector.

To this end the Administration created the Instituto de Fomento de la Producción de Fibras Textiles (Institute for the Development of Textile Fibre Production) in 1940, and authorised the founding of industrial corporations to gin cotton. With the incentives contemplated in these provisions and healthy cotton prices, cultivation quickly grew from an average of 41,000 ha. in 1941–5 to almost 350,000 in 1962, when 120,000 tons of fibre were produced. When imported fibre restrictions were eased in 1962, domestic production toppled, and cotton cultivation only continued in the most profitable irrigated areas.

Until 1962 the licenced companies mentioned earlier were exclusively responsible for the cotton growing industry, dividing among themselves the country's eleven cotton cultivation areas. These companies operated in their respective zones, monopolising demand and therefore having a controlling hand with farmers. Their position was strengthened even further by their strong mutual ties and their involvement in the Consejo de Administración del Instituto de Fomento de la Producción de Fibras Textiles (the Board of the Institute for the Development of Textile Fibre Production), an authority with the task of ensuring that all official provisions regarding domestic cotton production were carried out. Using their strong monopoly position, the licensed companies reaped tremendous profits for many years without fully complying with the obligations imposed on them by administrative provisions.

In view of an endless stream of protests and pressure exerted by Catalan industrialists, the system had to be changed when the 20-year licences expired in 1962. A Decree of 10 February 1962 redesigned the cotton exchange. Restrictions on the founding of new ginning factories were lifted, and farmers in each area became free to do business with the factories of their choice. With this freeing of the market, crops took a nose dive, and after a series of constantly changing regulations, Decree Law 927 of 13 February 1979 regulated the sector with a development plan aimed at securing 90,000 ha. and 76,500 tonnes of fibre by increasing mechanisation and the granting of aid to farmers.

Andalusia, the largest regional producer, represents 50% of total domestic production, followed by Extremadura, (almost 20%).

The expansion of *tobacco cultivation* from an average of 4,000 ha. in 1931–5 has been spectacular. The two most important tobacco growing regions are the Vera de Plasencia in Caceres (Extremadura) and the Vega de Granada (Andalusia). For fiscal reasons the state is involved in the cultivation, preparation, processing and distribution of tobacco. The Servicio Nacional del Cultivo y Fermentación del Tabaco (National Tobacco Cultivation and Fermentation Service) is involved in the first two of those stages, and the Monopolios de Tabacos, through Tabacalera SA, in the last two. This service, set up under a Law of 8 March 1944, reports to the Ministry of Agriculture and is responsible for technical, administrative and all other matters related to the farming, curing, fermentation and pricing of domestically-grown tobacco, including research and by-products.

Each year the Ministry of Agriculture issues an order regulating the tobacco harvest by establishing the kinds of tobacco cultivation which are permitted, as well as the farming areas and prices for each variety. In 1979 a 'Tobacco Development Plan' was approved with a view to raising annual production to 45,000 tonnes. Tobacco processing and sales are a monopoly regulated by the Act of 29 July 1921. This monopoly, which is under the control of the Ministry of Finance, manages the 'Compañía Arrendataria del Monopolio de Tabacos, Tabacalera SA' (Tobacco Leasing Company), which processes tobacco in factories within the monopoly, distributes domestic products and imports and collects taxes. The state has a controlling interest in this company. Only the Canary islands initially escaped the control of the monopoly; in the last decade, however, the Tabacalera has taken over most of the islands' huge tobacco industry. The contract between the Ministry of Finance and the Tabacalera was renewed in 1971 for a further twenty years, even though the contract will have to be annulled when Spain enters the Common Market.

7.6. *Livestock*. The development of livestock and cattle raising did not gain momentum in Spain until the second half of the nineteenth century and the first three decades of the twentieth. Antonio Flores de Lemus addressed this evolution in his famous work entitled *Sobre una dirección fundamental de la producción rural española* ('On the basic direction of Spain's rural production'), Madrid, 1923, in which he made the inaccurate prediction that this sector would greatly develop.

Between 1939 and 1960 the sector regressed for a number of reasons. First, the protection of wheat cultivation, achieved by high prices, increased wheat croplands and reduced both pasturelands and croplands used for feed grains (e.g. barley, corn and oats). Secondly, the protective measures surrounding the cultivation of natural textile fibres, beet and tobacco (all typical irrigated crops) reduced the possibility of enlarging fodder cultivation areas in new irrigated areas. Thirdly, the extent of the former pasturelands diminished as these were taken over by the State Forestry Trust for reforestation. Fourthly, the aforementioned three points, together with import restrictions, pushed up natural feed and fodder prices, discouraging livestock owners from increasing the number of their animals, given limited meat and milk demand. And finally, the gradual mechanisation of farming activities cut down the number of farm animals.

With this decline, food, wool and leather supply problems came to the surface, putting pressure on the country's foreign trade. At the same time, the reduction in the total quantity of livestock opened up a gap — even larger than the traditional one — between agriculture and livestock, thus running counter to the universal trend of bringing farming and livestock raising together. This trend was the result of the perfect coupling between mechanisation and livestock which is possible; farm machinery can only perform profitably if a farm also has income-producing livestock to take up the labour displaced by mechanisation, allowing part of the working hours saved by mechanisation to be invested. Moreover, soil and water maintenance practices are closely related to fodder cultivation, forming part of all efficient crop rotation cycles and the basis of sound livestock breeding. And food for human consumption needs to be upgraded, which means increasing the percentage of animal proteins. The

Table 3.11. LIVESTOCK CENSUS
(*adult head* × *1,000*)

| Livestock | 1970 | 1975 | 1980 | 1983 |
|---|---|---|---|---|
| Cattle | 4,282 | 4,335 | 4,495 | 4,956 |
| Sheep | 17,005 | 15,195 | 14,180 | 16,731 |
| Goats | 2,551 | 2,293 | 1,977 | 2,414 |
| Pigs | 7,621 | 8,662 | 11,263 | 12,364 |
| Horses | 282 | 251 | 242 | 250 |
| Mules | 533 | 314 | 199 | 162 |
| Donkeys | 363 | 266 | 188 | 175 |
| Poultry | 26,404 | 35,923 | 43,404 | 53,869 |

| Products | 1970 | 1975 | 1980 | 1983 |
|---|---|---|---|---|
| *Meat and poultry:* | | | | |
| Beef | 308 | 454 | 421 | 390 |
| Lamb | 127 | 136 | 127 | 128 |
| Pork | 492 | 602 | 986 | 1,170 |
| Poultry | 499 | 631 | 762 | 820 |
| Total | 1,426 | 1,823 | 2,296 | 2,508 |
| Cow's milk ($10^6$ litres) | 4,332 | 4,984 | 5,871 | 6,846 |
| Eggs ($10^6$ dozen) | 679 | 839 | 974 | 927 |

*Source:* Ministry of Agriculture.

evolution of livestock farming since 1970 in terms of size and yields is presented in Table 3.11.

*Cattle* raising, although marked by almost zero growth in numbers, has shown increasing unit yields; a growing specialised dairy sector; and a heavy concentration in the northern and north-eastern provinces. The large cattle deficits of the 1960s and 1970s were covered by frozen meat imported from Argentina, Uruguay, Cuba and Eastern European countries. The place of beef was taken by pork and poultry. In 1966 the foundations were laid for an increase in cattle numbers through incentives known as 'Concerted Action'; this was the provision of financing and subsidies to live-stock owners with more than thirty head. The results, however, were disappointing: natural pastureland and inexpensive fodder were difficult to secure; balanced feed was scarce and expensive and obstacles blocked the importing of select cattle, particularly breeding cows and feeder calves.

Since the mid-1960s, regulated pricing policies have been applied to cattle. A guaranteed price per kg./carcass was established for refrigerated slaughterhouses working in cooperation with the

SENPA. The pricing system for milk is more complex. A minimum price is set for milk processing plants and the rest of the industry. Annual prices varying from one region to another have often provoked conflicts between livestock owners and the Administration ('milk wars'). In Spain, as in all other countries, *sheep* occur with a density in inverse proportion to that of the human population. Their populations are densest in Extremadura, western Andalusia, La Mancha, Aragon and Old Castile. The *Mesta* (studied by Julius Klein), with powers only second to those of the King, protected the interests of sheep owners during the Middle Ages. Some 25,000 tons of wool are produced each year, but Spain has to import vast quantities of fine and medium-quality wool from Australia due to the shortfall of domestic production. After import barriers were lowered in 1962, the Spanish wool market entered a period of crisis, and only meat and milk prices have kept the sheep industry alive. Although sheep numbers are decreasing, the shortening of the production cycle with state-sponsored feedings is reshaping sheep farming, which would have otherwise have been abandoned. 'Sheep complexes' and milking machines provided by the state are additional incentives.

The decline in *goat farming* is even more glaring. Goats have been criticised for their destructiveness and for the Malta fever germs often found in their milk. But today the realisation that goats reduce the number of forest fires, together with animal sanitation measures, has enhanced their status. Goats are raised throughout the country, although they are most numerous in the provinces of Granada, Cáceres, Malaga, Ciudad Real, Badajoz, Murcia, Cadiz and Huelva.

*Pig breeding* produces high meat and fat yields with cheap feed, such as acorns, chestnuts and waste. Pigs represent the main source of animal protein for the human population. Pigs, raised and slaughtered domestically, are found in all parts of the country, but their numbers are highest in Extremadura, Galicia, western Andalusia and Salamanca. Pig meat production was formerly seasonal, since slaughtering occurred in winter months, but today refrigerated abattoirs make this work possible all year round. From 1962 to 1966 the African plague wrought havoc in this sub-sector, and it still returns occasionally to haunt the country. Pig farms are registered with the Ministry of Agriculture and prices are regulated, although most trading is conducted between meat producers and industries on a free market basis. Large feed companies stimulate feed sales by establishing service contracts with farmers for feed supply and pork purchases.

Until the 1950s *poultry* numbers were in constant fluctuation; feed availability and disease would directly influence the size of flocks within a relatively short period of time. However, once feed availability and disease were controlled, the 'poultry miracle' followed. In a space of seven years (1955–62), the quantity of egg-laying hens (those aged more than six months) rose from 23 to 40 million. This increase was attributable to the propagation of poultry farms, which came to represent 90% of the country's total (domestic and wild) in 1962 compared with 10% in 1955. Consequently, egg imports waned and heavily-subsidised egg exports sprang into existence. The poultry population is more evenly distributed than other groups of livestock, but their largest concentrations are located in Valencia, Catalonia and the northern *meseta*, with Reus and Valladolid being the principal centres.

Table 3.12.   FORESTRY, 1982

| Type of forests* | Under public control | Under private control | Total |
|---|---|---|---|
| High trees | 1,755 | 2,567 | 4,322 |
| Trees of medium height | 144 | 449 | 593 |
| River bank | 16 | 144 | 160 |
| Grazing | 44 | 1,589 | 1,633 |
| Low trees | 583 | 2,086 | 2,669 |
| Reforested areas | 1,432 | 983 | 2,415 |
| Total | 3,974 | 7,818 | 11,792 |

| Ownership* | Total | Wooded | Cleared | Density |
|---|---|---|---|---|
| State forests | 816 | 618 | 198 | 0.41 |
| MUP† under a consortium | 2,160 | 1,546 | 614 | 0.39 |
| MUP | 5,039 | 3,071 | 1,968 | 0.39 |
| Freely accessible forests | 1,639 | 607 | 1,032 | 0.36 |
| Private forests | 17,636 | 7,580 | 10,056 | 0.33 |
| Total | 27,290 | 13,422 | 17,633 | 0.37 |

| Products | 1970 | 1975 | 1980 | 1983 |
|---|---|---|---|---|
| Timber (10,000 cubic metres) | 8,627 | 11,340 | 11,892 | 11,760 |
| Firewood (10,000 cu. metres) | 12,639 | 3,979 | 1,474 | 1,300 |
| Resin (tonnes) | 43,083 | 38,224 | 26,374 | 26,000 |
| Cork (tonnes) | 109,512 | 82,497 | — | 80,000 |
| Esparto (tonnes) | 33,071 | 17,120 | 17,323 | 20,000 |

*Source:* Ministry of Agriculture.

* × 1,000 ha.

† MUP: *Montes de Utilidad Pública* (publicly-owned forest subject to special conservation regulations).

7.7. *Forestry.* The fact that 26,818,100 ha. of Spain's total area of
50,474,100 ha. is forest land (see Table 3.12) gives some idea of the
size of this sector. But the income it generates is negligible, with final
forest production representing at most 5% of total agricultural
income. Thus the average yield of Spain's forests in economic terms
is minimal. How has such a lamentable situation arisen, with 50% of
the country's surface area giving only trifling yields? This development is easily explained if we look at Spain's many treeless,
unmanaged and rudimentarily or uneconomically developed forest
lands. There is probably a grain of truth in the commonly-held belief
that Spain was once a country of great forests, which covered a great
area of land which today is bare. For centuries the abuse of the Mesta
through the hunger for sunny pasture lands for sheep, the effects of
the long War of Succession (1700–14), intensive coal production for
smelting purposes, and the use of timber for shipbuilding and many
other applications, diminished this natural resource. Ponz, in his
*Viaje por España*, completed during the reign of Charles III (*circa*
1760), described deforested regions, which coincide almost exactly

Table 3.13.   REFORESTATION

| | Reforested (ha.) | | Reforested (ha.) |
|---|---|---|---|
| 1940 | 792 | 1962 | 94,136 |
| 1941 | 10,486 | 1963 | 105,456 |
| 1942 | 20,018 | 1964 | 103,879 |
| 1943 | 30,842 | 1965 | 100,693 |
| 1944 | 37,414 | 1966 | 95,858 |
| 1945 | 48,834 | 1967 | 93,494 |
| 1946 | 52,488 | 1968 | 85,473 |
| 1947 | 38,139 | 1969 | 106,084 |
| 1948 | 44,155 | 1970 | 111,370 |
| 1949 | 43,972 | 1971 | 106,477 |
| 1950 | 38,344 | 1972 | 113,931 |
| 1951 | 45,790 | 1973 | 95,171 |
| 1952 | 72,785 | 1974 | 120,193 |
| 1953 | 111,888 | 1975 | 81,267 |
| 1954 | 108,806 | 1976 | 112,787 |
| 1955 | 127,418 | 1977 | 116,700 |
| 1956 | 129,816 | 1978 | 72,200 |
| 1957 | 135,987 | 1979 | 110,600 |
| 1958 | 87,605 | 1980 | 76,200 |
| 1959 | 120,560 | 1981 | 66,900 |
| 1960 | 88,002 | 1982 | 101,600 |
| 1961 | 105,340 | 1983 | 98,200 |
| | | Total | 2,829,937 |

*Source:* ICONA.

with similar regions found today. However, the worst damage was done in the nineteenth century. Forest resources were exhausted by the two stages of disentailment (1837 and 1855), civil wars, the breaking-up of forest lands for crop cultivation and destructive felling to create pastureland. Deforestation has yet to be studied to determine its political and economic causes and its effect on population growth, the economy and the countryside.

The total figure for forest lands, broken down in Table 3.13, tells very little about real timber stocks. Forests of maximum and medium tree-height, covering some 9,002,000 ha., represent the base of timber stocks, whose averages per hectare are under 16 cu. m. Spain's stocks are small when compared with those of other European countries (Austria 162, Germany 126, France 82, Italy 57, Portugal 69). The country's present felling average is 0.357 cu. m. of wood with bark per hectare, far below the European average of 2.2. Estimates have shown that if clearings were replanted and properly managed, average timber stocks per hectare of the forest areas would be 64 cubic metres, four times the present average. These 'ideal' stocks enable us to calculate the extent of 'national forest clearings'. If, out of a total of 13.44 million ha. of forest land, 2.6 million ha. have recently been replanted and 1 million (primarily farming land) sown or left fallow, then we are left with a total wooded area of 9.8 million ha., of which 2.4 million have an ideal density of 64 cubic metres per hectare. Thus approximately 5% of the country's total land surface in covered by timber forests. The difference between 9.8 and 2.4 million ha. consists of clearings and bare land. Spanish forest yields are given in Table 3.12.

Larger *timber* harvests are the result both of reforestation management, initiated in the post-war period, and of the age-old process of forest disinvestment. *Firewood* production, which is slowly being replaced by electricity and butane gas, is definitely in decline. The case of *resin* is similar. The development of synthetic resins and petrochemical solvents has precipitated a crisis in the turpentine and resin (colophony) markets throughout the world. The demand for *esparto*, used mainly as a cellulose fibre in paper mills, is also decreasing as supplies of other higher-quality raw materials improve. Last of all, *cork* is a clear example of the gradual substitution of a natural raw material by synthetics (buna rubber, plastic etc); nevertheless cork, the only Spanish forestry export, has experienced a recovery in recent years.

Turning to forestry policies, soil and timber could be considered forestry assets. If harvest volumes surpass annual growth, assets decrease, as has been the trend in Spain for centuries. When timber assets disappear completely — whether they are cut and sold, cleared for pastureland or burned to the ground by fire — the potential value of soil regeneration remains. Erosion, however, eats away at unprotected soil assets until they too disappear, leaving only rock in their place. The decrease and in some cases disappearance of timber assets and the slow loss of soil assets over hundreds of years have reduced Spain's forest lands to their present state and modified the country's environment by negatively influencing climate and water systems and creating unfavourable conditions for most sectors of agriculture. For this reason the long-term forestry policies of a country so bereft of forests must be aimed at expansion and replanting. Forestry expansion and restoration programmes require such long periods of time that they are only of interest to public agencies. At the beginning of the twentieth century, reforestation aspirations finally became a reality thanks to the creation of the Water-Forestry Divisions, which executed the first large reforestation projects in Spain. Though not very extensive, these projects set an example of how protection and conservation problems can be effectively dealt with.

In 1935 the reins held by the Forestry Divisions were handed over to the Patrimonio Forestal del Estado (PFE — State Forestry Trust), and Don José Larraz was appointed chairman of the preparatory committee for the forestry bill enacted on 9 October 1935. As soon as the PFE was founded, it set about preparing working programmes, which were interrupted by the Civil War. Preparatory work was resumed in Nationalist Spain in June 1938, and the first general reforestation plan was concluded in January 1939, calling for the replanting of 6 million ha. over 100 years at the rate of 60,000 ha. a year. The final details of this goal were published in 1940, and 792 ha. were symbolically replanted. Thereafter, reforestation activities evolved as shown in Table 3.13.

Since 1971, the hitherto separate activities of the National Soil Conservation Service and of other public agencies similar to the PFE were merged to form a new agency, the Instituto de Conservación de la Naturaleza (ICONA — Natural Conservation Institute), bringing together traditional reforestation activities and other environmental and wildlife activities (hunting, fishing and national parks).

The reforestation procedure followed by the PFE in the past and by ICONA today is as follows:

(*a*) First and foremost, reforestation of publicly acquired holdings.

(*b*) Reforestation, under a consortium system, of public or private holdings, whereby ICONA replants and manages the holding. When

## Fig. 11. ECOLOGICAL SPAIN

The title of this figure is not wholly inappropriate since ecology covers a much wider field. But its theme is a basic ecological issue, namely officially protected natural spaces. *National parks* (indicated by black triangles) are relatively large areas offering exceptional natural resources and extra-ordinary scenic beauty. To protect these parks, profit-making activities (lumbering, hydroelectric power-stations, mining, quarrying etc.) are either prohibited or severely restricted. At present Spanish national parks are small in both number and size (see Table 1.1). As a result, in practice they are seriously threatened by systematic and tenacious speculation.

*Possible future national parks* (white triangles) have been included with a view to guaranteeing the protection of many other areas of natural interest. Unfortunately, tourism and short-term hydroelectric or lumber business deals loom ominously on the horizon.

Black circles show existing and future *natural parks* (small in size and where certain kinds of development are permitted). And the shaded boxes represent sites of natural scenic beauty. Instead of the meagre number shown on the map, the country should have hundreds of these sites.

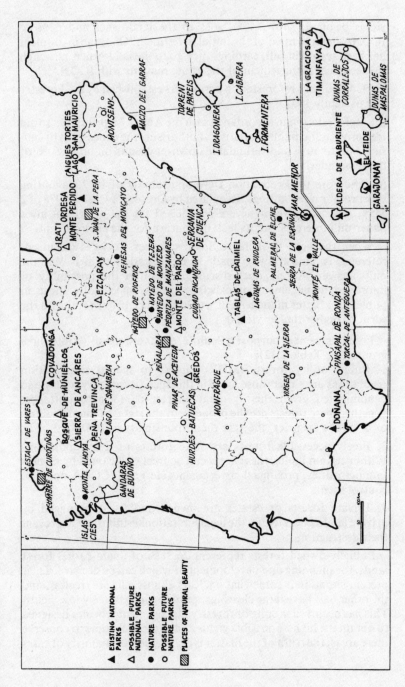

EXISTING NATIONAL PARKS
POSSIBLE FUTURE NATIONAL PARKS
NATURE PARKS
POSSIBLE FUTURE NATURE PARKS
PLACES OF NATURAL BEAUTY

yields begin to show, 40% goes to the landowner and 60% to ICONA in repayment of the initial investment. Once the investment has been repaid in full, earnings then go to the landowner, although the technical management of the estate remains with ICONA.

(*c*) Compulsory reforestation perimeters established by the Forestry Act of 8 July 1957.

(*d*) Reforestation in accordance with the Act of 7 April 1952, 'to aid free private and public initiative', authorising the concession of subsidies up to 50% and refundable down-payments on up to 50% of the remainder.

(*e*) The Forestry Production Development Act of 1977, favouring short rotation replantings. Regulated by Decree Law 1279/1978 of 2 May, this act has been severely criticised for the priority it gives paper-mill interests and its lack of concern for the environment.

When the need to increase Spain's timber stocks is discussed, reference is almost always made to reforestation, as if it were the only answer. Rarely does discussion turn to the possibility of improved management of existing forests, specifically those in public use. Better management would produce better results (in the form of higher timber yields).

For management purposes, Spain's forests are classified into three groups (see Table 3.12):

1. Public utility forests (MUP) subject to special conservation regulations are either those listed in this specific category or those so denominated given their general interest or social importance. Whether these forests are the property of the state, of municipalities or of public agencies, they are the responsibility of ICONA.

2. Freely accessible forests are state forests of less importance. Within certain limits, these areas can be freely developed by owners (municipalities, provincial governments etc.) and ICONA does not control them.

3. Private forests or estates are owned and freely managed by private landowners within the legal limitations established to prevent their destruction.

Publicly-owned forests represent 26.38% of Spain's total forest lands, the planning and development of which can be decisive. Their present situation is somewhat unclear: almost half are treeless, and the other half have large clearings, resulting in extremely low yields. This has occurred in spite of forestry management schemes designed to obtain the highest possible yields and at the same time to conserve these areas; the truth of the matter is that in the vast majority of cases

these schemes never reach completion. The law only requires that
15% of annual earnings be invested in conservation and improvements. This is far too little to do any good.

Where private forests are concerned, a law concerning holdings
which are obviously ripe for improvement must be enacted before
underdeveloped lands can be systematically expropriated and
replanted and managed. The scope of these operations, their
complexity and the control of the substantial investments needed,
calls for the reorganising of the state forestry administration as a
sub-secretariat or ministry.

Among the most recent legal provisions governing the forestry
sector is the Forest Fire Prevention Act of 5 December 1968, enacted
as a result of an outbreak of forest fires due to arson.

7.8. *Saltwater fisheries.*    Saltwater fisheries will wind up our discussion of the food and agriculture sector. Spain has 4,551 km. of
coastline, 770 on the Bay of Biscay, 1,541 on the Atlantic (including
the Canary islands) and 2,300 on the Mediterranean (including the
Balearic islands). Despite this tremendous water front, an underwater plateau adjacent to the Peninsula hampers fishing activities;
and a 400-metre isobar runs along the coast at an average of 30–50
km. out, only widening to 80–100 km. in the gulfs of Cadiz and
Valencia. The underwater shelf surrounding the Peninsula is relatively narrow, particularly on the Atlantic side; and low fish production in the Mediterranean limits the possibility afforded by a wider
continental shelf. Consequently, the Spanish fishing fleet has had to
enlarge its working area to include other sea areas (e.g. in the Irish
Sea, Newfoundland, Greenland, Mauritania and Senegal).

Fisheries have been one of Spain's fastest-growing sectors (see
Table 3.14). Nevertheless, the total volume since 1979 was down
compared with the year before, as a result of two serious developments. First, the depletion of fishing grounds close to the Spanish
coastline advances apace, with marine authorities turning a blind eye
to improper fishing practice, and secondly, the Spanish fishing fleet
is constantly being confronted with difficulties in its most
frequented offshore fisheries: the fishing agreement established for
the waters surrounding Morocco imposes severe restrictions, and the
same has occurred with Mauritania in waters to which Spanish
fishermen have traditionally had free access (the Saharan fishing
grounds). Since 1974 Canada, the United States and the EEC have
been limiting fisheries. The 200-mile limit has — dramatically —
become an established element in the law of the sea, and Spain itself
took the decision in 1978 of setting a 200-mile limit off its Atlantic

Table 3.14.    FISHING: TOTAL UNLOADED CATCH
(*annual averages*)

|        | (*1,000 tonnes*) | Index |
|--------|------------------|-------|
| 1927   | 230.6            | 100.0 |
| 1931–4 | 340.9            | 147.8 |
| 1941–5 | 475.2            | 206.1 |
| 1946–50 | 502.5           | 217.9 |
| 1951–5 | 523.6            | 227.1 |
| 1956–60 | 735.0           | 318.7 |
| 1961–5 | 786.0            | 340.8 |
| 1966–70 | 1,171.0         | 507.8 |
| 1971–5 | 1,273.8          | 552.3 |
| 1975–80 | 1,218.9         | 528.5 |
| 1981   | 1,207.1          | 523.4 |
| 1982   | 1,299.5          | 563.5 |
| 1983   | 1,206.3          | 523.1 |

## CATCH BY REGION

|                        | (*1,000 tonnes*) | | (*1,000 million ptas*) | |
|------------------------|------|------|------|------|
|                        | *1982* | *1983* | *1982* | *1983* |
| Bay of Biscay          | 121  | 125  | 22.3 | 25.1 |
| North-west             | 564  | 558  | 58.3 | 66.6 |
| South Atlantic         | 138  | 111  | 27.5 | 25.4 |
| Southern Mediterranean | 60   | 53   | 6.7  | 7.3  |
| Eastern Mediterranean  | 31   | 33   | 5.2  | 6.6  |
| Catalonia              | 85   | 81   | 11.8 | 13.4 |
| Balearic islands       | 5    | 5    | 1.4  | 1.7  |
| Canary islands         | 238  | 178  | 18.0 | 21.4 |
| Total                  | 1,242 | 1,144 | 151.2 | 167.5 |

*Source:* National Statistics Institute.

coast. All these developments have aroused a growing interest among Spaniards in their surrounding seas.

The characteristics of Spain's coastal fishery areas vary greatly, the most active areas being found in the north-west, the south–west and the Canary islands. The uneven north-west coast, particularly rich in its lower *rias* (small fjords), brings in the highest volume (one-quarter of the total) and the widest variety of species. Approximately half the Spanish fleet and the most advanced fish industries are based in this region. Galicia, especially Vigo and its *ria*, is the most enterprising area in this sector. The southern part of the Atlantic coast is the second most active sector and comprises the ports between Ayamonte and La Línea de la Concepción (namely Algeciras, Huelva and Cadiz); it is favoured by migratory schools of tuna and sardines and an abundancy of crustaceans. This area serves as a base for the many boats that fish the West African coast. The Canary archipelago, on the 25th parallel, is the southernmost Spanish fishing area and has often been used as an advance base for fleets working the waters off Morocco, the Western Sahara, Mauritania and Senegal, especially before the present-day restrictions came into force.

We should now look at the main kinds of fish caught. Cod fishing is the most modernised of the fleet; pair and side trawlers and seiners are used to work the cod fishing grounds, which are almost entirely in the North Atlantic. However, because of the financial investment it requires, only a few cod companies (e.g. MAR, Pescanova *et al.*) are involved in the complete fishing and drying process. Sardines continue to be the most important coastal fish, but cyclical sardine depressions have caused serious problems for fishing fleets and directly dependent canning industries. Tuna is the second most important fish after sardines for Spain's canning industry. Many of the nets used for inshore tuna fishing are the same ones that have been used for centuries.

Trawlers are used for catching white fish (hake, sole etc.) in the Irish Sea, the Bay of Biscay, the Portuguese coastal waters and the Cantabrian and north-west regions. Many other species are caught by the coastal fleet within a limited radius of action. White fish catches (primarily hake and whiting) have been revolutionised in recent years. The fishing fleet has invested huge sums to send fishing fleets, factory boats and freezer vessels to the South Atlantic and Antarctica.

The relatively recent evolution of catches, broken down by tonnage, value and distribution percentages, can be seen in Table 3.14 — which also shows the disquieting trend, mentioned earlier, towards stagnating production levels. Fish marketing and distribution are marked by certain peculiarities. A long process is involved in getting unloaded fish to consumers. Prices of fish at the ports fluctuate widely because the influx of fish at the marketplace is highly irregular. Fish are auctioned off in the markets,and only cod, porgy, corvina and deep-sea fish are not sold in this way — to the wholesale buyers that tend to monopolise local demand. Many salt-water fish are either canned, salted or dried. Galicia has 60% of the canning industry and most of the salting industry, followed by the south Atlantic region, the Cantabrian coast and the Canary islands.

Act 33 of 21 June 1980 created the Fondo de Regulación y

Organización del Mercado de Productos de la Pesca y Productos Marítimos (FROM — the Fund for Regulating and Organising the Market in Fish and Other Marine Products). The functions of this body, similar to those of the FORPPA in agriculture, are to control prices, report on import activities, and generally to support the fishing industry.

# IV. THE INDUSTRIAL SECTOR

## 1. *The industrialisation process*

In this chapter basic industries (energy, extractive, iron and steel and chemical), transformation industries (shipbuilding, engineering and metal transforming), and consumer goods industries (textiles, leather and footware, paper, publishing etc.) will be discussed, together with the construction industry, another well-defined subsector. But before separately considering each separate subsector, we should make some general remarks, beginning with an analysis of the historical background to the industrial process in Spain.

### 1.1. *The reasons for Spain's late industrialisation.*   It has been said that industrial development can be classified according to the operation of a certain set of factors at the start of the industrialisation process. These factors—a spirit of enterprise, technology, real capital (the set of productive and energy resources), financial capital (necessary to finance the mobilisation of real resources and to cover the weaknesses of any of the other factors) and the level of demand — can either drive forward the rate of progress or retard it. This model would seem to explain the industrial precocity of some countries and the backwardness of others.

While a *spirit of enterprise* was highly developed in England and the Netherlands by the end of the eighteenth century, in Spain it had fallen into decay following the great conquests and evangelising enterprises of the Spanish empire in the two previous centuries. But even during those two great centuries, the Spanish genius had tended to manifest itself in military adventure, discovery, art, religion and the search for gold and silver, but seldom in the search for genuine economic progress.

During this same period the second factor, the state of Spain's *technology* was in no better condition than the first. In the words of Ortega y Gasset, the celebrated Spanish philosopher (1883–1953), technology can be defined as 'the reform man imposes on nature to satisfy his needs'. More specifically, science usually precedes technology. Thus if Spain could only show meagre scientific development, its technology would inevitably be wanting too. Santiago Ramon y Cajal, the 1906 Spanish Nobel Prize winner in medicine, stated that 'Spain is an intellectually backward, not a decadent, country, where scientific development has never been advanced. . . .' In the nineteenth century, Spanish technological and educational levels were rather low. Engineering schools sprang up in the middle of the century, but there were few graduates. The country was shrouded in layers of ignorance: as late as 1887, 54.2% of men and 74.4% of women were illiterate. Of course, there were educated people, but they were few, and so exclusively tied to private interests that their influence was at best slight.

As for the third factor, *real capital*, although Spain's resources are respectable, there have been huge gaps. In the middle of the nineteenth century, copper pyrites, iron, lead, zinc and other mineral deposits could have laid the foundations for industrialisation, but the scarcity of energy sources was a formidable obstacle. Asturian coal, mined far from centres of activity, of poor quality and more expensive than British coal, was practically the only source.

*Financial capital*, or the monetary resources with which real resources are mobilised and industrial development (fundamentally the means to make foreign payments) is financed, was insufficient in Spain in the middle of the nineteenth century. Private individuals had their capital locked up; real estate, which rose enormously in value due to land speculation in both urban and rural areas, was the chief means to accumulate capital, which was none the less difficult to realise. Moreover, the financial situation of the state was parlous. The influx of gold from the Americas had been halted by the outbreak of the War of Independence in 1808, and civil and colonial wars, which quickly ate up the mediocre revenues of an ailing tax system, swelled the public debt to such an extent that state financial assistance for industrial development was impossible. And the private banking system, which should have mobilised national savings, remained ineffective at the national level until the start of the twentieth century.

Not having capital of its own to finance development turned Spain into what today could be called an underdeveloped country, whose only way out of economic penury would have been through huge investment in industry and agriculture; but the possibilities for investment were nil, since economic penury prevented capital formation. Thus a vicious circle was established which could only be broken by the influx of foreign capital — which was exactly what happened. Foreign investment and the repatriation of Spanish capital from Cuba, Puerto Rico and the Philippines at the end of the Spanish-American war in 1898 were decisive for Spain's industrial development.

Spain also lacked the fifth factor necessary for industrial development, namely an *adequate level of demand*. The country's population in 1797 was only 10.5 million but, more important, income levels and therefore purchasing power at that time were extremely low and greatly inferior to those of England and France. Hence the domestic market suffered arrested development.

The explanation given so far for Spain's slow industrial development may seem simplistic and even 'mechanistic'. Two more elements are needed to complete the picture: domestic and foreign political developments. Historically, it is obvious that the industrial revolution had to follow a *bourgeois revolution*. The absolutist and semifeudal political structure prevailing in Spain up to the later nineteenth century led to low levels of domestic consumption. Great areas of land were in mortmain, and guild-supported rigidity prevented the establishment or enlargement of industries. Moreover, trading mechanisms suffered from severe paralysis as mercantalist monopolies refused to die. Industrialisation was impossible without disentailment and industrial and commercial freedom.

In the mid-eighteenth century, under Ferdinand VI and Charles III, a movement began in these three directions. But after being discreetly encouraged by Charles III and his best ministers, this renewal was snuffed out under Charles IV when, after the beginning of the French Revolution in 1789, an atmosphere of resistance and distrust invaded Spain. The movement could have been rekindled with the application of laws and decrees issued by the Cortes of 1812 and 1813, but quite the opposite occurred. Ferdinand VII repealed all bills enacted by the Cortes which abolished guilds and promoted disentailment, in this way postponing Spain's modest industrial revolution for almost twenty years, till Ferdinand VII's death in 1833. Not until political liberalism began to break down barriers after that year could Spanish industrial development be set in motion.

Two foreign political developments also contributed to a slowdown in industrialisation: the War of Independence against Napoleonic France (1808–14) and the loss of Spain's American empire (1810–26). The long War of Independence reduced the best of what had arisen in Spain's pre-capitalist modern economy to ruin. The destruction of factories by troops under Napoleon and Wellington, the latter coming to Spain's 'aid', nipped industrialisation in the bud. The war also had a disastrous effect on the rest of industry: the fruits of a half-century of significant, albeit timid, industrial expansion had been laid waste, and smuggling became a way of life as Spain's traditional industry tried to rebuild itself, plunging the monetary system into chaos. The loss of its possessions in Central America and the whole of South America except Brazil also rocked the country's industrial foundations. Without its American markets and sources of raw materials, the metropolitan industry, which had finally seen the Seville trading monopoly broken in the late eighteenth century, was dealt a staggering blow.

1.2. *The mechanism behind industrial development up to 1936.* For development to get under way, there had to be political changes: the abolition of the Inquisition, the *Mesta* and the guilds; disentailment; and the laying of new foundations for the fiscal and monetary integration of the Peninsula's kingdoms. None of this happened until after the death of Ferdinand VII.

Spain also imported a spirit of enterprise, technology and capital, enabling industries (with the exception of Catalonian textiles) to get on their feet. Railways, mining and some public services were promoted; foreign investment also gave life to the chemical industry; the iron and steel industry was built by Basque entrepreneurs with the profits generated by iron exports to Great Britain; and the private banking system was developed by capital repatriated from the former colonies lost in 1898 (Cuba, Puerto Rico and the Philippines).

The new industry created to meet domestic market demand could not take shape without protective tariffs. Following an endless free trade *versus* protectionism debate, industrial protectionism was ultimately established in 1892 (and later reconfirmed with the 'Arancel Cambò' of 1922), and from that year industrialisation began an uninterrupted, foreign-capital-financed slow march ahead. By 1900 the involvement of the private banking system in this process was proceeding steadily. The two world wars, in which Spain remained neutral, caused supply difficulties which gave rise to import substitution.

Thus until the end of the nineteenth century, Spain's only industrialisation policy consisted of promoting foreign investment and raising protective trade barriers. Bills were only enacted to protect domestic industry early in this century. With the Act of 14 February 1907, all government contracts could thereafter only include goods made in Spain. The Comisión Protectora de la Producción Nacional (Domestic Production Protection Commission), created by this act, later helped prepare a series of new protectionist acts: that of 14 July 1909 to advance maritime transport and shipbuilding industries; that of 2 March 1917, to protect new industries and develop existing ones; that of 22 July 1918, to organise and nationalise industries; and that of 22 April 1922, to raise tariff barriers. When the Consejo de Economía Nacional (Council on the National Economy) was founded in 1925, the Comisión Protectora was absorbed by the new Council's department of industrial protection.

However, it was the supply shortages of the First World War that did most to stimulate new industries. We have just mentioned act of 2 March 1917 to protect new and existing industries; it also created the Banco de Crédito Industrial in 1920 to provide domestic industry with medium- and long-term loans, but the design of the bank prevented this task from being carried out, because loans were only granted to create or expand industry, never to respond to day-to-day financial needs. This initial problem was resolved by the Decree Law of 29 April 1927, which authorised the bank to confer both fixed and current asset loans. Later, the Decree Law of 23 June 1929 extended the maximum repayment period from fifteen to fifty years.

The Act of 1917, the Decree Law of 30 April 1924 (which regulated the first act) and the Act of 31 December 1927 (a rewrite of the first two laws) were precursors of today's industrial protection legislation. This protection coincided with an upturn in the economy, and industries did indeed grow. We can plot the evolution of industrial development between the turn of the century and the outbreak of the Civil War with the help of the general industrial production index, prepared by the Council on the National Economy for the period between 1906 and 1936. This index shows three different stages of development. The first stage, from 1906 to 1923, is marked by slow growth with recessions in 1908 and 1911. In the second stage, from 1923 to 1930 (coinciding with the dictatorship of Primo de Rivera), industries grew and production levels rose three times faster than in the previous period. During the 1930–6 period, industrial production reached record levels in 1931. Then in the two following years the worldwide economic crisis took its toll of Spanish exports and, consequently, on industry. A recovery began in 1934, but it was interrupted by the outbreak of the Civil War.

1.3. *Industrialisation, 1939–59: Autarky*.　Tariff barriers, the key to industrial development until 1939, became inoperative thereafter because the severe quantitative restrictions (import licences, quotas and exchange controls) made necessary by the war in Europe virtually sealed off the domestic market from industrial imports. The lack of international competition was the main factor driving forward industrial development. Paradoxically, foreign trade restrictions were the main obstruction on the road to industrial expansion.

In the stage of development ushered in around 1939, the state maintained and strengthened the industrial policy which had prevailed throughout the long preceding period. The prime objective of the new industrialisation policy was to achieve an advanced degree of economic autarky, along with a stronger national defence, by upgrading military industries and raw materials used for military purposes. This policy found its legislative expression in the Industry Acts of 1939 (on the Protection and Development of National Industries — the foundation for 'industries of national interest' — and on the Organisation and Protection of National Industries). To ensure that the objectives set forth in the Acts should be realised, the state intervened directly in production through the Instituto Nacional de Industria (INI — National Institute of Industry), established in 1941 to take the place of private initiative when that was not forthcoming, either because very large investment was needed or because profit margins were slight. However, for a number of reasons (basically foreign trade bottle necks), autarky could not be realised. Goals became so inaccessible that they were eventually renounced altogether, leaving mountainous errors in their wake: uneconomic companies too small to meet urgent foreign market needs, for which they had been designed; operations that sooner or later had to be abandoned because of the technology employed (substitute industries); and the costly collapse of public enterprises, turning people against state economic intervention and development planning. And when the financial system that was followed gave a stimulus to inflation and reduced the consumption levels of the working and middle classes, another problem arose. This was that the sacrifices that people had made over so many years did not earn their rewards, because industrial development was insufficient to improve the position of the working classes; rather, those people involved in the state monopolies became richer through the typical inflationary income redistribution mechanisms.

The period between 1941 and 1950 was one of slow growth, because the shortage of energy and raw materials (cement, steel and non-ferrous metals) strangled production. A change occurred in the economic cycle in 1950, largely due to better climatic conditions (the end of a long drought), United States economic aid in exchange for military bases in Spain, and the securing of credit facilities from certain European countries to purchase capital goods from Britain, France and Belgium. The inception of tourism, aided by the improvement in Spain's foreign relations from 1950 onwards, was also related to the upward trend. Thus from 1951 to 1957 the rate of economic growth was double what it had been during the Primo de Rivera dictatorship. It is also interesting to note that this second stage of development of basic industries was more important than the first.

The intensive industrial development reflected in the indices does not mean that any proper planning lay behind it. Throughout the 1950s there were absolutely no plans that included all the different sectors; there was merely a strong preference for industry over

Table 4.1.   INDUSTRIAL INCOME
( × *1 million ptas*)

| | Current ptas | 1970 ptas | Real growth Index (1955 = 100) |
|---|---|---|---|
| 1955 | 133,178 | 232,767 | 100.0 |
| 1956 | 149,984 | 249,879 | 107.3 |
| 1957 | 173,375 | 261,544 | 112.3 |
| 1958 | 197,941 | 277,717 | 119.3 |
| 1959 | 204,029 | 283,877 | 121.9 |
| 1960 | 210,360 | 291,135 | 125.0 |
| 1961 | 248,171 | 338,839 | 145.5 |
| 1962 | 279,917 | 370,772 | 159.2 |
| 1963 | 323,297 | 409,660 | 175.9 |
| 1964 | 377,987 | 462,045 | 198.5 |
| 1965 | 436,891 | 513,977 | 220.8 |
| 1966 | 503,611 | 575,713 | 247.3 |
| 1967 | 549,462 | 611,629 | 262.7 |
| 1968 | 596,480 | 644,801 | 277.0 |
| 1969 | 690,190 | 729,603 | 313.4 |
| 1970 | 767,112 | 767,112 | 329.5 |
| 1971 | 857,361 | 814,319 | 349.8 |
| 1972 | 1,029,759 | 930,668 | 399.8 |
| 1973 | 1,240,243 | 1,021,092 | 438.6 |
| 1974 | 1,547,782 | 1,093,696 | 469.8 |
| 1975 | 1,798,603 | 1,095,490 | 470.6 |
| 1976 | 2,181,705 | 1,133,940 | 487.1 |
| 1977 | 2,654,673 | 1,177,596 | 505.9 |
| 1978 | 3,146,295 | 1,198,793 | 515.0 |
| 1979 | 3,582,044 | 1,213,670 | 521.4 |
| 1980 | 4,054,874 | 1,216,097 | 522.4 |
| 1981 | 4,572,535 | 1,222,177 | 524.8 |
| 1982 | 5,204,672 | 1,228,755 | 527.8 |
| 1983 | 6,037,420 | 1,259,847 | 541.2 |
| 1984 | 6,876,700 | 1,292,792 | 555.4 |

*Source:* Banco de Bilbao.

agriculture. However, the industrial development that took place was not harmonious; basic sectors were neglected for years, logically leading to shortages and rising energy and industrial raw materials prices. Finally, state intervention compounded the typical problems of an antiquated industrial structure: limited scope, centralism, and poor distribution, not to mention the negative effects of monopolies.

1.4. *The National Institute of Industry (INI).*   The INI was established under the Act of 25 September 1941 with the object — as the legal texts state — of "fostering and financing, on behalf of the nation, the creation and recovery of Spanish industries, particularly those working towards national defence or autarky, by offering Spanish savings a safe and attractive investment''. Its main purpose was to protect the nation and develop self-sufficiency.

The INI has financial and legal status. Formerly placed under the office of the President, this agency was passed on in 1968 to the Ministry of Industry. By virtue of its founding law, it is responsible for promoting industries so that they can eventually operate within the private sector. The companies in which the INI is directly involved are scattered among the different sectors of the economy; it has, in fact, become a state holding company, with direct controlling interests in some 70 different companies and indirect controlling interests in another 100. It was initially (in 1941) endowed with 50 million pesetas and state-transferred bearer securities (except those of Campsa, Tabacalera and the Spanish National Telephone Company). Its funds came from different sources: subsidies advanced by the state (up till 1958 mainly from monetisable bond issues), profits generated by the holding company's own enterprises, and income produced by selling off companies to the private sector. The INI was also authorised to issue bonds, the sale of which has been its main source of income since 1958. Under its founding law, bonds had to be placed with savings banks (*Cajas de Ahorro* — see Chapter XIII/5), which was not necessarily the safest or most attractive investment for these state-controlled financial institutions.

It is reasonable at this point to ask what was the real purpose behind the INI. It has been said that one of its chief aims was to break the monopoly in certain sectors, but this is doubtful. The INI has never applied any prices lower than those set by private enterprises; in fact, it joined forces with private companies in a series of mixed public and private ventures of dubious general interest. The anti-trust effects of INI investments in the iron and steel industry were only appreciable at the end of the 1950s. When foreign competition stiffened in 1962, following the lowering of trade barriers, the institute sided with private companies in their request for protection and in the hope of maintaining high domestic prices. The INI has done even less in other monopolistic sectors. Its activities in cement production have been minimal and in paper production almost valueless; and in the nitrogenous fertiliser industry, the institute started up production at the very moment when the market was decontrolled, which did not lower market prices — indeed its fertiliser companies teamed up with other domestic manufacturers in a bid for higher prices.

The second legal purpose traditionally assigned to the INI was to achieve autarky, in which it also (fortunately) failed. And, with the exception of the navy, it was unsuccessful at creating and maintaining industries, a task that was not embarked upon till the 1980s, when it gave Spanish industry a military dimension.

Although the INI has not effectively tackled any of these three objectives, its true role has been that of direct state intervention to strengthen production — and this involvement alone justifies its existence. Its achievements in the areas of oil, iron and steel, electricity, shipbuilding, cellulose, transport etc. are respectable. However, the cost of this strengthening must also be weighed. Especially up to 1957, the INI financed itself with inflation — with compulsory savings that have weighed heavily on the working and middle classes. These measures have lowered levels of consumption, setting off spiralling price rises, fuelled by the monetisation of government bonds and, therefore, fiduciary expansion.

In spite of this criticism, we do not believe that the INI should be dismantled and its activities transferred to the private sector. But it should be reorganised so that its activities are redefined on the basis of present-day assumptions, leaving behind those of the 1939 autarky policy. The INI is no longer the only state holding company. First, the Ministry of Finance has for some time had a controlling interest in Tabacalera, the National Telephone Company and official banks. Secondly, since 1981 the Instituto Nacional de Hidrocarburos (INH — National Hydrocarbon Institute) has operated as a holding company in the oil and gas sector. And thirdly, in 1983 the state expropriated the private Rumasa group, made up of 400 companies. In 1984 the process of returning these companies to the private sector got under way. The problems of the INI and, in general, of all public enterprises are larger than any of the problems

---

Fig. 12 (*overleaf*). RANKING OF SPAIN'S 50 LARGEST
INDUSTRIAL COMPANIES
*(1983 sales figures)*

*Note*. Foreign capital has partial control of 3 of these companies and majority or complete control of 12, while the state, either directly or through the INI, has partial control of 4 companies and majority or complete control of 13. Consequently, private Spanish companies not closely involved with financial groups are in the minority among these leaders. All this goes to show that industrialism in Spain is either state capitalism (INI), foreign capitalism, or capitalism backed by a financial group. Independent industries are not among Spain's top companies.

| 1983 | 1982 | Company | Activity | Sales figure | Value added | Net profit (NP) | Investment | Own assets (OA) | Profitability (NP/OA) | No. of employees |
|---|---|---|---|---|---|---|---|---|---|---|
| | | | | ($\times$ 1 million ptas) | | | | | | |
| 1 | 1 | Campsa | Oil distribution | 1,299,713 | 35,018 | 6,885 | 12,001 | 36,979 | 0.186 | 8,908 |
| 2 | 2 | Empetrol | Oil refining | 605,675 | 53,864 | 2,065 | 9,806 | 72,375 | 0.028 | 5,667 |
| 3 | 3 | Cepsa | Oil refining | 448,900 | 38,442 | 2,133 | 9,066 | 41,004 | 0.052 | 4,422 |
| 4 | 4 | Telefónica | Public services | 313,422 | 336,927 | 27,536 | 175,520 | 668,275 | 0.041 | 66,830 |
| 5 | 8 | El Corte Inglés | Department stores | 215,053 | 54,634 | 4,678 | 3,873 | 81,775 | 0.057 | 21,776 |
| 6 | 6 | Iberia | Transportation | 209,217 | 72,164 | −29,965 | 9,369 | 43,696 | −0.685 | 24,240 |
| 7 | 5 | Fasa-Renault | Vehicles | 205,964 | 77,142 | 11,151 | 18,906 | 77,348 | 0.144 | 21,714 |
| 8 | 7 | Petronor | Oil refining | 191,783 | 13,252 | 2,973 | 16,532 | 36,759 | 0.080 | 654 |
| 9 | 9 | Explosivos Río Tinto | Chemicals | 187,836 | 36,668 | −14,984 | 4,011 | 26,556 | −0.564 | 9,253 |
| 10 | 10 | Iberduero | Electricity | 161,342 | 65,274 | 11,983 | 38,486 | 490,981 | 0.024 | 8,157 |
| 11 | 12 | Hidroeléctrica | Electricity | 157,580 | 58,440 | 18,485 | 97,705 | 489,213 | 0.037 | 6,725 |
| 12 | 14 | Tabacalera | Tobacco | 152,928 | 219,423 | 1,361 | 10,455 | 8,194 | 0.166 | 8,696 |
| 13 | 11 | Ensidesa | Iron and steel | 150,353 | 51,193 | −27,725 | 4,336 | 50,263 | −0.551 | 22,356 |
| 14 | 19 | Seat | Vehicles | 146,796 | 48,027 | −35,778 | 42,152 | 44,412 | −0.805 | 25,170 |
| 15 | 13 | Hispanoil | Oil prospecting | 143,407 | 10,778 | 1,596 | 9,815 | 6,839 | 0.233 | 266 |
| 16 | 15 | Endesa | Electricity | 141,997 | 88,722 | 24,866 | 49,173 | 171,812 | 0.144 | 5,987 |
| 17 | 17 | Dragados y Constr. | Building | 137,981 | 34,651 | 759 | 2,708 | 18,825 | 0.041 | 14,348 |
| 18 | 16 | Ford España | Vehicles | 136,691 | 31,535 | 3,399 | 7,893 | 39,396 | 0.086 | 9,373 |
| 19 | 18 | Unión Eléctrica-Fenosa | Electricity | 130,689 | 66,955 | 8,468 | 194,182 | 434,476 | 0.019 | 7,640 |
| 20 | 20 | Butano | Oil refining | 130,140 | 14,163 | −790 | 4,187 | — | — | 3,700 |
| 21 | 94 | General Motors España | Vehicles | 129,842 | — | — | 9,644 | 30,000 | — | 8,880 |
| 22 | 21 | Petrolíber | Refining | 119,648 | 11,043 | 508 | 2,799 | 16,334 | 0.031 | 834 |
| 23 | 23 | Renfe | Transportation | 119,585 | 46,958 | −94,773 | 118,230 | 272,178 | 0.348 | 74,964 |

| | | | | | | | | | | |
|---|---|---|---|---|---|---|---|---|---|---|
| 24 | 22 | Sevillana | Electricity | 111,531 | 61,955 | 3,982 | 62,943 | 201,025 | 0.019 | 6,373 |
| 25 | 24 | Petromed | Oil refining | 107,021 | 7,946 | 2,595 | 5,969 | 25,446 | 0.101 | 422 |
| 26 | 25 | Fecsa | Electricity | 104,221 | 45,382 | 7,439 | 95,161 | 303,296 | 0.024 | 6,293 |
| 27 | 27 | Citröen Hispania | Vehicles | 88,900 | 18,202 | -3,963 | 2,420 | 15,039 | -0.263 | 9,135 |
| 28 | 28 | Altos Hornos de Vizcaya | Iron and steel | 83,744 | 34,577 | -5,389 | 2,115 | 26,031 | -0.207 | 11,004 |
| 29 | 29 | IBM España | Hardware and software | 78,772 | — | 6,061 | 14,731 | 23,127 | 0.262 | 3,700 |
| 30 | 33 | EN Bazán | Shipbuilding | 76,382 | — | -3,931 | 835 | 10,298 | -0.381 | 14,087 |
| 31 | 32 | EN Autocamiones | Vehicles | 75,147 | 17,948 | -2,793 | 2,707 | 11,266 | -0.247 | 9,323 |
| 32 | 30 | Michelin | Rubber | 75,101 | — | — | — | — | — | 12,836 |
| 33 | 34 | Enagás | Public services | 74,986 | 21,952 | -1,267 | 6,520 | 45,752 | -0.027 | 541 |
| 34 | 31 | Agromán | Building | 74,750 | 21,633 | 203 | 3,951 | 9,498 | 0.021 | 11,000 |
| 35 | 43 | Dow Chemical | Chemicals | 71,684 | — | — | 2,034 | 17,971 | — | 1,076 |
| 36 | 40 | Promotora de Hipermercados | Department stores | 64,171 | 7,560 | 1,094 | — | 8,793 | 0.124 | 3,700 |
| 37 | 26 | Astilleros Españoles | Shipbuilding | 63,851 | — | -27,306 | 5,074 | — | — | 15,155 |
| 38 | 37 | Entrecanales y Tavora | Building | 62,000 | — | — | — | — | — | 9,500 |
| 39 | 39 | Nestlé | Food | 61,658 | 19,817 | 4,316 | 2,053 | 31,005 | 0.139 | 4,640 |
| 40 | 44 | Cindasa | Edible soils | 60,271 | — | — | 202 | 4,604 | — | 400 |
| 41 | 50 | Talbot | Vehicles | 55,446 | 20,240 | -8,022 | 3,004 | 21,345 | -0.375 | 9,101 |
| 42 | 42 | Galerías Preciados | Department stores | 54,719 | — | -7,300 | — | — | — | 11,404 |
| 43 | 46 | Cubiertas y MZOV | Building | 51,503 | 13,642 | 481 | 1,297 | 7,337 | 0.065 | 6,932 |
| 44 | 41 | Huarte | Building | 51,075 | 9,909 | 601 | 1,032 | 7,519 | 0.079 | 940 |
| 45 | 48 | Motor Ibérica | Vehicles | 50,767 | 14,066 | -5,774 | 2,237 | 16,159 | -0.357 | 7,432 |
| 46 | 45 | FOCSA | Building | 50,749 | 17,151 | 474 | 1,155 | 7,008 | 0.067 | 11,064 |
| 47 | 58 | Hunosa | Mining | 48,606 | 41,534 | -4,236 | 6,195 | 11,825 | -0.358 | 21,112 |
| 48 | 49 | Standard Eléctrica | Electronics | 47,758 | 33,034 | -1,674 | 1,569 | 19,685 | -0.085 | 16,133 |
| 49 | 38 | Ford Credit | Finance | 46,784 | 3,472 | 501 | 15 | 1,760 | 0.285 | 126 |
| 50 | 137 | Hoechst Ibérica | Chemicals | 46,550 | — | — | — | — | — | 1,310 |

*Source: Fomento de la Producción, 1984.*

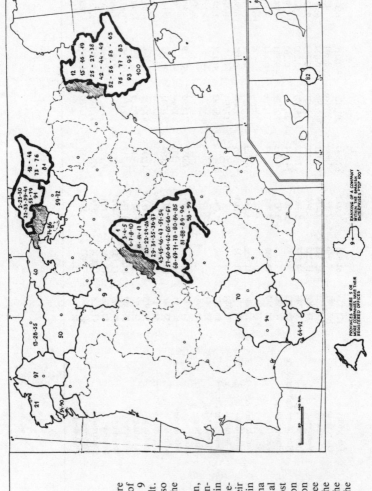

Fig. 13.
HEAD OFFICES
OF SPAIN'S
50 LEADING
INDUSTRIAL
COMPANIES

These companies are numbered in order of importance. E.g., no. 9 represents Fasa-Renault. (Data refer to 1980 and so are not consistent with the ranking in Fig. 12.)

Like the population, major companies are concentrated in three main centres (Madrid, Barcelona and Bilbao). Of their head offices 45% are in Madrid, 20% in Barcelona and 10% in Bilbao, a total of 75%. Thus the most important decisions on investment and expansion are mainly taken in three areas (also the home of the main stock exchanges, the financial oligarchy and the industrial bourgeoisie).

encountered hitherto. Public enterprises have problems with control, the regionalisation of investment, the decentralisation of activities, employee participation, conflict of interest, the acquisition and disposal of property and many other factors that affect performance. All these issues are addressed in the public enterprise by-laws bill announced in the Moncloa Agreements of 27 October 1977. Although they were not subsequently enacted, the possibility of their being introduced increases as the economy becomes modernised. The essential elements are as follows:

(*a*) *Parliamentary control.* Given the problems of public enterprises, parliamentary control would be exercised by a specific subcommission within the Economic Commission of the Congreso de los Diputados (House of Representatives) in the Cortes.

(*b*) *Government control* in accordance with the following points: — Joint coordination and organisation by an agency within the Administration; — External financial control in accordance with budgeting by–laws; — Internal control by authorised ministerial departments.

(*c*) *Regionalisation of investment* to advance less developed regions and earmark percentages for each area.

(*d*) *Decentralisation of activities* as far as possible in accordance with the general guidelines laid down for public enterprises.

(*e*) *Employee participation.* Recognition of employee participation in the government agencies within public enterprises through trade unions and with channels for consumer or user consultations.

(*f*) *Acquisition and disposal* of companies or stock by the public sector at competitive prices.

(*g*) *Conditions affecting performance.* Avoidance of discriminating situations by matching the conditions affecting the performance of both public and private enterprises.

1.5. *Current problems of industrial policy.* The first symptons of a basic change in autarkic industrial policy could be seen in the way industrial policy lagged behind trade policy. While import restrictions were lifted in the trading sector in July 1959, the industrial sector still held to the rigid system established by the laws of 1939. Finally, in 1963, the industrial sector began to loosen up. In January of that year new factories, relocations and expansion were (with some exceptions) permitted without previous authorisation. Production capacity minimums were set in each sector for new industrial plant to avoid excessively small companies from coming into being (had this measure been taken earlier, the industry would

## Fig. 14. MAJOR INDUSTRIAL CENTRES

This figure presents the leading industrial centres of the major companies in eleven different sectors. Eighty factories operate in 29 provinces. With the exception of Gerona and Alicante (bases for many small- and medium-size companies), the remaining 31 provinces have no major factories. Nor are there any sizeable industrial centres in the western strip, in the Iberian System or on part of the *meseta*.

This map also shows how dependence influences location. For example, with the exception of Puertollano, all oil refineries are situated on the coast to receive imports of crude. The same occurs with iron and steel industries, which are increasingly dependent on sea transport for their basic inputs. On the other hand, the more flexible automobile industry has set up shop in a variety of areas, such as Valladolid, Linares, Madrid, Zaragoza, Barcelona, Pamplona, Almusafes (Valencia), Figueruelas (Zaragoza), etc.

It is also interesting to note the migratory trend of factory centres as companies expand. For example, the Michelin company started up operations in the outskirts of San Sebastian (Lasarte) and then branched out towards the south, first in Vitoria and later in Aranda de Duero. The same pattern has been followed by Firestone and Standard Electric (a subsidiary of ITT).

A diversity of working centres can usually be traced back to the founding of a company. If a large company is formed by the merging of several smaller ones, wide distribution of offices or factories is often the result. This is true of Astilleros Españoles, SA (AESA), with factories in Bilbao, Seville and Cadiz; it was constituted when the Empresa Nacional Elcano, Astilleros de Cádiz, SE de Construcción Naval and Euskalduna were consolidated in the 1960s.

OIL REFINERIES
COPPER
ALUMINIUM
INTEGRATED STEEL MILLS
SHIPBUILDING
AUTOMOBILE INDUSTRY
TYRE FACTORIES
NITROGENOUS FERTILISERS
PETROCHEMICAL FACTORIES
CELLULOSE PRODUCTION
TELEPHONE PRODUCTION

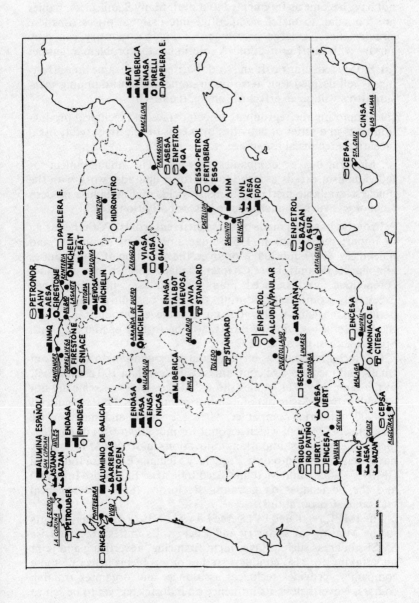

not have become as fragmented as it did). Many Spanish companies are too small to match competitive international prices. In these circumstances, a large percentage of Spain's industry can only survive with tariff protection. A solution to this problem might be:

(*a*) Slowly reducing tariff and trade barriers, at the same time effecting a well-defined long-term programme and anti-dumping measures (this will be an effect of joining the EEC).

(*b*) Promoting the regrouping of companies and technical production units in a series of activities by means of selective credit, fiscal incentives, technical assistance etc.

(*c*) Modernising as companies regroup. The abandonment of individualism breeds a desire to improve, upgrade, work with the quickest available methods, increase yields and maximise modern technology, such as microelectronics, robotisation etc.

Progress has been made on these different fronts. With the easing of import restrictions in 1959, huge amounts of equipment and machinery were imported. Moreover, the reduction of import duties and market decontrol (see Chapter V) made Spanish industry more competitive, and induced many companies, which had been excessively comfortable during the previous ultra-protectionist period, to reorganise. This goal, partly achieved through GATT and the unilateral lowering of tariffs, will be further encouraged with Spain's accession to the EEC.

Our recommendations on industrial consolidation do not rule out small- and medium-size companies (with less than 100 employees), in the same way that studies show that economies of scale are not enough to bring Spain out of its more serious crises. Of the country's 350,000 industrial companies, 90% are small- and medium-size enterprises (SMSEs), which account for more than 50% of employment. The two most important innovations in official SMSE policy have been the Instituto de la Pequeña y Mediana Empresa Industrial (IMPI — Small- and Medium-Sized Industrial Enterprise Institute) and the Sociedades de Garantía Recíproca (SGR — Reciprocal Guarantee Corporations).

The IMPI, regulated by Decree Law 1114/1978 of 2 May, reports to the Ministry of Industry and Energy. Its duties are to advise SMSEs in areas such as investment financing, advertising and joint undertakings; it also conducts studies on problems affecting these companies, provides technical assistance, and organises training courses. Nevertheless, its influence on industry has yet to be felt to any important extent.

The SGR was created under Decree Law 1885/1978 of 26 July for the purpose of 'providing collateral security or any other legally acceptable guarantee to its members' to secure credit that would be unobtainable on an individual basis. But SGRs, 22 of which were established in 1978–81 with 2,300 million ptas in capital assets and 15,000 million in collateral security, are required to have a 'second collateral' before financing can be raised. To this end the Decree of 10 April 1981 established the 'Sociedad del Segundo Aval' (the Second Collateral Corporation) with public and private capital (state/SGR). In spite of the SRG's attractiveness, private banks and savings institutions continue to be the main sources of credit.

To provide a clearer picture of Spanish industry today, two foreign relations problems must be broached. First of all, Spanish industry is dependent on foreign technology. If we look at the leading companies in different sectors — automobiles, motorcycles, electrical machinery, electronics, computer science, food, pharmaceuticals etc. — most are producing goods in Spain under foreign patents and licences. It would be naive to aim for complete self-sufficiency, but Spain's degree of dependence is frequently excessive and detrimental to export activities, since patent-owners prefer to authorise their use exclusively for the domestic market. Despite the mediocre results of this policy, Spanish businessmen, with some honourable exceptions, prefer to acquire patents the easy way instead of seeking scientists and technicians to study and build new prototypes; it is almost as if Miguel de Unamuno's grotesque maxim 'Let others invent' was making itself felt among the country's entrepreneurs. And the state has done little to put this situation right, and thus encourage exports and industrial expansion. Apart from some outdated patent legislation (a new bill was presented to the Cortes in 1982 but its enactment has been delayed due to EEC complications), no effort has been made to create an official scientific and technical research centre to work directly with industry. Most developed countries invest 2–4% of their GDP in research; Spain invests 0.3% in bureaucratised agencies, such as the Consejo Superior de Investigaciones Científicas (CSIC — Council for Scientific Research). In recent years the restrictions of foreign technology on exports have eased up, as a result of foreign capital consolidations in Spanish export companies. Today cars, telephone equipment, household appliances etc. are exported.

There was some concerted action in the 1960s and '70s — state loans and other aid to modernise complete sectors and the subsidising of industrial growth areas and individual industrial estates (see Chapter 16). Then came the international industrial crisis set off in 1973, which reached Spain in 1975. But because of the policy followed during the transition to democracy, countermeasures did not immediately tackle the situation in its entirety. A broad approach could have been achieved in the Moncloa Agreements of October 1977, but the country fell into a 'drop by drop' policy — yesterday one company, today a second, tomorrow a third — without solving any of the overall problems. The most that happened was that a series of government/employer/trade union agreements were made in specific sectors (e.g. iron and steel and shipbuilding); however, follow-up was insignificant.

In an attempt to tackle the matter more systematically, after so much time had passed that the scope and intensity of the problem highlighted the situation, Decree Law 9/1981 of 5 June 'on industrial reconversion measures' was published. It established a framework for economic aid to be given to large sectors in crisis through reconversion plans (one per sector), negotiated by the Administration, employers' associations and trade unions. Most of the aid was given in the form of tax relief and soft loans. Later the Socialist Government emphasised the importance of reconversion by adopting Decree Law 8/83 of 30 November, promoting the organisation of 'sectorial reconversion enterprises' and 'job creation funds'; it also made 'horizontal' or geographical reconversion possible for 'areas in urgent need of industrial reconversion' to assist the traditional industrial areas most affected by the crisis. Industrial reconversion plans have been most dramatic (often precipitating social upheaval) in the iron and steel and shipbuilding sectors.

1.6. *Industrial net income.*  Gross industrial product is the gross value of production minus the value of raw and other materials employed; it is the added value generated by industry. And by further subtracting depreciation and indirect taxes, we obtain the industrial net income figures shown in Table 4.1.

This chapter covers the fourteen industrial sectors recognized in the National Accounts, starting with basic industries (energy, extractive, iron and steel, construction materials and chemicals), later moving on to consumer goods (textiles, leather and footware, paper etc.), an intermediate group of transforming industries (including shipbuilding, railway materials, vehicles and machinery) and durable goods.

## 2. *Basic industries*

2.1. *Energy.*  The size and possibilities of a country's energy sector can make or break economic development, and in the past, energy deficiencies were partly responsible for Spain's industrial backwardness. The country's energy possibilities consist in mining domestic coal beds, importing enriched uranium for nuclear power plants, purchasing crude oil (domestic production is limited) to be refined domestically, and harnessing hydroelectric power. Our discussion of the energy sector will centre on the current structure of production and on the coal, fuel and electricity market.

A new energy policy began to take shape during the Moncloa Agreements (1977), when the various political parties involved agreed on a diagnosis of the situation. In their opinion, Spain's energy crisis was particularly serious for three reasons: excessive energy consumption in relation to GNP and an irrational use of primary energy; a scarcity of domestic energy sources, resulting in a disproportionate reliance on foreign sources; and, lastly, the adverse effect of energy imports on Spain's balance of payments.

To correct this situation, it was agreed that the Cortes would be presented with a new National Energy Plan, in harmony with environmental concerns, with a view to diminishing the intensity and elasticity of energy consumption.

PEN 78/87 (Plan Energético Nacional, updated for 1981/90 and later for 1984/93) was finally debated in Congress in 1979 and adopted as follows:

(*a*) Approval of the energy balance sheet, with emphasis on nuclear energy.

(*b*) Fixing prices high enough to cover costs, and the adoption of energy conservation measures.

(*c*) Research on new energy sources, particularly solar energy and the recycling of waste.

(*d*) Nominal control of the public sector, but without taking power away from UNESA (see page 113) and thus becoming involved in high-tension networks and load distribution systems.

(*e*) The creation of a Nuclear Safety Council as an agency under the Ministry of Industry and Energy.

(*f*) An agreement to encourage the use of coal, hydrocarbon research and a greater consumption of natural gas (turning this goal into a reality was somewhat doubtful, given the PEN's polarised treatment of the nuclear alternative).

(*g*) A set of *social relations* promises concerning consumer and environmental protection.

Developed in the 1978/83 PEN were, as envisaged, the nuclear and coal power plant programmes and the four acts summarised below (among others):

(*a*) The Act of 15/1980 of 22 April, creating the Nuclear Safety Council, the only agency given powers in connection with nuclear safety and radioactive protection matters.

(*b*) Modification of the Mining Act, under Act 54/1980 of 5 November, giving special attention to mineral energy resources. It modifies the Mining Act of 21 July of 1973 by founding a new section (called 'section D') encompassing coal, radioactive minerals, geothermal resources, bituminous rock and all other energy-related mineral resources, as agreed on by the government or required by the economy for national defence. The text defines the special zones and sets forth application procedures and the period during which exploration and research permits and mining leases shall be valid. The Act also governs the terms under which the government itself may develop these resources.

(*c*) Act 82/1980 of 30 December is designed to strengthen energy conservation activities. It governs the profits derived by individuals and businesses engaged in any of the activities contemplated in the text and in the agreement endorsed by the Administration.

(*d*) Act 7/1981 requires customers to pay an Electricity Tax (or *bribe*) to municipalities for the use of nuclear installations. The proceeds of the tax are distributed according to the capacity of the coal, hydraulic or nuclear energy electrical power plant authorised in each province.

The PEN was revised in 1984 under the approving eye of the Socialist government in the following manner: nuclear energy was given less importance, with the inauguration of the Lemoniz plant (in the Basque country) being postponed for political reasons and the construction of three other plants being delayed; the state took control of the National Grid (the high-tension network) of the national electric power system; the oil sector was reshaped; and the state decided to intervene in the distribution of electric power company dividends to ensure their financial reorganisation.

2.1(*a*). *Coal.*  Coal mined in Spain is on the whole of less good quality and more expensive than the average imported coal. It has a low calorific value and a high percentage content of ash and sulphur, and thus very little can be used for coking. Coal production is costly for three reasons: first, the layers of many anthracite and hard coal deposits are thin and scattered, with an average thickness of 50–60 cm.; secondly, unlike most large foreign mining operations, the coal mining process in Spain must also include coal washing; and thirdly, Spanish coal is friable, or fine, which is not a positive selling point. Its most successful use is at *in situ* power plants located alongside the

Table 4.2.  COAL PRODUCTION

| | Anthracite 10³ tonnes | Hard coal 10³ tonnes | Lignite 10³ tonnes | Total 10³ TEC (*) |
|---|---|---|---|---|
| 1931–5 | 633 | 5,980 | 317 | |
| 1940–5 | 1,370 | 8,395 | 1,136 | |
| 1946–50 | 1,467 | 9,187 | 2,336 | |
| 1951–5 | 1,858 | 10,225 | 1,691 | |
| 1956–60 | 2,274 | 10,576 | 1,934 | |
| 1961–5 | 2,694 | 10,284 | 2,525 | |
| 1966–70 | 2,798 | 9,357 | 2,755 | |
| 1971 | 2,876 | 7,811 | 3,081 | |
| 1972 | 3,013 | 8,051 | 3,068 | |
| 1973 | 2,989 | 6,976 | 2,999 | |
| 1974 | 2,948 | 7,391 | 2,882 | |
| 1975 | 3,154 | 7,469 | 3,380 | |
| 1976 | 3,548 | 6,969 | 4,150 | |
| 1977 | 3,730 | 8,010 | 5,810 | |
| 1978 | 3,801 | 7,598 | 8,257 | |
| 1979 | 3,654 | 7,829 | 10,542 | |
| 1980 | 3,864 | 8,820 | 14,964 | |
| 1981 | 4,644 | 9,517 | 20,606 | |
| 1982 | | 15,500 | 23,200 | 20,200 |
| 1986 | | 17,200 | 22,500 | 21,200 |
| 1990 | | 20,400 | 22,600 | 23,800 |
| 1992 | | 21,400 | 22,900 | 24,700 |

*Sources:* 1931–81, Ministry of Industry; 1982–92, National Energy Plan (1982, revised figures; 1986–92, forecasts).

* TEC = *Toneladas equivalentes a carbón* (equivalent in tonnes of hard coal).

mines themselves. Production figures appear in Table 4.2.

Spain has three major coal mining areas. In the north the Asturias-Leon region (including Palencia and Burgos) produces hard and anthracite coal, in Galicia lignite is plentiful around La Coruña, and large new deposits were found in Orense in 1982. In the south, hard coal deposits are mined in the provinces of Ciudad Real, Córdoba, Badajoz and Seville. The third area is Catalonia and Aragon, where lignite and hard coal reserves are worked.

Because of the unfavourable conditions surrounding coal production, mining has always been protected by the state. By the end of the Civil War, the coal situation had changed greatly from that of 1936; tight import restrictions due to shortages of foreign currency and industrialisation requirements forced a growth in domestic production. In 1941 the Coal Distribution Commission was established to determine selling areas for coal companies and quotas for different consumers — for both domestic and foreign coal.

From 1940, coal production was stimulated by a series of measures: military service exemptions for miners, cooperative stores subsidised by coal companies, housing programmes in coalfields, special prices for surplus production, etc. But with the 1959–61 Stabilisation Plan, which liberalised imports and suppressed fuel consumption restrictions, stagnation overtook domestic production because of low productivity, a small specialised labour force and the substitution of coal for electricity and petroleum-based products. Productivity was also undermined by sector fragmentation; at one time there were more than 500 mining companies, which gave few opportunities for development, since mining leases, resources and technology were limited. In 1967, to increase productivity, a mixed capital corporation was founded under the name of Hullera del Norte, SA (Hunosa), which was to reshape the mining operations of the leading companies (Duro-Felguera, Mieres, Industrial Asturiana, Hullera Española etc., as well as the INI). However, the INI and private enterprise made strange bedfellows and after two years the INI had to make huge outlays to buy out its private partners. Moreover, the employer-employee relationships of a state-run company are not the most suitable for such an unhealthy, dangerous and isolated activity as coal mining. Absenteeism and collective conflicts inevitably ensued. If possibilities of joint management and a time-table allowing more days off do not receive study, Hunosa will continue to chalk up losses year after year.

Prompted by the energy crisis, a movement got under way in October 1973 to review the measures of the period, now ended, of 'abundant and cheap energy'. To this effect, private initiative (specifically Fenosa) and the INI threw their energies into lignite mining to fuel the Sebon (La Coruña), the Puentes de García Rodriguez (La Coruña) and the Andorra (Teruel) thermal power plants. In 1978 the PEN laid down the foundations for coal power plants, envisaging higher production and consumption levels. The ecological consequences of this are dangerous, for the discharge of contaminants, particularly $SO_2$, could give rise to acid rain.

2.1(*b*).  *Oil.*  Because Spain was a non-oil-producing country up to the 1960s, the long chain of activities between extraction and consumption was nationalised as much as possible. This policy was started by setting up a state domestic distribution monopoly. Later, crude was transported by a fleet of Spanish-built tankers, to be refined at home. Faced with the possibility of fuel shortages, the synthesising of hydrocarbons from poor quality coal and bituminous slate was studied, but later abandoned (in 1962).

Until 1927, the Spanish oil by-products market operated with almost no intervention, but in this year, the Monopolios de Petróleos was constituted under the Minister of Finance, José Calvo Sotelo. This was done with two purposes in mind. The first was fiscal: the *de facto* private monopoly was to be replaced by a public monopoly which, by absorbing distribution earnings, would prevent tax evasion and increase revenue. The second aim was economic: the domestic economy was to be emancipated by acquiring foreign oil fields, building a fleet of tankers, and constructing a crude oil refining industry. Monopolio de Petróleos is involved in importing all kinds of industrial handling operations and warehousing, and in the sale of liquid mineral fuels and their derivatives. The agency works under the Ministry of Finance and its services are diffuse: it has jurisdiction in forty-eight provinces excluding the two provinces of the Canary islands. Its administrative activities are controlled by the Compañía Arrendataria del Monopolio de Petróleos, SA (Campsa). Campsa satisfied a fiscal purpose by carrying out distribution, which it often did ineffectively. Dividing out its duties among both public and private companies, Campsa relegated industrial development to a backseat position.

In 1984, with the reshaping of the energy sector and the preparations for Spain's entry into the EEC, the 'new Campsa' was formed by various Spanish oil groups, with the Instituto Nacional de Hidrocarburos (INH — National Hydrocarbon Institute) retaining a controlling interest. Although this public-private company will lose its commercial distribution monopoly when Spain becomes part of the EEC, it will continue to dominate the market. During a conference held by the present author at the Escuela de Minas in Madrid in the winter of 1973/4, the need for a coordinated hydrocarbons policy was pointed out. But bureaucratic delays, battles between different interest groups and the like prevented any decisions from being taken until the 1979 PEN was published; and three more years passed before Decree Law 8/1981 of 24 April was pronounced and INH itself was created; it is responsible to the Ministry of Industry and Energy. This law also limited the responsibilities of the various public authorities in matters concerning hydrocarbons.

The INH was set up as a public agency to coordinate and promote the hydrocarbon-related activities of public enterprises, in accordance with government guidelines. Its assets were the following:

(*a*) An initial endowment of 300 million ptas.

(*b*) State interests and rights in the two public/private refining companies, Petroliber (54%) and Hispanoil (100%).

(*c*) The interests and rights of the state and the Banco de España in Campsa (54%).

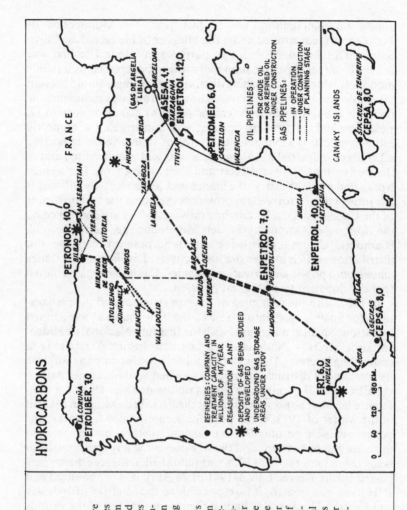

## Fig. 15. ENERGY

The first map in this Figure on hydrocarbons indicates the country's ten petroleum refineries, crude oil and finished products pipelines and gas pipelines (completed, under construction and still at the planning stage).

The second map shows nuclear power plants in operation, under construction and with future construction authorised. For cooling purposes, all the plants are located on the coast or alongside major rivers. With the exception of the Lemoniz plant, well-known for its many political start-up problems, the zones chosen for nuclear power plants are sparsely populated.

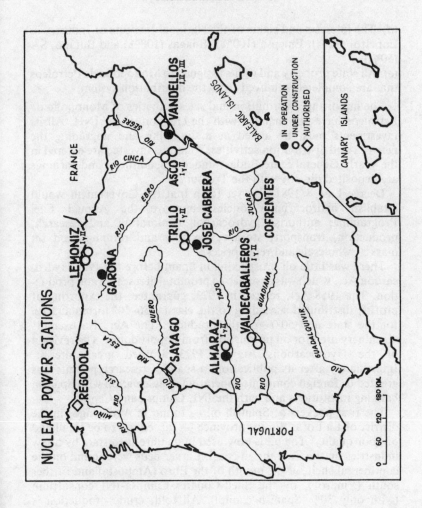

(*d*) The interests and rights of the National Institute of Industry in Enpetrol (92%), Eniepsa (100%), Enagas (100%) and Butano, SA (50%).

(*e*) All state property and rights assigned to Monopolio de Petróleos that are completely removed from the distribution system.

The importing, distribution and sales activities of Monopolio de Petróleos have not changed with the creation of the INH. All its investments must be aimed at maintaining and upgrading the network and distribution activities. Amounts invested are entered in the yearly General State Budget under expenditures, and earnings are deposited directly with the Treasury.

Decree Law 8/1981 also set forth that the Government would establish hydrocarbon policies; approve the Annual Fuel Programme; authorise hydrocarbon exploration and research, production, transport, storage, cleaning and refining; and set market, wholesale and retail prices.

There was little oil prospecting in Spain before the 1958 Hydrocarbon Act, which was designed to promote oil research and production. The 1958 Act, revised in 1973, guarantees the exporting of profits, distributed according to the classic '50–50' formula: 50% for the state and 50% for the producer. The Act also exempts machinery used for oil production from import duties. The revision of the Hydrocarbons Act in 1973 aroused great interest. Immediately after its publication, a spate of research permits was granted to foreign companies operating in association with Spanish banking institutions and with the INI, Campsa and Cepsa.

The first pockets of Spanish oil — found in Ayoluengo, in the district of La Lora, Burgos province — turned out to be small and of poor quality. The oil is now used in its unrefined state by a few industries on the Cantabrian coast. Larger beds were found on the continental shelf, at the mouth of the Ebro (Amposta) and further south (Vinaroz), by the Shell-Coparex-Campsa-INI consortium (with only 30% Spanish capital). All told, crude production is expected to reach some 3 million tons annually. Lastly, the Cantabrian Shelf discoveries off the Asturian coast are not as large as was initially hoped. Most productive will probably be the natural gas deposits on the continental shelf in the Gulf of Cadiz and the Aragonian Pyrenees (Sabiñánigo). Hispanoil's foreign prospecting activities (currently 100% INI) also show some promise.

Neither prospecting efforts nor synthetic hydrocarbon production have yielded satisfactory results. For this reason, most investment has been in imported crude oil refining. The following oil refineries have been built in Spain: Cepsa in Santa Cruz de Tenerife, the oldest and one of the most productive; Petrolíber in La Coruña, promoted by the Grupo Fierro and 52% state-owned; Riotinto in Huelva, founded by Minas de Riotinto, SE; the 'Gibraltar' refinery in Algeciras, promoted by Cepsa, the Banco Central and international oil interests; Petromed, in Castellón, owned by the Banco Español de Crédito; and Petronor, in Bilbao, financed by Campsa, Basque savings institutions and Petromex (a Mexican state-run enterprise).

The three remaining refineries in Puertollano, Cartagena and Tarragona belong to Enpetrol, within the INI group. Spain's refining capacity is approximately 70 million tonnes of crude, with a surplus of 20–25 million tonnes. Total consumption has dropped due to the economic crisis, energy conservation measures and oil substitution. Recent oil consumption figures (in thousands of tonnes) are as follows:

|  | 1975 | 1980 | 1984 |
|---|---|---|---|
| Domestic production | 1,166 | 1,602 | 2,318 |
| Imported crude | 48,506 | 49,412 | 41,718 |
| *Total* | 49,672 | 51,014 | 44,036 |

2.1(c). *The electric power industry.* Spain's first power-station was built in 1873 by Xifré and Dalmáu in Barcelona to feed many establishments, including the 'Maquinista Terrestre y Maritima (Land and Marine Machinist) enterprise. In 1890 the Compañía General Madrileña de Electricidad, in cooperation with the German firm AEG, constructed the first power-station in Madrid. Between 1890 and 1912, large private electric power companies emerged as the only protagonists in this sector until the INI companies were created: the Companía Sevillana de Electricidad in 1894; Hidroeléctrica Ibérica (which later became Iberduero) in 1901; Hidroeléctrica Española in 1907; the Barcelona Traction (today Fecsa) in 1911; and Unión Eléctrica Madrileña (today Unión Eléctrica Fenosa) in 1912. By 1914 the five major companies that today control 60% of the market were already in a state of expansion.

Capacity and production grew slowly (see Table 4.3). In 1936 electric power capacity was 1,909,000 kw. (25% thermal electric and 75% hydroelectric), with a production level of 2,800 million kwh. In the 1940–53 period, new features emerged in the domestic electric power market: uniform rates, increased state intervention and joint management of the electrical power network. In 1953 a flat rate went

Table 4.3.    ELECTRIC POWER PRODUCTION
*(millions of KwH)*

|      | Hydraulic | Thermal | Nuclear | Total   |
|------|-----------|---------|---------|---------|
| 1931 | 2,381     | 300     | —       | 2,681   |
| 1936 | 2,598     | 203     | —       | 2,801   |
| 1940 | 3,687     | 270     | —       | 3,957   |
| 1945 | 3,365     | 1,019   | —       | 4,384   |
| 1950 | 5,344     | 1,842   | —       | 7,186   |
| 1955 | 9,204     | 2,912   | —       | 12,116  |
| 1960 | 15,625    | 2,989   | —       | 18,614  |
| 1965 | 19,630    | 12,020  | —       | 31,650  |
| 1970 | 27,990    | 27,571  | 923     | 56,484  |
| 1971 | 32,747    | 27,246  | 2,523   | 62,516  |
| 1972 | 36,458    | 27,695  | 4,751   | 68,904  |
| 1973 | 29,524    | 40,203  | 6,545   | 76,272  |
| 1974 | 31,347    | 42,285  | 7,223   | 80,855  |
| 1975 | 26,448    | 48,490  | 7,543   | 82,481  |
| 1976 | 22,508    | 60,759  | 7,555   | 90,822  |
| 1977 | 40,990    | 46,610  | 6,360   | 93,960  |
| 1978 | 41,497    | 50,388  | 7,649   | 99,534  |
| 1979 | 47,611    | 51,623  | 6,700   | 105,934 |
| 1980 | 30,830    | 75,010  | 5,210   | 111,050 |
| 1981 | 23,270    | 78,342  | 4,568   | 111,180 |
| 1982 | 25,641    | 68,707  | 8,364   | 102,712 |
| 1986 | 33,970    | 50,327  | 29,660  | 113,957 |
| 1990 | 38,990    | 52,110  | 39,080  | 130,180 |
| 1992 | 40,380    | 57,531  | 40,970  | 138,881 |

*Sources:* 1931–81, Ministry of Industry; 1982–92, National Energy Plan (1982, revised figures; 1986–92, forecasts).

into effect for each category of consumption (low-voltage metered lighting, low-voltage lighting *à forfait* without a meter, domestic lighting and uses, industrial uses and rural electrification). Of course, to unify rates was not easy. With a flat rate system, thermal power production (with the jump in fuel prices) and the new hydro-electric power stations (the expenses of which were also growing), costs were not fully covered. Therefore, the Oficina Liquidora de Energía (Ofile — Energy Settlement Office) was created to make up for these differences with premiums, the funds for which were drawn from a surcharge, paid by consumers, known as factor 'R'.

From 1939 onwards, the state directly intervened in the electrical power industry through the INI, which constituted various national electric power companies. Thermal electric power is produced by the

Empresa Nacional de Electricidad, 'Gas y Electricidad' (Mallorca), the Empresa Nacional Eléctrica de Córdoba and Unelco (the Canary islands). Hydroelectric power is generated by the Empresa Nacional Hidroelectrica del Ribagorzana (ENHER), which manages part of the Catalan Pyrenees (the Noguera-Ribagorzana area) and the lower Ebro river. A move towards joint management was made in 1944 when the leading electrical power companies founded Unidad Eléctrica, SA (Unesa): they did this to avoid, or at least ease, the serious consumption restrictions imposed in that year and intermittently thereafter till 1958. The different companies then tried to act as one by maximising the use of all available sources of electricity. To this end, Unesa set up a load-redistribution system in Madrid.

A new phrase began in 1954, which at first appeared to be no more than a continuation of the previous period. Consumption, state intervention, joint management efforts and production all increased, as can be seen in Table 4.3. Moreover, in 1955 France and Spain linked up their electricity networks, which enabled Spain from then on to buy and sell energy from and to other European countries. The need to change the rate-fixing system arose in 1967, in the wake of Ofile's serious deficit problem. Consequently, the 'block consumption' system (with differential rates for the first, second and third time-blocks) was replaced by a two-tiered rate system, consisting of one constant fixed according to the maximum capacity contracted by the consumer and another depending on real consumption.

Nuclear power companies such as Cenusa, Nuclenor and Hifrensa, together with Unión Eléctrica (whose nuclear plant in Zorita began operation in 1968) and Hidrola are today building a number of plants. Stations already in operation include the Zorita de los Canes plant (Guadalajara) of 175,000 kw., and the Santa María de Garoña plant (Burgos) of 500,000 kw., both employing enriched uranium; and the Vandellós plant (Tarragona) of 500,000 kw., where heavy water and not enriched uranium is used in the reactor. Also, two 500 mw. groups are operating in Almaraz (Cáceres). The start-up of the Lemoniz plant (Vizcaya) has been held up by the nuclear moratorium adopted in 1984. Construction work on the Valdecaballeros, Ascó II and Trillo II plants has been shut down since electric power demand was falling far behind the 1978–87 PEN estimates. On the other hand, work continues on the Ascó I (Tarragona), Cofrentes (Valencia) and Trillo I (Guadalajara) plants.

Economic concentration in the electric power industry has been growing, according to a series of indicators. In production, the five leading companies own almost 50% of power and production

## Fig. 16. THE NUCLEAR FUEL CYCLE

This diagram shows the steps involved in converting uranium into electricity. This long cycle can be broken down into three main stages: the obtaining of $U_3O_8$ concentrates; the converting of $U_3O_8$ into uranium hexafluoride ($UF_6$); and the enriching of uranium hexafluoride (which should contain $U_{235}$). Spain, with its mining base, can obtain concentrates, but it lacks the technology to produce fuel, a process only carried out in a few countries. Enusa,* together with French, Italian, Belgian and Iranian state-run companies, is engaged in the Eurodif project (with 11.8%) designed to obtain enriched uranium from a plant built by this state-run multinational in Tricastin (France).

It is one thing to obtain enriched uranium and quite another to obtain the fuel. At present Spain buys from the United States (which employs light water reactor technology) and, to a much smaller degree, France (which employs heavy water reactor technology) for its nuclear plant in Valdellós. The fuel produces nuclear fission, which generates heat; heat then converts water to steam to power the turbo-alternators, which ultimately create electricity.

Spent fuel (having had only 40% of its energy content burned up) is reprocessed (a technology Spain has yet to develop), yielding recovered uranium, which is put back into the system; plutonium, which is used for military purposes and as a breeder reactor fuel; and radioactive waste, which must be carefully disposed of, for many particles may live for up to 24,000 years. The risks implied are sharply criticised by ecologists, on the grounds that if the longest-surviving political system to date was the Roman Empire, which lasted for barely 2,000 years, it is impossible to imagine a system lasting 24,000 years.

* Empresa Nacional del Uranio, within the INI group.

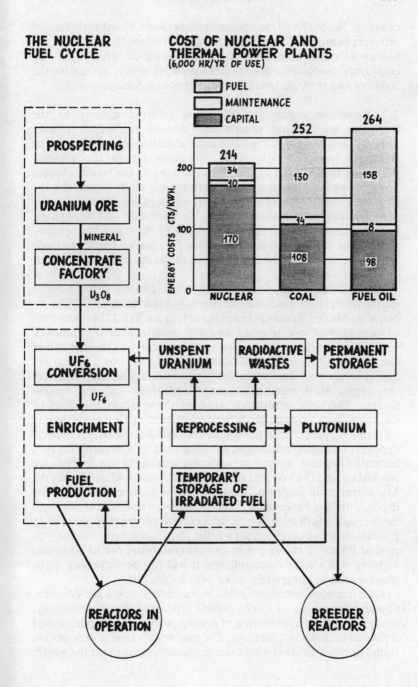

THE NUCLEAR
FUEL CYCLE

COST OF NUCLEAR AND
THERMAL POWER PLANTS
(6,000 HR/YR OF USE)

FUEL
MAINTENANCE
CAPITAL

PROSPECTING

URANIUM ORE

MINERAL

CONCENTRATE
FACTORY

U₃O₈

UF₆
CONVERSION

UF₆

ENRICHMENT

FUEL
PRODUCTION

UNSPENT
URANIUM

RADIOACTIVE
WASTES

PERMANENT
STORAGE

REPROCESSING

PLUTONIUM

TEMPORARY
STORAGE OF
IRRADIATED FUEL

REACTORS IN
OPERATION

BREEDER
REACTORS

capacity. Secondly, close connections between board members of different companies have strengthened the formal association of the twenty-six major companies in Unidad Eléctrica, SA (Unesa), an employers' association that studies the major issues confronting the industry and presents overall proposals to the Administration.

**2.2. *Extractive industries.*** We have referred already to the legendary wealth and present-day lacunae in Spain's mining industry. But in spite of the latter and the exhaustion of many of the country's best deposits, some Spaniards ignore the present, preferring to recall the golden age of mining of the late nineteenth and early twentieth centuries. Modern mining really began with the extremely liberal Mining Act of 1869, which paved the way for perpetual mining concessions granted to nationals and foreigners, provided that they paid the fees required by the state. The application of this Act, passed at a time when free markets and free trade were popular, placed the best mines in the hands of foreign capital.

**2.2(*a*). *Metallic mineral mining.*** According to the 1970 estimates of the Programa Nacional de Investigación Minera (PNIM — National Mining Research Programme), Spain had 272 million tons of proven *iron ore* reserves and 400 million tons of unproven reserves. Iron ore production is determined solely by the demand of the domestic iron and steel industries, and has shown a zero net export balance in recent years. Major iron ore deposits are located in the north, north-east, south-east, south-west, and the Iberian System. The most productive areas are the northern provinces of Cantabria and Vizcaya, the latter region holding first place despite its shrinking deposits. In the south, Granada has the largest mineral deposits, including magnetite, in the district of Conjuro. Teruel's hermatite deposits in the Sierra Menera (in the Iberian System) are worked to feed the iron and steel blast furnaces of Altos Hornos del Mediterraneo in Sagunto. In the south-west, there are magnetite deposits around Fregenal de la Sierra, between northern Huelva and Seville, and south of Badajoz. In 1982 the government decided to provide the means to construct a pellet plant in this area with the support of Presur, a mixed public-private enterprise, but its economic viability was always doubtful, and it will not be surprising if the plant should be completely taken over by the INI.

*Lead* has been mined in Spain since ancient times. Lead deposits, abundant and easy to work, require little capital and technology, thus giving rise to a splintering of mining property, multiplication of wells and decrepit installations. The peninsula's largest deposits are found in two areas that were once recognised throughout the world:

Linares-La Carolina in Jaén and Cartagena-Mazarrón in Murcia. The latter reserve, a typical marginal mining area, is probably the richer, but its expensive extraction and mining operations are only undertaken when international prices are high. Two lead foundries handle almost the entire market. The French Sociedad Minero-Metalúrgica de Peñarroya, the more important of the two, works the Peñarroya, Cartagena and Linares mines. The La Cruz foundry, part of the Banco Central group, is near Linares.

Of domestic *zinc* production 95% is mined in Santander and Murcia. Reocín in Cantabria has by far the largest veins, which are worked by the Real Compañía Asturiana de Minas (RCAM). Reocín zinc, whose grade (58%) is one of the highest in the world, represents more than two-thirds of total domestic production. As with lead, the zinc deposits in the mountains of Cartagena are scattered, and the grade of this area's mineral (50% at best) is lower than that of Reocín. Zinc mining and metallurgy are closely linked to the history of the RCAM, created in 1833 with Belgian capital. Thanks to the Reocín zinc bed, the RCAM unlawfully obtained a monopoly in the Spanish market up to the 1960s, when Espanola del Cinc (part of the Banco Central group) was set up to work the mines in Cartagena.

Of the *copper* on the Spanish market only 50% is domestic, although almost all the copper used in blister copper production is mined in the province of Huelva. Huelva's ferrous copper pyrites beds are mined by, among others, Unión Explosivos Río Tinto and the Compañía de Azufre y Cobre Tharsis. More copper is obtained from the recovery of scrap and imported raw material (blister) than from mining itself. Production is basically controlled by Ibercobre, an association of the country's former leading smelting and manufacturing firms.

*Aluminium* production dates from 1929, when Aluminio Español (whose founding capital was put up by the French Pechiney financial group) switched on electrolytic installations in Sabiñánigo (the Aragonian Pyrenees). In 1943 the INI (with a small investment of private capital) established the Empresa Nacional de Aluminio, SA (Endasa), which today operates in Valladolid and Asturias (Avilés and San Juan de Nieva). A new company, Aluminio de Galicia, later added its name to the list of aluminium producers. Up until 1979, Spanish aluminium production was only involved with the second stage of the production process, consuming huge amounts of alumina imported from France, Ghana and Guinea (Conakry). Bauxite is now directly imported (for alumina and aluminium production) to the mixed public-private processing plant of Aluminio Español in San Ciprián (Galicia) to satisfy its 500,000-ton capacity. This plant has turned Spain into a leading aluminium exporter.

Few of the important *tin* deposits along the Spanish-Portuguese border have been worked since 1959, when the bottom fell out of the tin market with the easing of import restrictions. Tin is produced from domestic and imported cassiterite (from Portugal, Britain and Belgium) and by means of detinning.

As regards *ferroalloy metals*, domestic wolfram and manganese ore production has run into problems, given the marginal nature of the deposits, which can only be mined during times of high prices (i.e. in war-time). Carburos and Hidronitro are the two major Spanish enterprises in this field.

The largest cinnabar (mercury ore) deposits are those of Almadén (Ciudad Real), which have been mined since 400 BC. Information on Almadén's production dates back to 1499 (7 million flasks of 34.5 kg. each up to 1960). Estimated reserves indicate that cinnabar mining activities should be able to remain at their present level for another 200 years. Given the grade of Almadén's mercury ore (almost 3%), these mines are by far the richest in the world. The state owns these mines, having almost always worked them directly. However, for most of the nineteenth century and the first two decades of the twentieth Spanish cinnabar exports, together with those of Istria in Italy and California, were controlled by the Rothschild family, which thus possessed an effective world monopoly. In December 1921 the Minister of Finance, Cambó, put an end to this situation by placing full control of mercury exports in the hands of the Board of the Almadén and Arrayanes Mines (an agency under the Ministry of Finance), which had been dealing with all mining matters since 1918. The Empresa Nacional de Minas de Almadén, also responsible to the Ministry of Finance, was set up in 1982, and at the same time a modernisation programme was launched. Spanish mercury production (fluctuating between 1,500 and 2,000 tonnes) depends on foreign demand, for 90% of the metal is exported. Since the early 1970s demand has been declining, due to the campaign against the use of mercury by environmentalists given its harmful effects on the environment.

2.2(*b*). *Non-metallic mineral mining.*    Spain is rich in *common salt* (sodium chloride), with considerable rock salt deposits and ideal conditions for obtaining salt from seawater. Domestic common salt production and exports are constantly on the increase.

Cantabria is the leading rock salt producer; and its large centres of Polanco de la Sal, Cabezón de la Sal and Monte Corona supply the Solvay Salt Company (near Tarragona) and other chemical industries in the area. The main centres of sea-salt production are the salt works of Torrevieja, in Alicante, followed by Denia, Sagunto, San Pedro del Pinatar, Mar Menor, Cabo de Gata and San Roque, all of which are on the Mediterranean coast. The salt works of the south Atlantic region include San Fernando, Puerto Real, Chiclana and Puerto de Santa María. There is also salt production in the Balearic and Canary islands, but on a much smaller scale. Spanish sea-salt production is concentrated in a few tightly-knit companies, one of which, the Unión Salinera de España, produces 50% of the country's total.

*Potassium salt* ($K_2O_4$) is primarily used for the production of fertilisers. There is large potassium basin in the Ebro Valley, extending from Catalonia to Navarra. In Catalonia, Minas de Potasa de Suria, a subsidiary of the Belgian Solvay Company, works a salt mine discovered in Suria in 1913, while Explosivos Rió tinto mines the Cardona salt works. Potasa de Navarra, SA, was founded in 1957 with more than 95% of its capital being provided by the INI, to work the Navarra salt basin. This company's operations did not start till 1964, and from the outset there were economic difficulties. The quality of the salt has been so disappointing that in 1984 it was decided that this mine would gradually be shut down. These three potassium concerns work closely together through Potasas Españolas, a sales and distribution cartel that operates both domestically and internationally.

*Phosphates*, used as a basic raw material in the production of superphosphates, have a $P_2O_5$ content that makes them one of the basic groups of mineral fertilisers. Spain has a few such deposits; but those in Murcia, Almería and Albacete are economically insignificant. The phosphate mines in Caceres, the only ones ever in operation, have been closed for some time now. All phosphates used in the production of phosphorus fertiliser are imported from Morocco in ever-increasing volume. In November 1975 Morocco saw its position further strengthened: Spain's transfer of control of the Western Sahara (in complete disregard of the inhabitants' wishes) shortly before the death of Franco put large reserves of phosphates (formerly mined by Fosbucrá of the INI group) within Morocco's grasp. With this transfer Spain's ownership interest in Fosbucrá fell from 100 to 35%, as Morocco took absolute control. Then the Saharan war impeded mining activities, and in 1980 operations were finally suspended altogether. In 1982 work was resumed, but only symbolically.

Superphosphate production is possible, first of all because of the vast domestic reserves of pyrites, which is necessary for producing sulphuric acid for the treatment of natural phosphates, and secondly

## Fig. 17. MINING IN SPAIN

The *Mining Map of Spain*, published by the Geological and Mining Institute, was used to prepare this Figure.

For simplification, we have omitted those mines that have been abandoned, those that have smaller deposits of main minerals and those that are widely disseminated and of little economic importance (bauxite, kaolin, mica, sodium sulphate, titanium etc.).

Details of the activities of the mines presented here are given in Section 2.2. We should mention that Spain has a great variety of minerals, some of which are found in vast quantities (iron, lead, zinc, pyrites, mercury, magnesium, potash, fluorspar, uranium, rock salt and sea salt) and that mining zones occur at the edge of the *meseta*.

The formation of the *meseta* and the Ebro and Guadalquivir depressions in the Tertiary and Quaternary ages produced negligible mineral wealth when compared to the rougher, more ancient areas of Spain, such as the Northern Corniche, the Spanish-Portuguese borderlands, the Sierra Morena, the Sierra Nevada and the Iberian System.

COALFIELDS
PIT COAL
LIGNITE
ANTHRACITE

OIL
IRON MINERAL
IRON PYRITES
LEAD, ZINC
TIN, WOLFRAM
POTASH (SALT)
FLUORSPAR
PHOSPHORUS
URANIUM
ANTIMONY
MANGANESE
MAGNESIUM
KAOLIN
MERCURY

GOLD
SILVER
SULPHUR

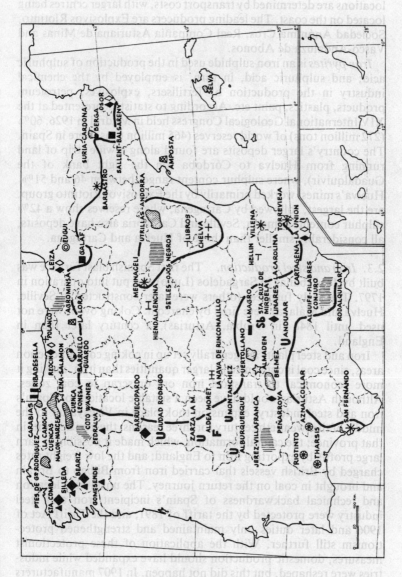

because of the proximity of the North African deposits. Factory locations are determined by transport costs, with larger centres being located on the coast. The leading producers are Explosivos Ríotinto, Sociedad Anónima Cros, Real Compañía Asturiana de Minas and Vasco-Andaluza de Abonos.

*Iron pyrites* is an iron sulphide used in the production of sulphuric acid; and sulphuric acid, in turn, is employed by the chemical industry in the production of fertilisers, explosives, petroleum products, plastics, paint etc. According to statistics presented at the XIV International Geological Congress held in Madrid in 1926, 60% (272 million tons) of world reserves (465 million tons) were in Spain. The country's larger deposits are found along a wide strip of land running from Huelva to Córdoba (on the right bank of the Guadalquivir), where sulphur content ranges between 46 and 51%. Huelva's mines, worked primarily by the Explosivos Ríotinto group, are the largest, followed by Cartagena, where reserves show a 42% sulphur content. Almería, Seville and Cantabria also have deposits, all considerably smaller than those of Huelva and Cartagena.

2.3. *Iron and steel production.* The first Spanish blast furnace was built by José Ibáñaz in Sargadelos (Lugo) and put into operation in 1797. The early furnaces (others were later constructed in Seville, Huelva and Málaga) were fired by charcoal. Coking ovens were not used until 1848 (in Trubia, Asturias), a century later than in England.

Iron and steel plants are generally set up in coking coal production areas, since coal is consumed in larger quantities than iron, making it more economical to transport iron ore or scrap to coal zones. Although Asturias would have been a suitable location for Spain's iron and steel industry, expansion took place in Vizcaya up to the middle of the twentieth century for three reasons: the iron deposits in that province; the capital formation, which made it possible to earn large profits by exporting iron to England; and the low freight rates charged by British vessels that carried iron from Bilbao to Britain and brought in coal on the return journey. The unsuitable location and technical backwardness of Spain's incipient iron and steel industry were protected by the tariff of 1891, and the Tariff Act of 1906 and later duties only maintained and strengthened protectionism still further. With the application of these protectionist measures, domestic production should have expanded while industries were reshaped, but this did not happen. In 1907 manufacturers founded the Central Siderúrgica de Ventas (later called the Central Siderúrgica, SA, and today Unesid — Unión de Empresas y Entidades Siderúrgicas) to restrict competition by fixing common

Table 4.4.  PRODUCTION OF SOME BASIC INDUSTRIES

| Types of Industry | 1950 | 1960 | 1970 | 1975 | 1980 | 1981 | 1982 | 1983 | 1984 |
|---|---|---|---|---|---|---|---|---|---|
| Steel production (1,000 tonnes) | 815 | 1,920 | 7,380 | 11,136 | 12,672 | 13,106 | 13,280 | 13,009 | 13,484 |
| Shipbuilding (1,000 tonnes draft) | 35 | 100 | 318 | 1,703 | 557 | 602 | 547 | 464 | 438 |
| Automobiles (× 1,000) | — | 38 | 442 | 697 | 1,028 | 855 | 927 | 1,141 | 1,176 |
| Tractors (units) | — | 8,639 | 19,513 | 38,258 | 18,613 | 17,418 | 20,209 | 15,524 | 16,550 |
| Cement (million tonnes) | 2.9 | 6.2 | 15.4 | 21.7 | 26.0 | 29.0 | 29.0 | 28.0 | 24.0 |
| Cotton fabrics (1,000 tonnes) | — | 78.9 | 120.6 | 123.3 | 107.0 | — | — | — | — |
| Wool fabrics (1,000 tonnes) | — | 9.4 | 33.2 | 31.0 | 16.6 | — | — | — | — |
| Paper (1,000 tonnes) | 158.0 | 342.1 | 1,183.5 | 1,855.8 | 2,489.0 | 2,268.0 | 2,683.0 | 2,754.0 | — |
| Shoes (millions of pairs) | — | 27.6 | 69.7 | 127.0 | — | — | — | — | — |
| Housing (finished units × 1,000) | 55.0 | 144.0 | 308.0 | 374.0 | 259.0 | 235.0 | 215.0 | 199.0 | 139.0 |

*Source: El Pais Yearbook.*

prices for all production, centralising the sales of all associate companies and laying down production quotas. The monopoly was largely responsible for the low production levels of 1910–23.

During the dictatorship of Primo de Rivera (1923–30), which coincided with a period of world prosperity, an annual production of 1 million tons of steel was reached (1929), a record that remained unsurpassed for the next twenty-five years. Between 1939 and 1959 there was stagnation as a direct result of the monopolistic structure of supply and the difficulties involved in importing equipment, coke and scrap iron. As demand increased, so prices shot up, prompting the government to intervene by establishing prices and distribution procedures. To ensure compliance and to coordinate other official measures taken in this sector, the Delegación Oficial del Estado en la Industria Siderúrgica (DOEIS — the Official State Iron and Steel Authority) was created in December 1940 under the Ministry of Industry; it introduced rationing to cope with the severe shortage of iron and steel products. Faced with a scarcity, the state decided to get to the root of the problem, namely production, and set up the Empresa Nacional Siderúrgica, SA (Ensidesa) to build a factory in Avilés (Oviedo), with a view to producing 1,400,000 tonnes of steel in the first stage and 2,500,000 tonnes by the end of the second. In the 1960s the Unión de Siderúrgicas Asturianas (Uninsa) emerged to become eventually part of Ensidesa. In the early 1970s Altos Hornos de Vizcaya (AHV), the country's leading iron and steel company since the nineteenth century, turned its old Sagunto factory into a new company, Altos Hornos del Mediterráneo (AHM). Due to faulty planning and the general crisis, the INI ended up in 1980 owning 100% of AHM.

Turning to industrial location, factories are found in Vizcaya, Cantabria, Asturias and Valencia. Vizcaya, traditionally leading production, has fallen into second place after Asturias, where Ensidesa operates the largest integrated plant in the country (Avilés-Veriño). In Sagunto (Valencia) the third complete iron and steel complex was designed to produce 6,000,000 tonnes of steel. Nevertheless, as a result of the plans to reshape the industry, it was decided that the Sagunto blast furnaces would be shut down, and that these installations would specialise in cold-rolled steel production. The reconversion of Ensidesa and AHV not only provoked social unrest but also ran into difficulties stemming from a dramatic drop in demand and poor planning. Total capacity of the iron and steel industry is of some 16 million tonnes, but real production during the last years of crisis was never much more than 13 million tonnes (see Table 4.4).

2.4. *Cement and other construction materials.* The Tudela-Veguín Corporation began modern cement production in Oviedo at the end of the nineteenth century. Today there are some sixty factories with a joint production capacity of 30 million tonnes, guaranteeing domestic market supplies and export expansion. From 1939 to 1960, during the autarkic period, the cement industry was officially controlled by the Delegación del Gobierno en la Industria del Cemento (DGIC — the State Cement Industry Authority), an agency responsible to the Ministry of Industry with duties similar to those of the DOEIS for iron and steel. Intervention was necessary because of domestic cement supply shortages (resulting from post-war stagnation in the industry) and because of a greater demand for cement from the construction industry (due to a shortage of wood, iron and steel products). The present-day structure of the industry is oligopolistic, with a few groups of companies forming closely-knit corporations. The most important of these groups is headed by the Asland Corporation. All manufacturers belong to the Asociación de Fabricantes de Cementos (Oficemen), in which joint decisions are taken on pricing, market distribution etc. This framework naturally gives rise to high prices when market conditions in the construction sector are favourable. The jump in production levels in the late 1970s and early 1980s (reaching some 30 million tonnes) was in response mainly to foreign market demands. While in Spain itself housing and public works construction languished at the end of the 1970s, North African and Gulf countries became Spain's primary customers for cement (see Table 4.4).

Also on the list of construction materials are prefabricated cement slabs, fibre cement, cement floor surfaces and linings, ceramic materials (tiles, flat tiles, porcelain, roofing tile and brick), gypsum, glass and plumbing fixtures. While the production of cement by-products, ceramic materials and gypsum is splintered among small, unorganised and economically-limited companies, the manufacture of fibre cement, glass and plumbing fixtures is concentrated in a small number of companies which have complete control of the market: Uralita (fibre cement) Cristalería Española and its subsidiaries (glass), which belong to the French state-owned St Gobain group, and Roca Radiadores (plumbing fixtures).

2.5. *The chemical industry.* The development of a chemical industry depends on three factors: the availability of raw materials and the degree of industrial and scientific and technical development in the country concerned. Spain has such abundance of some basic raw materials employed by chemical industries, such as pyrites, sodium chloride and potash, that surpluses are exported. In the case of hard coal, an essential part of all coal-based chemical processes in the past, production has been inadequate and quality poor; and almost all oil, which plays an important part in petrochemical industries, is imported. Industrial and agricultural progress stimulates the chemical industry, and consequently the slowness in Spain of industrialisation and modernisation in agriculture held back the chemical industry for many years. However, the autarky policy on industry from 1939 to 1959 drove the chemical industry forward at a faster rate than ever before through import substitution.

Spain's modern chemical industry emerged in 1872, the year in which the Sociedad Española de la Dinamita was founded in Bilbao, with Nobel patents, to manufacture explosives for the military, mining and public works sectors. The demand for mineral fertilisers for agricultural purposes gave rise to the Union Española de Explosivos (1891) and the Sociedad Anónima Cros, which began production in 1904. At around the same period the manufacturing of soda and chlorine, to meet the demands of paper-mills and the soap industry, was undertaken by two companies: the Sociedad Electroquímica de Flix, founded in 1897 with German capital, and the Solvay Company, constituted in 1908 with Belgian capital, which built its main factory in Torrelavega (Cantabria). The production of gases for metal welding, oxygen and acetylene was also undertaken by Carburos Metálicos (in 1904 in Barcelona) to supply the mechanical construction industries of Catalonia. Dyes and primings required by the Catalonia textile industry were first produced from coal tar by another Barcelona enterprise, in 1885; in time, this company merged with others to form the Sociedad Fabricación Nacional de Colorantes y Explosivos.

Almost all chemical companies founded in this early period enjoyed tariff protection, which was practised without reservations from 1892 onwards. Once the domestic market was assured by means of tariff protection and locational advantages, the Spanish chemical industry grew and consolidated itself. Consolidation, in fact, took place during the 1914–36 period when production of nitrogenous fertilisers began; the already existing companies increased production and new companies sprouted up using raw materials or imported intermediate goods in their production processes. Thus the national chemical industry broadened its scope, even though it depended on foreign companies for a large part of its supplies. This absence of initial and intermediate links in some production processes led to serious difficulties in the wake of the Civil War, when import restrictions were stiffened; these barriers promoted the movement to complete the technical chain. Basic intermediate goods that had previously been imported began to be manufactured domestically. The Unión Química del Norte de España (Unquinesa) was set up in 1939 in Bilbao to produce phenol and formol (from tar and coke provided by Altos Hornos de Vizcaya), compounds used in the manufacture of plastics and other products. Another carbon-chemical centre similar to that of Unquinesa sprang up in La Felguera (Asturias), where Proquisa (a subsidiary of Duro-Felguera) used the by-products of the Duro-Felguera iron and steel factory. Carbide and urea electrochemical production was developed by Energía e Industrias Aragonesas in Sabiñánigo and Hidronitro Española in Monzón del Río Cinca. These and other new installations in the basic chemical industry allowed not only for continuity in existing product lines but also for the appearance of a wide variety of new products.

After the Civil War, the pharmaceutical sector made swifter advances than the basic chemical industry. When pharmaceutical supplies from other European countries, particularly Germany, were cut off by the Second World War, Spanish pharmaceutical companies, most of which were representatives and bottlers of imports up to 1936, became manufacturers, producing a broad range of items. Production was also stimulated by the establishment of a national health service in 1943.

Spanish chemical companies tend to be small, a handicap which becomes apparent when Spain is compared with other countries. Imperial Chemical Industries in the United Kingdom alone produces twice the volume of all Spanish chemical companies combined. Hoechst, Bayer and BASF in Germany each have production levels above Spain's entire chemical industry, and this is to name only a few. Of course the industry has been trying to consolidate itself around Explosivos Riotinto (ERT) Cros and Cepsa, but the plans for expansion of the first two suffered setbacks from the crises of the 1970s and '80s.

The foundations of Spain's petro-chemical industry were laid in 1963 with the decision to build two petro-chemical plants, one in Puertollano (Ciudad Real) and another in Tarragona. The Puertollano plant (owned by Enpetrol) and refinery receive 4.4 million tons of crude each year through the Málaga-Puertollano oil pipeline. In Puertollano, the Paular, Calatrava, Alcudia and Montoro companies manufacture plastics, fibres and synthetic rubber. The Tarragona plant (next to which a new oil refinery was built in 1969) belongs to Industrias Químicas Asociadas (IQA), formed by domestic (ERS and Cepsa) and foreign (Shell and Hoechst) companies. Tarragona's basic products include polyethylene, estirene, polypropylene and synthetic rubber.

The last organic chemical plant is that of Algeciras, at Cepsa's highly specialised petro-chemical refinery. Cepsa subsidiaries also work at these installations: Petresa (alkibenzine and linear paraffin), Carbesa (carbon black for tyre manufacturing etc.) and Induquímica. Cepsa is associated in Petresa, with Continental Oil (Conoco) and in Carbesa with Continental Carbon and United Carbon.

### 3. *Capital and durable goods manufacturing*

All the industrial activities in this sector use metal, particularly iron and steel, as a basic raw material to build ships and capital goods (machinery, railroad equipment and industrial vehicles) and manufacture durable consumer goods, such as cars, motorcycles and electric home appliances.

**3.1.** *Shipbuilding and railroad equipment manufacturing.* Most shipbuilding activity has been traditionally carried out on the north and north-west coasts. Andalusian and Levantine shipyards only began to be important in the 1950s. The main shipyards in the north belong to Astilleros Españoles, SA (Aesa), an INI company, and are located in Vizcaya. In the north-west, the Empresa Nacional Bazán de Construcciones Navales Militares, also part of INI, works for the military in the navy shipyards of El Ferrol. Astilleros del Noroeste (Astano), originally part of the Banco Pastor group and today 100% INI, is also located in El Ferrol. Shipbuilding for fishing fleets on the Vigo *Ria* was a prosperous business before 1973. In the south, ships are built in Cádiz and Seville. The Matagorda and La Carraca yards in Cádiz, the most important shipbuilding centre today in Spain, belong to Aesa. On the Mediterranean coast the military shipyards of Cartagena are also rented to the Empresa Nacional Bazán; the shipyards of El Grao (Valencia) are worked by the Unión Naval de Levante, which specialises in passenger ships; and the small shipyards of Tarragona and Barcelona repair and build small vessels. Palma de Mallorca and Las Palmas in Gran Canaria also have small shipyards.

Spain has a total of thirty shipyards building steel hulls and some 200 shipwrights who make wooden hulls. In 1970, following laborious negotiations, various public and private companies were merged into Aesa, in which INI initially owned 50% of the capital and private stockholders the other 50%. But, as happens time and again in loss-making nationalised enterprises, the INI eventually took over Aesa. As soon as the most important of Aesa's projects, namely a new shipyard in Cádiz with a 1.5 million dwt. capacity per year, was completed, it was crippled by the 1973 crisis. Total shipyard capacity is estimated at 2.5 million dwt., a level reached because of the glowing prospects for shipbuilding in the 1960s, when the oil sector was growing and the demand for tankers was increasing. Since the 1973 crisis, the shipbuilding industry, not surprisingly, has experienced a dramatic downturn, producing losses and making recoversion plans a necessity (see Table 4.4). Reconversion, finally decreed in July 1984, means a severe cutback in building capacity and huge layoffs of labour. These measures have set off strikes and demonstrations, particularly in El Ferrol and Vigo (Galicia). Unless a new line of construction is introduced, reconversion will not be enough to enable Spanish shipyards to compete with Korean and Japanese industries.

Although Spain has no specific railway equipment manufacturing industry, many companies (the Maquinista Terrestre y Marítima, Ateinsa, Material y Construcciones, Compañía Auxiliar de Ferrocarriles, Babcock and Wilcox, Aesa etc.) devote part of their activities to this kind of construction, which includes electric and diesel locomotives, box and passenger cars and signalling equipment, and the repair and maintenance of rolling stock. Railway equipment exports are respectable, but the industry depends heavily on the railway modernisation plans of the Renfe, Feva and the Autonomous Communities. The steady decline of railways puts this industry in a difficult situation.

3.2. *The motor industry.* The motor manufacturing industry (cars, industrial vehicles, motor-cycles and tractors) did not begin to unfold until the 1950s when Spain achieved two prerequisites: an industry capable of producing the quality and quantity of the special steels and alloys required, and a large enough market to make a domestic car industry worthwhile.

The first year in which the Sociedad Española de Automóviles de Turismo (Seat) manufactured passenger cars in Barcelona was 1950. Seat, working first with Fiat and today with Volkswagen patents, is controlled by the INI. Fabricación de Automóviles, SA (Fasa), technically associated with the Régie Renault company, started manufacturing passenger cars at Valladolid in 1955, and Citroën Hispania in Vigo's foreign trade zone in 1957. In 1965 Barrieros, in association with the Chrysler company, began manufacturing American-type and Simca cars. Chrysler later moved out, the French SPA-Peugeot-Citroën group moved in, and the Company's trade name was changed to Talbot. In 1967 the British Motor Corporation (BMC) started building Morris cars in its Pamplona factory (first belonging to Authi and then Leyland). Later BMC left Spain and sold its factory to Seat.

Encouraged by domestic market growth and export possibilities, Ford set up shop in Spain in 1971. Decree 3339/1972 of 30 November set forth new guidelines for car manufacturing, whereby the degree of nationalisation in this sector was reduced in exchange for high export levels. With this decree in force, Ford built a 240,000-car capacity plant in Almusafes (Valencia), and in April 1979 General Motors was given permission to build a 300,000-car capacity assembly plant in Figueruelas (Zaragoza), which started production in 1983. Total production at present is about 1 million vehicles a year (see Table 4.4).

The main characteristics of the automobile sector in the 1980s can be stated as follows:

(*a*)  Seat passed through a serious crisis when Fiat decided to pull out for good in 1981. Since that time, it has been launching models designed within the company and by Volkswagen.

(*b*)  It was necessary to lay off a minimum of 20,000 workers in companies throughout the sector, with a view to bringing production levels more in line with demand in the least costly way possible, and to introduce robots to bring manufacturing costs down to Japanese levels.

(*c*)  It was necessary to reduce the number of models manufactured and enlarge the series, which means signing complementarity agreements between firms.

(*d*)  The car industry crisis has inevitably dragged down ancillary industries with it. These are faced either with outright closure, or with difficult reconversion plans or with the risk of being absorbed by stronger industries, as occurred with Femsa (specialising in electrical parts for cars and other vehicles), which was swallowed up by the Spanish subsidiary of the German firm Bosch.

As with passenger cars, domestic industrial vehicle manufacture also employs foreign capital and technology. Four Spanish companies work with foreign patents and capital. Mevosa, a Mercedes/Volkswagen subsidiary, builds vans in Vitoria and Madrid. Motor Ibérica of Barcelona produced its 'Ebro' trucks for many years with Ford Motor technology, then (in 1969) with the British firm Massey-Ferguson, and later (in 1983) with the Japanese firm Nissan. The Empresa Nacional de Autocamiones (Enasa, created in 1946), produces various kinds of 'Pegaso' buses and trucks (with 6-to 35- ton load capacities) at its Barcelona and Madrid factories. Enasa's two factories can turn out 20,000 units a year in two shifts, putting it in fourth place in Europe, despite its minute size compared with its foreign competitors, such as Berliet-Saviem (France) and Iveco, the multinational holding company headed by Fiat. Like Seat, Enasa has been a bad example of how to plan and manage a company. Barreiros-Diesel trucks hit the assembly line in Madrid in 1959. In 1968 control of Barreiros fell into the hands of Chrysler España, and in 1978 of SPA Peugeot-Citroën. Special vehicles, such as those that can handle all kinds of terrain, are manufactured under British (Land-Rover) and Japanese licences by Santana in Linares (Jaen) and Motor Ibérica in Barcelona.

There are tractor factories in Madrid (John Deere) and Barcelona (Motor Ibérica), which work with foreign patents and capital (Motor Ibérica with Massey-Ferguson, John Deere with its American parent company). Spain also produces walking tractors for vineyards and small farms (see Table 4.4).

In the motor-cycle sub-sector, the strength of the more important companies, the possible growth of the domestic market and the prices and quality achieved (on a par with those of other European countries) indicated a rosy future. After a series of adjustments, however, domestic companies (Sanglas, Bultaco, Derbi etc.) lost ground to Yamaha and Honda in Spain, while Moto Vespa (originally Italian) succeeded in enlarging its scooter and moped market share.

3.3. *Machinery.* The construction of non-electrical machinery in Spain is spread over a large number of small and medium-sized companies with a wide range of models. The textile machinery industry, based in Catalonia, has successfully designed and produced an assortment of spinning, weaving and knitting machines. A few domestic companies (Alfa, Sigma) manufacture a variety of top-quality home and industrial sewing-machines; and in the office-machine sector, Hispano Olivetti has a clearly dominant position in the market.

Most electrically-powered machinery is manufactured by companies that either have foreign capital (AEG, Siemens, General Eléctrica Española etc.) or are publicly-owned (Maquinista, Babcock and Wilcox etc.). Products include hydraulic turbines, alternators and almost the entire gamut of electrically-powered industrial machinery and installations. Production of machine tools in Spain started in 1939, due to the difficulty of securing imports from Britain, Germany, Czechoslovakia etc. A dozen new machine tool companies emerged in 1940. At present there are more than 250 such companies established in Guipúzcoa, Barcelona, Vizcaya, La Rioja and Zaragoza. In 1963 the leading machine tool companies founded the Asociación Española de Fabricantes de Máquinas-Herramientas (the Spanish Machine Tool Manufacturers Association), which addresses itself to common fiscal, quota, tariff and promotion (trade show) problems. However they have never embarked on a genuine production coordination programme, despite overlapping among firms.

3.4. *Other metal transforming sectors.* The crisis also reached the electrical home appliance sector, with plummeting demand, closures, regrouping of companies and restructuring with state aid. Following an agreement between state companies, trade unions and the state in 1981, the market was divided among five groups of companies: Unelsa (Balay and Fuyma); the Orbaiceta-Zanussi group (formerly Super-Ser, Corcho, Ibelsa, Crolls and Agni); the Basque holding company comprising Fabrelec (working under Westinghouse patents), Sagarduy (Far and Thimsel) and Mayo (under the Otsein trademark); and lastly, the Ulgor Cooperative group (Fagor) of Mondragón. A decree of 26 September 1981 set in motion the Electrical Home Appliance Sector (white line) Reconversion Plan, establishing the legal and financial framework to achieve product specialisation, thus making the sector more competitive with a view to entering the Common Market.

Although the *toy industry* does not properly belong in this section, it should be mentioned. This industry is promoted through advertising, primarily on television, which speeds up in November and December in response to seasonal sales peaks. Toy manufacturing in Spain is not a new sector when we remember that the products of Payá were an attractive export item even before the Civil War. The company has been modernised, introducing each year new models, often inspired by (they say 'copied from') German and Japanese originals. Toy factories are concentrated in Ibi (Alicante), home of the annual Toy Trade Fair.

The Secoinsa and Telesincro group are leaders in the *data processing equipment* sector. Secoinsa, head of the group, was founded in March 1975 with 27% INI capital, 27% Telefónica, 30% Fujitsu Ltd and 2% from various Spanish banks (Central, Banesto, Hispano, Santander, Popular, Bilbao, Vizcaya and Urquijo). With its factory in Málaga, Secoinsa is engaged in the manufacturing and marketing of information processing and communications equipment, while Telesincro (representing 60% of Secoinsa) works primarily in the mini-computer subsector. The American company IBM, with factories in Fuente del Jarro and Puebla de Vallbona (Valencia) and a research centre in Madrid, produces computer sub-assemblies. Hispano Olivetti and Standard Eléctrica also have a diverse line of computers and telephone equipment. In 1984 Telefónica reached an agreement with ATT — (American Telegraph Telephone) — to manufacture chips in Spain.

*Aircraft* (for military training programmes and rapid take-off transport) are produced by Construcciones Aeronáuticas SA (Casa). Casa's most advanced products, the Aviocar and the CN235, are exported to many countries, including the United States. This company is also associated with state enterprises in Indonesia and India and with the multinational European Airbus project.

Turning to arms production, Eibar in the Basque country manufactures and exports hunting rifles and pistols. Till recently, military weapons have been manufactured in state factories in Toledo, Trubia, Plasencia de la Armas etc., and to a smaller extent in private enterprises. Since 1959 the INI has been in charge of running state factories, all of which became part of the Empresa Nacional Santa Bárbara in 1960. This production sector is in full swing today, powered by the political heat of Spain joining NATO. In 1983, Spain exported $700 million worth of arms.

## 4. *Consumer goods industries*

It is interesting to note the characteristics common to non-durable consumer goods industries, most of which have been producing basic commodities for decades. This sector includes clothes manufacturing, furniture, films and handicrafts.

The *food industry* is extremely important since all its products are basic commodities: sugar, flour, oils, canned foods, concentrates, wine, beer, alcohol and tobacco. Most countries are largely self-sufficient in these items. This is also true of Spain, although specific branches of food production (dairy products, canned vegetables and juices, oilseed oils, instant coffee, baby food etc.) have been penetrated by foreign capital and technology.

Most of Spain's *cotton industry* is in Catalonia (90% of spinning and 80% of weaving), making Barcelona by far the leading province in the region. The factories are on the Llobregat, Cardoner, Besós and Tordera rivers and on the coast; major factories are found in Barcelona itself and Manresa. Outside Catalonia, there are isolated cotton textile centres and factories in Levante, the Balearic islands, Andalusia and Extremadura. The factories in Andalusia and Extremedura are a recent development, using local raw materials.

The cotton textile industry grew under strong tariff protection, which reserved the markets of the metropolis and its last overseas possessions (Cuba, the Philippines and Puerto Rico). The loss of the latter in 1898 dealt a harsh blow to the industry, from which it could only recover by exporting to other countries. Consequently, for many years cotton textiles were the only true Spanish exports, although its main market was always the domestic one; foreign markets were usually secondary and used for surplus absorption. The highest export levels have been reached during times of war, when other textile industries have been unable to operate normally. The possibility of opening new export markets narrowed as many former purchasing countries developed their own textile industries to the point of exporting. This development harmed Spain as well as other traditional exporters, but it also forced the reshaping of the industry, which would otherwise have collapsed. Since 1959 the Ministry of Industry has fostered a series of relatively effective modernisation plans, the latest of which were included in the 1981 reconversion plans.

The *wool textile industry* has the longest tradition in the textile sector. Supplied with top-quality merino wool, this industry flourished in medieval Spain in centres such as Béjar, Medina del Campo, Palencia, Medina de Rioseco, Segovia, Sabadell and Tarrasa. At the beginning of the nineteenth century, the activities of these factories slackened, and the industry had to consolidate itself in a small number of points, particularly Barcelona, Sabadell and Tarrasa (Catalonia). Other wool centres are spread throughout the Peninsula: some of them, like Béjar and Alcoy, are quite active, while others, like Palencia, Logrono, Antequera and Morella, are past their prime.

Almost half the potential of the *leather industry* is located in Catalonia, particularly in the province of Barcelona (Igualada being the leather capital), followed by Valencia, Castellón and La Coruña. Sectorial modernisation plans have boosted exports in recent years. The *footwear industry*, centred in the region of Valencia and the Balearic islands, is extremely fragmented. The reasons are threefold: first, the capital-product ratio is one of the lowest in industry; secondly, new factories do not require large initial investment, since equipment can be rented; and thirdly, footwear has a very large informal economy. Factory modernisation and the lowering of raw material import barriers and trading opportunities abroad drove export levels to new heights in the 1960s, but, as with textiles, the Spanish export market was eroded by the economic crisis, with a subsequent decline in consumption and stronger protectionism, and by the emergence of new exporters (Brazil, Mexico, Argentina *inter alia*), employing cheaper raw materials and labour. It is largely due to the informal economy that Spanish exports have recovered over the last few years.

Modern technology was not introduced in Spain's *pulp and paper industry* until 1841, when the first cylinder paper machine mill was built in Burgos — forty years after the technique had been introduced in France. Until then, paper had been made in small mills distributed along the main rivers. Given the country's limited forestry resources and dependence on Scandinavian pulp imports, the first papermills appeared in Guipúzcoa and Vizcaya, and only later in other coastal provinces, notably Barcelona. Before 1936 Spanish pulp manufacture was insignificant, with only one mill, that of La Papelera Española in Rentería, producing pulp from *pinus insignis*, which had been introduced with modern forestry methods. Post-war import restrictions gave rise to a pulp industry using domestic raw materials — such as wood, recycled paper, chaff, esparto, rope and rags.

Spain has some 200 paper mills, half engaged in the entire production process (from pulp paper) and half exclusively in paper production. Domestic paper shortages are largely due to the monopoly held by La Papelera Española, which produces 30% of domestic paper and controls Central Papalera and Consorcio Papalero. Other cartels have been formed around Papelera Reunidas de Alcoy, Cepal (Central de Papaleras Libres) and Unión Papelera (created in 1962 by a large number of small concerns). Concerted action measures in the 1960s enabled the paper industry to upgrade itself and increase capacity. And the decontrolling of imports spurred the sector towards reorganisation, even though many monopolistic practices are alive and well (see Table 4.4).

Faced with the need to enlarge its market, and its inability to break into the domestic market, the book publishing industry has taken to exporting on a large scale. Its export activities began in the early eighteenth century, when the first books were shipped to the Americas. The Spanish-speaking American countries remain of great importance for Spain, but although the market's demographic base is massive, the *per capita* absorption capacity is lower than in Spain itself. Of Spain's 500 publishing houses, 80% are in Barcelona and Madrid. Aguilar, Espasa-Calpe, Bruguera, Planeta, Salvat, Plaza y Janés, Orbis, Sarpe and Alianza Editorial, some with branch offices in Latin America, are leaders in this sector; and Anaya and Santillana are important school book publishers. The distribution network consists of some 1,300 bookstores and 500 used-book dealers.

## 5. *The construction industry and housing policy*

The construction industry encompasses activities ranging from water projects to housing construction and represents 15% of gross industrial product and 5% of gross domestic product. This industry is also an important materials user and employer, with construction workers making up nearly 10% of the national workforce.

Spain has more than 10,000 construction companies, and the major ones (Agromán, Huarte, Dragados y Construcciones, Entrecanales y Távora, Cubiertas y Tejados Focsa, Cycsa, Comylsa and others now integrated in Seopan, the pool of major building and civil engineering firms) have considerable capital and technological backing, and do much of their work abroad. Financing is of course vital to construction companies, especially when a project requires sizeable investments. For this reason, the state provides developers and customers with long-term loans. State loans for housing construction are granted through the Banco Hipotecario de España, a state bank.

Shortly after the Civil War ended in 1939, the housing problem became acute for a variety of reasons: population growth, the lack of construction projects and destruction of buildings during the war and, above all, negligible construction activity once the war was over. In this period, also one of inflation, the lack of materials and construction projects caused leases to be frozen. Migration from the countryside to areas of industrial development, namely the coal fields of Asturias and Vizcaya, and Madrid and Barcelona, only aggravated the problem. The state responded by attempting to promote housing construction with direct and indirect aid provided through the Instituto Nacional de la Vivienda (INV — National Housing Institute), created under an Act of 19 April 1939 and through sponsored housing legislation. Experience of this housing policy and a more exact diagnosis of the problem with figures provided by the 1950 Population and Housing Census (indicating the need for 1 million new housing units) enabled the state to embark on a new phase, this time avoiding past problems. A Decree of 1 July 1955 approved a 5-year National Housing Plan to build 550,000 housing units at the rate of 110,000 units a year. Seventy-seven percent of the plan's founding goals were reached, a respectable percentage bearing in mind that at this time greater impetus was given to the so-called Social Urgency Plan of Madrid, reshaping subsidised housing throughout the country. When the first 5-year National Housing Plan (1956–60) expired, a new 16-year national plan (1961–76) was approved (broken down for budgeting purposes into 4-year periods).

Far too little attention was given to urban development: if Cerdá and Castro (the two leading urban planners of the nineteenth century) could see the growth of Barcelona and Madrid in the twentieth century, they would turn in their graves. The root of the problem is land speculation, which leads to the building of over-crowded and poor-quality tower-blocks. In a capitalist economy, it is hard to turn this situation around, as was seen by the ineffectiveness of the 1956 Land Act and its 1975 revised version. Concerted urban development in 1973–7 also failed to resolve anything; on the contrary, this brand of urban development brought large cities a step closer to serious overcrowding. Fortunately, this trend was arrested with the arrival of democracy in 1977, and city planning became more rational.

In the Moncloa Agreements (October 1977), a range of agreements on housing policy was adopted, but they were unsuccessfully executed due to negligence and indecision and to the government's monetary policy. With housing construction waning, Royal Decree Law 4 'on the streamlining of urban management' was enacted in March 1980, creating the Instituto para la Promoción Pública de la Vivienda (IPPV — State Housing Development Institute), gradually to replace the INV, and the Sociedad Estatal de Promoción y Equipamiento del Suelo (SEPES — State Land Development and Equipment Corporation), eventually to replace the INUR (Instituto Nacional de Urbanización). These two new agencies were to become developers of officially-sponsored housing units (the IPPV) and land (the SEPES) on terms favourable to private developers, municipal sponsorship and cooperatives. In order to speed up formalities,

Table 4.5.   HOUSING
(*1,000 units finished*)

| | | | |
|---|---|---|---|
| 1961 | 135.4 | 1973 | 350.0 |
| 1962 | 162.4 | 1974 | 359.0 |
| 1963 | 206.6 | 1975 | 374.3 |
| 1964 | 256.9 | 1976 | 319.8 |
| 1965 | 283.4 | 1977 | 324.3 |
| 1966 | 270.1 | 1978 | 332.6 |
| 1967 | 208.7 | 1979 | 252.3 |
| 1968 | 248.1 | 1980 | 258.8 |
| 1969 | 270.2 | 1981 | 234.6 |
| 1970 | 300.0 | 1982 | 215.0 |
| 1971 | 318.9 | 1983 | .199.0 |
| 1972 | 336.2 | 1984 | 139.0 |

*Source:* Ministry of Public Works and Urbanism.

some of the periods specified in urban development legislation, particularly regarding municipal licences, were drastically reduced. However, Royal Decree Law 4/1980 was crippled by the abundance of previous legislation on housing loans. This forced the government to establish the 1981–3 3-Year Plan to construct 571,000 housing units with 1.22 billion ptas in financing. But results did not come up to the forecasts because of economic depression (see Table 4.5). This pattern may be repeated with the 1984–7 Plan.

In the Spanish Constitution of 1978, article 47 promotes a speculation-free and just housing policy. Although the attainment of these goals is still nowhere near realisation, the policies of municipalities and provinces are aimed at more rational long-term urban development of a more progressive and more human character.

# V. PROTECTING THE SYSTEM OF PRODUCTION

Spain's system of production is protected from foreign competition by a series of institutional mechanisms, the most important being customs tariffs, the exchange rate and trade regulations. The evolution of protectionism has helped to shape the spirit and mentality of businessmen and to foster economic development — or stifle it, as free trade supporters would say. A supporting column of the economy's institutional framework, protectionism, has been the subject of heated debate.

## 1. *Customs tariffs*

Tariffs became an issue in Spain following the first impact of the industrial revolution. Instead of restricting imports so that the old factories at Segovia, Burgos, Medina and elsewhere, razed during the War of Independence in 1808–14, would once again flourish, their purpose was to protect modern domestic industries — first the textile industry of Catalonia, and later Basque iron and steel and Asturian coal. Castilian wheat also became involved in the debate when it was threatened by cheaper American grain, as a result of transport upgrading.

The free trade-protectionist debate of the nineteenth century unfolded in four different stages: (*a*) a protectionist trend up to 1841; (*b*) a transition to free trade with the 1841 and 1849 tariffs; (*c*) the 'Figuerola Tariff' of 1869 (also known as the free trade proclamation) and the incidents that weakened the initial force of this movement; and (*d*) the ultimate triumph of protectionism in 1891 and its later consolidation. In this chapter we will avoid the many complex episodes that occurred during this period and focus on the factors that contributed to the triumph of protectionism.

### 1.1. *The triumph of protectionism.*

Following the free trade enthusiasm of the 1868 Revolution, resulting in the 1869 'Figuerola Tariff', protectionists began towards 1880 to catch a glimpse of the first-fruits of their support in the restoration of the Bourbons. The Act of 6 July 1882 and the Tariff of 1886 were the last gasps of free trade, whose followers were losing faith daily. Industrial and farm workers abandoned the cheap bread of naive free trade in search of a solution to their problems in their own (socialist and anarchist) organisations. Intellectuals, who had yet to join the socialist and anarchist ranks, had mostly moved away from free trade by the early 1880s. Moreover, the posture of Catalonian textile workers, led by Bosch and Labrús under the protectionist banner to promote national production, was strengthened by the interests of Asturian coal miners, represented by Adaro, and Basque iron and steel workers, headed by Chávarri and Zaracondegui.

The insistent request for a protectionist policy from various sectors prompted the President of the government, Cánovas del Castillo, to appoint a commission in 1889 to study the possibility of revising tariff policies. Its report, submitted to the government in November 1890, recommended that existing tariff legislation be repealed, that favourable trading agreements and most-favoured-nation clauses be revoked, and that all coasting trade be reserved for nationals. In 1890, Cánovas also published his famous work entitled *De cómo he venido yo a ser doctrinalmente proteccionista* (How I became a doctrinal protectionist), which led to protectionism becoming a dogma of the conservative party. The commission's report and the atmosphere created by protectionists and conservatives culminated in the Royal Decree of 24 December 1890, which abolished the fifth condition of the Figuerola Tariff of 1869, and envisaged the slow, systematic reduction of all tariffs. The Decree of 31 December 1891 approved a new tariff, eliminating exemptions and raising duties to such an extent that, with the jump in price of some items, it was dubbed the 'Hunger Tariff'. Years later fervent free trade supporter and democrat Gabriel Rodríguez, commenting on the influence major economic groups had on the preparation of the tariff, said that the names of public figures could have been written next to each item.

After 1891 some Liberal attempts were launched to make the tariff more free-trade-oriented, but Catalonians and Basques reacted swiftly, particularly the Basques, who established the Producers League of Viscaya. The colonial débâcle of 1898, forcing the Spanish economy to turn inwards, drove home tariff protection even further, and so in 1904 the Junta de Aranceles (Customs Board) took a public opinion poll on the existing tariff system and concluded that 'the dominant position in the country is decidedly protectionist. The universal evolution against the free trade doctrine has crystallised in Spain . . .' The Tariff Act of 1906 settled the 50-year-long trade-protectionist debate once and for all. With the publication of this Act and the 1907 Act on the Protection of National Industry, the Spanish economy was decidedly sheltered.

1.2. *Tariff policy, 1906–1960.* The Tariff Act of 1906, in force till 1960, was to be reviewed every five years. The first review took place in 1911 and resulted in lower tariffs. There was no review in 1916 because the First World War upset normal trading patterns. Due to supply difficulties, all duties levied on agricultural imports were removed during the four years of the war; at the same time, domestic industries grew as import substitution gained momentum. At the end of the war, the demand from expanding industries for adequate protection against the renewed competition of foreign products ushered in a review of customs duties on 26 November 1920, the publication of the Provisional Tariff of 17 May 1921, and the issue of the 'Cambó Tariff', which taxed some goods up to 10% of their value.

The intensive economic development which took place under the dictatorship of Primo de Rivera (1923–30) was made possible by the strengthening of the tariff of 1922, raised again in 1926, 1927 and 1928. According to a League of Nations study on the levels of protection in different countries, Spanish tariffs topped the list. Peseta exchange control, initiated with moderation at the end of the 1920s, was tightened from 1931 onwards, with import quotas coming into play in 1933. Exchange control and quotas represented an extreme protectionist policy that made tariff reviews unnecessary. This situation, compounded by a move towards absolute bilateralism, remained unchanged until 1957. Meanwhile, GATT (1947) and the OEEC (1948) emerged on the international scene with a view to lifting quantitative restrictions; this was a new context in which tariffs regained their full value. When it looked as if Spain was going to join a multilateral system of liberalised trade, the country felt the need to return to tariffs as an instrument of trade policy. The commissions appointed by the Tariff Review Board (created under the Decree of 24 June 1957) took three years to prepare the new tariff, which authorised the Act of 31 April 1950, within the context of the Stabilisation Plan (Section 4, below).

1.3. *The tariff of 1960 and the present-day tariff and trade structure.* The tariff of 1960 included two innovations regarding nomenclature and schedules. First, the adoption of the Brussels nomenclature simplified the formalities inherent in the international exchange of goods, laying a solid, uniform foundation for international negotiations, customs agreements and international comparisons. Secondly, the tariff of 1960 only had one column of duties, unlike that of 1922 with its two columns (one that was general and another applied to countries with which Spain had signed no commercial treaties). While the second column of the 1922 tariff offered few advantages, the 1960 tariff allowed for supplementary duties (of up to 100% of normal duties) to be levied on the goods of countries that had no trade agreement with Spain; this second 'theoretical' column, in fact, has never been applied. In the 1960 tariff schedule, most duties are *ad valorem* (imposed on the value declared at customs); there are also some specific and mixed duties, allowing for flexibility.

In economic terms, the 1960 tariff is the outgrowth of that set out in article 4 of the Act of 1 May 1960. The fifth clause of this article states that 'in the absence of reasons of genuine national interest calling for an exception to be made, customs duties will be set at coordinated levels, in amounts proportional to the value added and the cost of raw materials, the means of production and other factors, bearing in mind the suitability and development of production in Spain and consumption requirements.' Unlike the Tariff Acts of 1869 and 1906, the Act of 1960 does not have guidelines to apportion degrees of protection and set ceilings, for the 1960 legislator preferred to rid the tariff of limitations. Having no basic protection criteria, the new tariff was the product of a casuistical examination of the situation and expectations of Spain's system of production and of interest-group pressures.

The fact that the new tariff was protectionist surprised no one. While free trade could not be approached as ingenuously as it had been by nineteenth-century Spanish Liberals, slowing down economic development with it, the 1960 tariff was admittedly overprotective in certain cases. In any event, in response to economic development, unilateral and GATT-negotiated tariff reductions have been effected over time, relaxing Spain's tariff schedule to a certain degree. In 1961, the first year when the new tariff was fully in force, average customs duties were 12.71%; in 1965 this ratio dropped to 8.82%. If we exclude monopolised imports and goods shielded under special tariff laws (state trade, temporary imports etc.), average duties were as follows: 14.98% in 1961 and 11.71% in 1965 (7.4% being the Common Market average in 1964, before the 30% across-the-board reduction agreed during the Kennedy Rounds). In 1960 the mean average of duties was 23.75%, falling to 16% in early 1966. In the March 1972 issue of the magazine *Información Comercial Española*, Luis Gamir published a new paper on the evolution of tariff protection between 1961 and 1970. Protectionism eased after 1970 for four reasons: first, tariff reductions resulting from the Preferential Agreement signed with the EEC in 1970; secondly, a 10% reduction in general duties effected in 1977 to counter inflation; thirdly, the fulfilment of the GATT agreements reached during the Tokyo Rounds, starting in 1979; and finally agreements with EFTA countries (1981), similar to those previously signed with the EEC in 1970. Spain's accession to GATT in August 1963 was a milestone in Spanish tariff history; duties established in favour of member-countries can only be raised if a related concession is made. As when it joined the OEEC/OECD (liberalisation, quotas etc.) and the IMF (parities etc.), Spain, when it signed the GATT agreement, accepted an international discipline in the area of tariffs.

Spanish territory is considered a free trade area comprising three different customs territories: (1) the Peninsula and the Balearic islands, where the General Tariff Schedule shelters the production of 48 provinces; (2) the Canary islands, which are under a 'free port' system (the islands are actually a tax-exempt territory, for most imports are subject to a 5% local *ad valorem* municipal tax, used to finance the Canariot island and municipal governments; and (3) the North African enclave-cities of Ceuta and Melilla, which operate under a free port system similar to that of the Canary islands. There are absolutely no restrictions on trade between these three customs territories; goods produced in the Canary islands, Ceuta or Melilla are exempt from duty when shipped to the Peninsula and Balearic islands, and *vice versa*. Trade is also wide open between the Canary islands, Ceuta and Melilla. This peculiar tariff system was recognised as a genuine free trade zone in Spain's GATT protocol of accession, and the same happened at the EEC (see chapter XVIII).

## 2. *Exchange rates*

While tariffs directly protect national production by taxing imports, exchange rates used for foreign trade operations are equally decisive to economic defence. An exchange rate should be reasonable (giving just enough protection) and stable (avoiding fluctuations that constantly change the degree of protection of the system of production and upset business forecasts).

Following the creation of the peseta in 1868, the establishment of a peseta exchange rate provoked a crisis which lasted from 1890 till 1898. The financing of the colonial wars greatly increased the amount of notes in circulation, thus raising prices and depreciating the peseta's value. Consequently, from 1899 onwards the government concerned itself with stabilising the exchange rate. However, this concern did not result in controls until 1930. Up until this time the government tried to hold up the rate by different means, none of which involved limiting the buying and selling of currency on the free market. Since the peseta was virtually fiduciary, its value fluctuated widely in response to changes in the balance of payments and to speculation.

By 1925 the need for effective intervention was recognised. With Morocco being pacified in that year after giving Spain a series of economic headaches, the exchange rate became more stable, improving in 1926 as a result of a healthy export balance; the peseta appreciated from 33.6 to 32.8 against the pound sterling. Believing that the peseta would continue to climb, foreign banks and speculators bought up pesetas, so pushing up the value of the currency until it stood at 26.80 to the pound. This upward trend halted in the spring of 1928, when foreign speculators started to get rid of their pesetas, either because they lost hope in the revaluation of the Spanish currency or because the United States was exerting monetary pressure, and banks were cancelling loans used to make currency purchases (a premonition of the crash of 1929). Repatriation produced a surplus of pesetas and a demand for foreign currency, both of which lowered the peseta's value. The government reacted by creating the Comité Interventor de los Cambios (Exchange Control Board) in June of 1928, an agency formed by representatives of the state and the Bank of Spain and presided over by the Minister of Finance, José Calvo Sotelo. The board, entrusted with sufficient authority to operate on the market as it saw fit, had a 500 million ptas gold fund at its disposal in order to buy up currencies to keep down domestic money supplies and to control the value of the peseta. The board's main purpose was to stabilise the exchange rate with a view to adopting the gold standard, then thought to be the only possible way of eliminating foreign exchange rate fluctuations and the peseta's slow, steady depreciation. Given the implications of this issue, a commission was appointed in January 1929 to determine the applicability of the gold standard and, if appropriate, how it would be implemented. Don Antonio Flores de Lemus, a professor of economics at the University of Madrid, was appointed chairman of the commission and as such played a leading role in preparing the final recommendations. (The latter have been recorded in the annals of Spanish economics as among his best works.) The immediate effect of the commission's opinion was to abandon the proposal to adopt the gold standard, and this, together with the turn taken by the international economy and Spanish politics in 1929, led ultimately to a decision to stop controlling the exchange rate and to dissolve the control board.

After the dictatorship of Primo de Rivera fell in January 1930, the next government under General Berenguer let the exchange rate fluctuate freely. But when the value of the peseta then dropped, the Centro Regulador de Operaciones de Cambio (Exchange Regulatory

Agency) was set up. This agency's actions were, however, inadequate as was pointed out by Julio Wais, Minister of Finance in the cabinet of Admiral Aznar, who took over from General Berenguer. Wais attacked the problem of the exchange rate with resolution: to prevent operations on the same entry from multiplying, he prohibited the buying and selling of foreign exchange unless a genuine need was shown. Nevertheless, he believed that to exercise real control, the Exchange Regulatory Agency had to be replaced by a new agency that would be the exclusive buyer and seller of foreign currency. This agency would centralise all operations so that adjustments could be made, exact volumes known, and balance of payment figures obtained (at that time no statistical basis existed to determine the balance of payments).

August 1930 marked the conception of the Centro Oficial de Contratación de Moneda (Official Currency Exchange Office), which remained in operation during the Republic and was the precursor of the Instituto Español de Moneda Extranjero (Spanish Foreign Currency Institute), founded in 1939. Thus exchange control became part of Spain's economic tissue as a necessary means of controlling the value of the peseta and protecting domestic production by limiting imports.

The exchange policy of the Second Republic as embodied in its proclamation of April 1931 did not stray from the course set in the previous period, except that control now became absolute. The Decree of 29 May of that year divided foreign exchange operations into three groups: prohibited operations (speculation and capital flight), operations requiring previous authorisation (permissible financial transactions) and others (commercial operations) which, although technically free, required the agency's authorisation. This decree legally established the system regulating foreign trade operations; all foreign payments and collections had to pass through the agency, which could delay foreign currency transfers and so prevent depreciation of the peseta.

Currency exchange was fully controlled from 1939 till 1959, a period that can be broken down into three different stages. During the first stage (1939–48) the official exchange rate was fixed and special accounts were opened enabling exporters to use part of their foreign currency earnings in import operations; this combination gave exporters a favourable real exchange rate, far above the unrealistic official rate. The second stage (1948–57) saw the adoption of a multiple exchange rate system, simplified in 1950 and 1951. Finally, after a frustrated attempt to standardise exchange rates in April 1957 — prompting the re-emergence of multiple exchange rates through export premiums and import levies in July 1959, in accordance with the Stabilisation Plan — the peseta was fixed at a par value in relation to gold (namely 60 pesetas to the dollar), and this remained constant until the peseta was devalued in November 1967 to 70 pesetas to the dollar.

The international monetary crisis, starting in 1971, had a number of effects on the peseta. When the dollar was first devalued in December 1971, the peseta (maintaining its 1967 gold parity) underwent a *de facto* 8.57% revaluation, with the official exchange rate being set at 64.4737 ptas to the dollar; at the same time, the former 1% band was increased to 2.5% (65.93 and 63.03). In the light of widespread international instability (preceded by problems in Britain, Denmark, Italy and France), the decision was taken on 22 January 1974 to let the peseta float. Thus, with the exception of minimal intervention by the Bank of Spain (taking over the former functions of the defunct Spanish Foreign Exchange Institute), the peseta exchange rate was set in accordance with free market forces.

In February 1976, there was a *de facto* devaluation and inflationary pressures were mitigated, situating the exchange rate at 70 ptas to the dollar (the Villar Mir devaluation), but few benefits resulted because, contrary to certain affirmations, no complementary measures were taken. With an IMF-type devaluation in July 1977 being ruled out, the new democratic government (headed by Adolfo Suárez) decided to depreciate the peseta, fixing the official exchange rate at 87 ptas to the dollar. From that time on, the fall of the dollar in international markets improved the peseta exchange rate (registered at 65 ptas to the dollar in the summer of 1979). In 1980, however, the dollar began to climb again, and ever since Reagan's decisive 1980 high interest rates policy, it has grown increasingly. In December 1985, the official exchange rate was around 55 pesetas to the dollar and 125 to the ECU.

The Bank of Spain, operating through appointed private banks, absorbs and transfers the foreign currency involved in all foreign transactions.

## 3. *Quotas and clearing agreements*

Quotas limit the amount of a certain commodity that can be imported or exported over a specific period. France imposed the first import quotas as a result of the Great Depression, since they were the quickest way to provide domestic producers with the additional protection they needed in the wake of the 1929 crash in international prices and ineffective tariffs. All of France's trading partners retaliated by applying the same restrictions to French imports; and slowly but surely this new system was extended to all international relations. Import quotas were authorised in Spain by the Ministries of Agriculture, Industry and Commerce under the Decree of 23 December 1931, the preamble to which clearly stated that quotas were a retaliatory and not a protective measure. Nevertheless, quotas soon became a means to protect the national economy from foreign competition. Their protectionist role, together with tariff policy, was kept intact during the second half of the Republican period (1933–6), and in 1939 the quota system developed into Spain's main form of protection.

As in the case of quotas, the clearing agreements emerged as a transitory measure to solve international payment problems. When the gold standard was abandoned after the crash of 1929, many countries supported their currencies by not making good their debts to other countries, including Spain, blocking export balances, emigrant remittances, capital returns etc. Consequently, in 1932 the Official Currency Office saw its balances frozen in a number of countries. These difficulties were cleared up on a case-by-case basis through agreements to unblock frozen funds by quickly tying together the transitory problem of repayment with trading and quotas. The prototype of these clearing agreements was the Spanish-British agreement of 1935 which, apart from listing quotas for both countries, established a bilateral payment scheme. Each country had a clearing house where domestic importers paid amounts owed and collected amounts due. Credit balances were periodically settled between the two clearing houses (in this case the Bank of England and the Banco Exterior de España).

The clearing system, eventually adopted by all Spain's trading partners, was strictly bilateral, which meant that a credit balance shown in one country could not be used to cover a deficit in another; and currency convertibility virtually disappeared, for conversion could only be effected through free foreign exchange markets, where currencies were generally converted at a loss. The bilateral trend of foreign trade conceived in the Republican period was consolidated in the 1939–59 period, which began with the setting of one official exchange rate, and later adopting a complex system of multiple exchange rates and special accounts.

## 4. *The 1959 Stabilisation Plan; Patterns of trade*

The Stabilisation Plan broke away from the protectionist methods followed from 1933 to 1959, attacking on three different fronts:

(*a*) bilateral quantitative restrictions, by liberalising imports;

(*b*) the multiplicity of exchange rates created by premiums and goods returned for credit by establishing the IMF gold parity; and

(*c*) the general situation, by revising tariffs, which had fallen into oblivion in 1933.

In a memorandum sent to the OEEC and the IMF, the Spanish government pledged that it would slowly transfer as many goods as possible from state trade to private trade, from bilateral trade to general trade and from general trade to free trade. On joining the OEEC (which became the OECD in 1961) in 1959, Spain adopted the foreign trading pattern set forth in this organisation's Merchandise Liberalisation Code, specifying the following categories:

(*a*) *Free trade* is practised on imported goods from specific trading areas that were initially OECD member-countries, having since grown. Goods included under this heading (under which goods may be freely imported on presentation of an appropriate 'import declaration') were indicated on successive 'lists' of liberalised goods. The countries involved in liberalised imports were also administratively indicated in successive ministerial orders. At the time of writing, 90% of all imports fall under the free trade heading.

(*b*) *Global trade* involves quantitative import restrictions. Annual ceilings are distributed among petitioners, who are granted import licences for specific amounts. Countries that may import under general quotas (indiscriminately instead of bilaterally) are the same countries that benefit from liberalised goods trading patterns.

(*c*) *Bilateral trade* operates on a quota system established under bilateral agreements. Goods imported under this system require that licences be raised before importing.

(*d*) *State trade* is practised on officially classified goods, including oil, tobacco, meat, vegetable oils, cotton, sugar and some grains. These products either belong to state monopolies for fiscal reasons, or fall under officially regulated domestic trade, in which the SENPA or other state agencies or dealers intervene. Goods subject to state trade are imported directly by state agencies or dealers (Tabacalera, Campsa etc.) or by means of contracts between the Administration and competitively-selected professional importers. State trade is in the process of being returned to the private sector.

*Exports* are currently regulated by Royal Decree 2426/1979 of 14 September, which establishes two basic mechanisms:

(*a*) *Customs export declarations*, a simplified document that speeds up formalities, permitting firm sales, consignment shipments (at a fixed price, a best price or a minimum guaranteed price) and shared sales.

(*b*) *Different types of export licences*:
— *by operation*, on a case-by-case or one-shot basis;
— *general*, which can be staggered for harvested and steady exports;
— *open*, in the case of stable customer relations and specific customs houses;
— *special operations*, in the case of barter operations and foreign capital investments;
— *without foreign currency or settlement*, when no payment for equivalent amounts is generated;
— *temporary exportation*, for goods that will eventually be returned.

## 5. *The promotion of exports*

Along with tariffs, exchange rates and trade regulations, exporting is also a means of defending a country's system of production. The measures adopted to promote exports can be grouped into two categories: tax and tariff privileges and credit facilities.

The most important export *tax privilege* is tax relief, under which 'state taxes, indirect taxes, local levies, semi-fiscal charges and levies and other indirect taxes are returned to exporters.' Actually, the total value of all these taxes combined is considered to be equal to countervailing taxes imposed on foreign goods so that imports will be on the same footing as domestic goods in regard to taxes. There are four kinds of *tariff privileges*: temporary admission, whereby raw materials are imported duty-free for the manufacture of export goods; temporary imports, similar to temporary admissions, which refer to finished goods; fiscal restocking which involves the duty-free entry of raw materials in amounts previously used in exported goods; and lastly, customs drawbacks, which are the repayment of duties paid on goods used to manufacture exports.

The state initiated its export promotion policy by providing *credit facilities* in 1923 when, at the request of the Congreso Español de Comercio de Ultramar, it founded the Banco Exterior de España. The control of export credits changed hands under the Banking Act of 1971, which turned the Instituto de Crédito Oficial (ICO — Official Credit Institute) into the new export credit agency. And export credits are not complete without export credit guarantees. According to the legal definition, these guarantees 'provide technical assistance and cooperation in foreign trade by offering insurance against bad debts'. Export credit insurance was reorganised under Act 10/1970 of 4 July, which created the Compañía Española de Seguros de Crédito a la Exportación, in which the state had a 51% controlling interest. Export insurance covers up to 75% of the value of a loan in the case of commercial risks and up to 65% in the case of political risks.

We should mention in conclusion that the Ministry of Commerce issues *letters of recognition* on an individual and collective (sectoral letters) basis when certain export conditions, such as minimum export volume etc., are met, and the granting of these letters increases the chances of recipients receiving export aid.

# PART THREE
# THE DISTRIBUTION SYSTEM

## VI. THE TRANSPORT SYSTEM

Goods manufactured within a system of production are carried to their final destination (consumption, investment or export) through specific channels of distribution, which can be seen from two different perspectives. First, there are the physical means of transport, which we review in this chapter (see Table 6.1). And secondly, there are commercial channels making up domestic trade, which will be looked at in Chapter VII.

### 1. *The railway network*

The first Spanish railway lines were built from Barcelona to Mataró in 1848 and from Madrid to Aranjuez in 1851. Railway legislation got under way with the Railway Act of 1855, which guaranteed minimum interest on capital invested and established a 99-year limit on railway concessions to operate lines. At the end of this term, concessions had to be returned to the state, which also reserved the right to recall concessions at any time. Under the protection of the 1855 Act, major railway companies (Compañía del Norte, MZA, Isabel II etc.) were founded with French, English and Belgian capital. The 1877 Railway Act, which left the 1855 act virtually unchanged, remained in force till 1941, the year when concession recalls were put into practice to create the Red Nacional de los Ferrocarriles Españoles (RENFE — Spanish National Railway Network).

The present-day problems of RENFE can be traced back to the way the network was built. From the beginning, little capital was invested in track, and consequently the infrastructure was poorly constructed. Moreover, the belief common in the late nineteenth century that railways only needed heavy initial investment, and that thereafter capital only needed to be allocated to operational expenses, led to little investment in material turnover. This trend was also due to the financial difficulties which beset railway companies from their inception; time and time again inflexible rates were cut down by chronic inflation. Also, light traffic attributed to heavy losses.

The creation of RENFE in 1941 was fully justifiable. The unsound

151

economic situation of railway companies before 1936 was aggravated by the Civil War, as railways were misused and damaged. Former railway companies, unable to face the difficult problems of reconstruction, welcomed the rescue with open arms. In its first period, RENFE tried to reconstruct the network and attain pre-Civil War levels, but insurmountable problems, namely the gravity of the damage and the Second World War, which made it impossible to import equipment, got in the way. Thus the many reconstruction and modernisation plans launched between 1940 and 1960 were unable to guarantee adequate services, and traffic shifted from the railways to the road system, which developed by leaps and bounds. Spain is now being forced to abandon trunk and branch lines registering a huge deficit. (In October 1984, the Government decided to shut down 3,500 km. of the country's 13,500-km. network.).

Basic data on railways and roads is presented in Table 6.1. The network is radial in its structure, with Madrid in the centre and the more important terminals in La Coruña, Gijón, Santander, Bilbao, Irún, Port Bou, Valencia, Alicante, Málaga, Algeciras, Cádiz and Lisbon (see Fig. 18). This radial network, completed with branch and spur lines, maximised connections with a minimum number of lines. The most acute infrastructural problem today is that the track width in Spain does not match that of other European countries. If regular Spanish trains could reach Paris in 24 hours, Hamburg in 40 hours and Copenhagen in 48 hours, exports from the Levante coast would acquire a new dimension. Fleets of carriages with interchangeable axles are contributing to a solution.

As regards locomotive power sources, as late as 1971 steam (with coal or diesel) was used to drive 34% of the sector. By 1974, however, steam locomotion was done away with and, instead of a conversion to diesel fuel, as recommended by the World Bank in 1962 in view of the energy crisis, a 3,000 km. electrification plan for major trunk lines was set in motion. In the 1980s, electricity powers almost 5,500 km. of track, a figure which should reach 7,000 km. by the time the project is completed. At present, Spanish railways have a sufficient number of adequately modernised carriages in their fleet. Turning to cargo classification stations, the sixteen stations currently in operation will have to be reduced to six to facilitate the movement of direct long-distance freight trains. The present number of regular loading stations is also excessive on the grounds that many of them are uneconomic.

In general, therefore, Spain's rail system is in an unfavourable position, for traffic is light with the result that operational costs outdistance earnings (this was why 1,000 km. of low-traffic track were closed in 1985). Today's infrastructure could, if properly

## Table 6.1.  TRANSPORTATION

### 1. *Interurban passenger traffic\**

|  | 1975 | | 1980 | | 1983 | |
|---|---|---|---|---|---|---|
|  | Million passengers/ km. | % | Million passengers/ km. | % | Million passengers/ km. | % |
| Road | 158,585 | 88.03 | 198,217 | 90.59 | 206,891 | 90.53 |
| Railway | 17,643 | 9.79 | 14,826 | 6.77 | 16,237 | 7.11 |
| Air | 3,928 | 2.18 | 5,762 | 2.64 | 5.398 | 2.26 |
| *Total* | 180,156 | 100.0 | 218,805 | 100.0 | 228,526 | 100.0 |

\* Data on maritime passenger traffic unavailable, but an estimated 10 million passengers (1% of the market) travel by sea.

### 2. *Internal freight traffic*

|  | 1975 | | 1980 | | 1983 | |
|---|---|---|---|---|---|---|
|  | Freight tonnes/km. | % | Freight tonnes/km. | % | Freight tonnes/km. | % |
| Road | 84,533 | 67.81 | 98,898 | 68.50 | 118,235 | 72.83 |
| Railway | 11,079 | 8.89 | 11,300 | 7.82 | 11,019 | 6.79 |
| Pipes | 2,118 | 1.70 | 3,005 | 2.06 | 3,240 | 2.00 |
| Maritime | 26,870 | 21.56 | 31,125 | 21.55 | 29,784 | 18.34 |
| Air | 55 | 0.04 | 74 | 0.05 | 62 | 0.04 |
| *Total* | 124,655 | 100.0 | 144,402 | 100.0 | 162,340 | 100.0 |

### 3. *International freight and passenger traffic (%)*

|  | Freight, 1981 | | | Persons, 1982 | | |
|---|---|---|---|---|---|---|
|  | Arrivals | Departures | Total | Arrivals | Departures | Total |
| Road | 4.96 | 15.10 | 8.03 | 64.75 | 92.18 | 71.57 |
| Railway | 0.64 | 3.80 | 1.60 | 5.15 | 2.03 | 4.37 |
| Maritime | 94.12 | 80.80 | 90.09 | 3.39 | 0.32 | 2.63 |
| Air | 0.27 | 0.30 | 0.28 | 26.71 | 5.47 | 21.43 |
| *Total* | 100.0 | 100.0 | 100.0 | 100.0 | 100.0 | 100.0 |

*Source*: Transport Commission.

maintained, handle twice its present traffic density; if this were to happen, the railways would receive a much-needed economic boost. Meanwhile, deficits on operating accounts were accumulating due to road transport undercutting official rates. To halt this decline, the

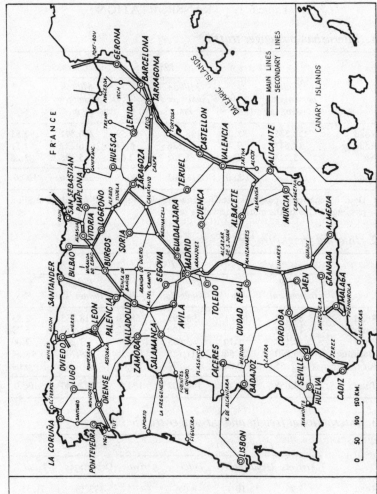

Fig. 18.
RAILWAYS

This figure shows RENFE (Spain's national railway system) in 1980. The most heavily travelled freight line (12,200 freight tonnes/km.) runs from Venta de Baños to Palencia, in contrast to other lines that have almost no traffic whatsoever. Some lines, where freight traffic was minimal, were devoted primarily to passenger traffic (e.g. the 'Ruta de Plata' from Astorga to Plasencia, near the Portuguese border — some 1,000 km. or 8% of the total system, were closed to traffic in 1985.

first state/RENFE contract programme was approved in January 1979 and in 1981 the go-ahead was given to a 10-year 1.2 billion ptas investment plan which, with the prospect of a long energy shortage, could have given the first incentive in decades. Unfortunately, the goals of the plan were soon overtaken by an ever–growing deficit, standing at 200,000 million ptas in 1982, and more than 180,000 million in 1983. In 1984 a second contract programme was proposed with a view to closing many of the trunk and branch lines showing a deficit (the 3,500 km. already mentioned).

## 2. Road transport

Road transportation, the only means of inland transportation before the advent of the railways, lost much of its importance with the building of the railways, but later regained it with the appearance of motor vehicles (see Table 6.1).

Of all vehicle traffic in Spain, 80% uses the country's radial road system, which has six axes passing through Madrid. On the other hand, regional and local road systems are far too extensive for many areas, which itself impedes their development. While Spain has 25 km. of highway for every 100 square km. of surface area and 4 km. of highway for every 1,000 inhabitants, the averages for the rest of Europe are 55 and 9, respectively, or twice the density.

The problems with the highway system were sharpened by the shift in traffic brought about by the Stabilisation Plan, which suddenly raised railroad rates by 50%; this made it necessary to rework highway policies with a long-term approach, in the form of the 12-year General Road Plan (1962–73). This was broken down into three 4-year periods. Development Plan I (1964–7) included the corresponding part of the 1962–73 General Road Plan. Development Plan II only called for a simple 4-year programme, at the same time as two new specific plans were started up: the REDIA Plan (la Red de Itinerarios Asfálticos — Asphalt Roadway System), designed to upgrade and standardise 4,928 km. of heavily used roads in 6 years (1967–72); and the PANE (Programa de Autopistas Nacionales Españolas — Spanish National Highway Programme), under which 3,000 km. of toll roads were to be built in 11 years. The only such expressways that were completed run from La Junquera to Alicante, from Bilbao to Behovia, from Bilbao to Burgos, from Villaba to Adanero, from Seville to Cádiz, and through the Ebro Valley (see Fig. 19).

In the wake of the 1973 crisis, road transport fell far below traffic forecasts, and the PANE was suspended. In late 1983, in an atmosphere marked by the nationalisation of expressway concessionaires threatening bankruptcy, the MOPU (Ministry of Public Works) announced a preliminary *national freeway plan* to build 5,000 km. of highway that required a smaller budget and that would have less environmental impact.

## 3. The merchant marine

Spain's inland water transport is negligible, but 80% of all transport to and from Spain is seaborne.

The domestic coasting fleet comprises three large transport groups: normal coasting, free coasting or tramps, and oil tankers. Normal cabotage is faced with a structural crisis due to the growing competition of road transport, which provides a door-to-door service that coasting cannot match because of its slowness in adopting the modern container system. Moreover, in an effort to control smuggling, coastal trading ships are required to carry excessive documentation, leading to considerable administrative and other costs. Tramps, which are primarily used to carry coal, ore, cement, wood etc., have a series of peculiar problems, such as fleet obsolescence (tramps being the last refuge for the oldest ships of the Spanish navy) and inefficiency at domestic ports, which increases demurrage beyond reasonable time-limits. Campsa and other oil tanker operators have no problems with competitors or rates; since Campsa is under monopolistic control, fluctuations in the domestic freight market are automatically absorbed.

In shipping, as in other sectors of the Spanish economy, there are an excessive number of companies, many having less than 100,000 DWT capacity and only one ship engaged in coasting. Sectoral fragmentation is one of the causes of obsolescence in smaller ships: most small coasting and tramp shipping companies lack adequate financial means to replace worn-out ships. The only solution to this problem would be for these small lines to regroup, thus increasing tonnage capacity and broadening their field of activities.

All shipowners of any significance belong to the Asociación de Navieros Españoles (Anave — Spanish Shipping Association), formerly the Oficema, created under the 1951 Shipping Agreement. Until freight rates were partly decontrolled in 1960, Oficema operated as a freight distributor, giving preference to Spanish ships. Today maximum rates are in force only for domestic coasting and for imports used in state trade. All other freight is contracted on the competitive international market, in accordance with shipping agreements or shipping conference rates. Aside from official rates,

## Fig. 19. ROADS

This Figure presents planned toll-road concessions. The Plan de Autopistas Nacionales Españolas (PANE — Spanish National Road Plan) is an attempt to break with the traditional Spanish radial transport system and strengthen the most used roads: along the Mediterranean coast, along the Cantabrian Corniche, and from Cadiz (via Seville, Caceres, Valladolid and Burgos) to the French border.

The drawback of the plan is that toll-roads give rise to huge administrative costs and thus higher operating costs. This was said to be the only viable system 'since the state lacked sufficient funds to assume responsibility for such a huge project'. However, the political group in power in 1965–76 was incapable of, or not interested in, reforming the tax system to generate the revenue needed to build these works, even though they are typical public services. When the energy and economic crises broke in 1973, the PANE was shelved, and in 1984 a National Freeway Plan of some 5,000 km. was substituted.

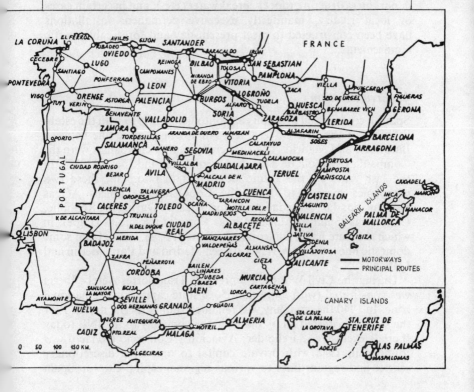

Spanish shipping lines also receive shipping premiums. With the economic crisis, the state had to execute the mortgages corresponding to many ships built since the mid-1970s with almost 100 per cent of funding provided by the state (Naviera Letasa, Euroflot group etc.). Moreover, the state recalled the concession made to Cía Transmediterranea, a private company. The largest shipowner today is the Banco de Crédito Industrial, which has been forced to attach numerous liens to ships in order to recover money owed to it.

Spain's coastline is dotted with 200 ports, of which Barcelona, Bilbao and Valencia are autonomous, 23 others are semi-autonomous (managed by Port Works Juntas), and the rest are controlled by the Comisión Administrativa de Grupos de Puertos (Administrative Commission for Port Groups), under the Ministry of Public Works and Urban Development. The ten most important ports (Cartagena, Santa Cruz de Tenerife, Bilbao, Barcelona, Gijón, Avilés, La Luz, Huelva, Valencia and Seville) handle 75% of all traffic. Since the 1960s, a large investment has been made in port infrastructure (docks, breakwaters etc.), and in certain cases of local rivalry, manifestly excessive permanent installations have been constructed to meet present-day and foreseeable traffic requirements.

## 4. *Civil aviation*

Spanish commercial aviation came into being in 1919 with the establishment of the first Government Air Postal Service line between Barcelona and Madrid. The first civil aviation companies were the Compañía Española de Tráfico Aéreo (Ceta) and Iberia (1927). In the last years of the Primo de Riverá dictatorship, these two companies merged to form the Concesionaria Líneas Aéreas Subvencionadas, Sociedad Anónima (Classa). During the Republic, Classa was renamed Líneas Aéreas Postales Españolas (Lape), in which the state had a controlling interest of 55%. Aside from some domestic lines, the Lape flew between Madrid and Paris, Berlin and Lisbon.

During the Civil War the Empresa de Transportes Aéreos Iberia was constituted (with more than 50% state capital) in the national zone. In 1940 the company was renamed simply Iberia, and in 1941 the state transferred all its shares in the company to the INI, today Iberia's exclusive shareholder. Aviación y Comercio (Aviaco) was founded in 1948 with private capital to operate a discretionary service and regular lines to various regional capital cities in Spain and North Africa. The INI has also become Aviaco's exclusive shareholder.

Domestic air freight and passenger lines connect almost all major Spanish cities to Madrid and Barcelona. Iberia flies to all South American countries, as well as to North, West and South Africa, the Gulf of Guinea, Beirut, Tehran, Kuwait, Jeddah and Cairo. Foreign lines link Spain with all important Western European and some Eastern European cities. On the average, 65% of passenger capacity is used on domestic lines and 50% on international lines. In general, services could be greatly improved.

Spain's sprawling geographical conditions foster air transport — in direct contrast to Belgium, Holland and Switzerland, which have strong domestic airlines but limited surface area — and thus domestic traffic is much denser than international traffic. Both railways and shipping lines steadily lose traffic to the airlines. Domestic traffic (the exclusive domain of Iberia and Aviaco) is less profitable, for domestic fares are lower than international ones. Since domestic lines work with a higher utilisation factor, service falls short of satisfying demand at peak times of the year.

In the 1970s, Iberia seemed to hold up well despite the crisis. In 1982, however, losses were reported to be almost 7,000 million ptas and in 1983 they were 30,000 million. This situation was attributed to the drop in traffic on South American lines (given that continent's financial crisis); also to blame were faulty administration, structural deficiencies, labour problems and so on. The strike of pilots and maintenance technicians in the summer of 1984 riveted public attention on the disastrous state of Iberia. We can only hope that Iberia has reached the bottom and will re-start its ascent.

While domestic traffic is handled exclusively by Spanish airlines, foreign traffic is controlled in accordance with the regulations of the International Air Transport Association (IATA), generally with airline pools. Charter flights have yet to be maximised by Spanish airlines. These flights are extremely popular in the high season, given the limitations of regular service. Although Iberia and Aviaco organise some charter flights, and one private company (Spantax) was set up for this purpose, Spain's potential in this field has not been fully exploited.

Fifty airports are currently open to civil aviation traffic, the busier airports of Madrid, Palma de Mallorca, Barcelona, Las Palmas de Gran Canaria and Santa Cruz de Tenerife being under-equipped to handle the recent expansion in this sector.

# VII. DOMESTIC TRADE

The strength of domestic trade can be measured through company accounts, national accounts and working population polls. According to national accounting, wholesale and retail trading represents 12% of gross domestic production, this percentage being equal to overall marketing cost. The trade sector employs 14% of the Spanish working population, with a sizeable number of young women and girls working for lower-than-average wages.

## 1. *The marketing of capital goods*

Most capital goods are sold directly by manufacturers to the industries that actually use them. No middlemen get involved in the wide range of capital goods, for manufacturers have commercial departments or divisions that conduct market studies, customer relations and so on. In some capital goods manufacturing subsectors, manufacturing associations have recently emerged with a view to sales promotion, particularly in foreign countries. Such is the case of Sercobe (Commercial Service for Capital Goods Manufacturers), Construnaves (Shipbuilders Technical-Commercial Service, now a division of the INI), the Association of Machine Tool Manufacturers etc. The most recent development in capital goods sales has been in companies that design and sell key-turn factories and provide financing and technical assistance.

Financing has taken on tremendous importance in the marketing of capital goods in the domestic market and throughout the world. Since capital goods generally have a long technical life, industrial buyers are often forced to pay on the instalment plan. For this reason, either the buyer or the seller must secure financing, a task usually left to the seller who must compete with the favourable terms offered by foreign suppliers. Consequently, capital goods manufacturers have the choice of tying up vast amounts of resources or resorting to credit. Naturally, it is the second option that is normally taken up by securing (18-month) commercial loans or long-term credit provided by industrial or business banks or official credit institutions.

The domestic capital goods trade also has its own showcase, namely its trade shows, the most important of which is the International Trade Show of Barcelona, followed by other national and international shows in Valencia, Bilbao, Seville and Zaragoza. Spain also holds shows for mining, footware, graphic arts, construction and machinery. Industrialists and technicians attend these shows to check on recent advances and to prepare for future purchases. Since 1980, Madrid has become an important stage for commercial exhibitions and showrooms, through the Institución Ferial Madrileña (IFEMA — Trade Show Organisation of Madrid).

## 2. *Marketing foodstuffs*

The marketing channels for Spanish fruit and vegetables (we considered meat and fish in chapter 3) can be drawn as follows:

*Channel 1*: Producer — Wholesale exporter — Retailer — Consumer.
*Channel 2*: Producer — Commission merchant — Wholesaler (wholesale market) — Retailer — Consumer.
*Channel 3*: Producer — Retailer — Consumer.
*Channel 4*: Producer — Consumer.

Of these four channels, 1 is for exports and 4 is uncommon. Spain (with the exception of a few cities, such as Madrid, where it occurs sporadically) has been unconcerned with direct consumer sales. The reasons behind this phenomenon can be easily summarized: the perishability of foodstuffs, which require quick marketing channels, and the economic limitations of farms, which are incapable of handling commercial activities. Channel 2 is the most commonly used. In large cities such as Madrid, Barcelona, Bilbao and Seville retailers must buy at central wholesale markets.

All along the marketing channel, middlemen successively widen the margin on the original price of a product. Mark-ups vary between 200 and 500% and thus the overall margin on vegetables and fruit is greater in Spain than anywhere else in Europe. According to OECD reports, fruit and vegetable consumer prices throughout the rest of Europe are only three times farm prices. The situation in Spain is approximately as shown below:

|  | *Price level* |
|---|---|
| Retailers | 350–500 |
| Producer | 100 |
| Commission merchants | 150 |
| Wholesalers | 200 |

Spain has an estimated 35,000 retailers; this large number is due to low sales averages, which in turn affect prices, for demand is inelastic, and retailers (aspiring to make a living) have small local monopolies. This situation has changed greatly with the spread of supermarkets, hypermarkets etc.

Non-perishable foodstuffs can be stored for relatively long periods (and always longer than a crop year). Intervention forms part of non-perishable foodstuff marketing, in order that supplies do not flood the market after harvests and knock down prices. Since 1968, intervention has been centralised by the Fondo de Ordenación y Regulación de Precios y Productos Agrícolas (FORPPA — Agricultural Commodities and Commodity Price Regulatory Fund), under the Ministry of Agriculture.

The state-run enterprise Mercados Centrales de Abastecimiento, SA (Mercasa), promotes the creation of new central wholesale markets; and, at another level, the state-run enterprise Mercados en Origen, SA (Mercorsa), groups agricultural supplies in small local markets.

## 3. *The marketing of durable consumers goods*

For these products customers pay either in cash or with bills of exchange, particularly in the case of home appliances, furniture and cars. Abuse of the customer has been great in this area: aside from strictly banking interests, merchants often obtain large additional profits. In today's economic climate, the growing use of the instalment plan has prompted the Government to lay down time-limits and downpayment minimums.

If a producer offers merchandise to a retailer at a fixed selling price, the retailer is prevented from offering discounts to increase sales. In Spain, unlike other countries, fixed selling prices are not prohibited by law. When prices are not fixed, manufacturers usually allow for trade and customer discounts.

## 4. *Domestic market competition*

Commercial practices restricting competition are as old as trade itself. It is natural for manufacturers or dealers in a specific product to agree to set common selling prices or to adopt other practices to avoid trade wars. All developed countries have passed copious legislation promoting effective competition and curbing restrictive trade practices. The Restrictive Trade Practices Act 110/1963 of 20 July prohibited price control in Spain. Article 3 of the act specifically banned price and production cartels, the creation of market and supply source 'rings', local price discrimination, trade discrimination against third parties and the exaction of extra conditions beyond the terms of the contract.

Of course, there are many cases in which competition cannot

work, whether due to natural monopolies (such as public utilities) or to the wastage which competition can produce. Spanish law, in general, follows Common Market guidelines, specifically articles 85 and 86 of the Treaty of Rome which list a number of cases in which restrictive practices are permissible. These cases are grouped into two categories:

(*a*) *Excluded restrictive practices*, which are those authorised by legal provisions. This category comprises natural monopolies and the monopolistic activities of the Senpa, Campsa, Tabacalera, RENFE etc.

(*b*) *Exceptive practices*. In specific cases, competitive restrictions may be advisable. To study these cases and, under certain conditions, eventually authorise such limitations, the Act of 1963 established the following exceptive practices:

(i) *Streamlining cartels*. Manufacturers and dealers set up these cartels to fix common standards and types, with a view to raising productivity. This may occur in the manufacturing of standardised packaging, uniform ceramic pieces, tools listed in the same catalogue etc.

(ii) *Structural adaptation cartels*. When the supply capacity for a specific item exceeds real demand, agreements may be reached between manufacturers to adapt supply to demand over the long-term. This is the case at present with the flour and cotton textile industries.

(iii) *Export cartels*. This is the typical case when some domestic producers band together to form a common front when dealing abroad. The Competition Defence Court has authorised such a cartel: the Spanish Potash Cartel.

(iv) *Cartels for sectors depressed by a steady drop in demand*. The difference between this heading and that of number two is not well defined in the act. An example of this situation would be coal mining; coal steadily lost its demand to technological advances during the 1960s.

Lastly, the act makes it possible for industries in a given sector to establish their own sectoral regulations on competition concerning a series of aspects of domestic trade, such as terms of payment, terms of delivery, fair competition guidelines and maximum price reductions in accordance with quantities.

Individuals or companies harmed by the ban on certain restrictive practices or interested in seeing certain exceptive practices authorised may submit their case to the Competition Defence Court. This court has unappealable final rulings, nationwide jurisdiction, considerable power to penalise (with warnings and various fines) and even the authority to turn a case over to the penal court system. The task of the Competition Defence Service, under the Ministry of Commerce, is to prepare the documents to be examined and judged by the court. The Competition Defence Council studies and either approves or rejects sectoral regulations on competition.

## 5. *Commercial areas*

In Spain, with its mountainous terrain and provincial administrative divisions which strongly influence commercial structures (it should be noted that all provincial capitals are the centres of the most important trading areas), studies on trading areas employ the more accurate method of direct surveys. The team set up by the Chambers of Commerce, Industry and Shipping, headed by Fontana Tarrats, to prepare the *Atlas Comercial de España* (Madrid, 1963), instead of using Reilly's model on economic gravitation, proceeded to conduct a direct survey. Staff in the 9,200 municipalities of that time were asked to cooperate by filling out questionnaires regarding *where* residents bought uncommon items (home appliances, furniture, books, clothing, cosmetics, gifts etc.). The *Atlas Comercial de España*, the fruit of these questionnaires, presents 101 clearly marked commercial areas with 170 sub-areas and their corresponding sub-centres. This atlas represented the country's first serious study of the spatial structure of the domestic market, and became an essential tool for regional and domestic companies in their studies on stock locations, sales promotion, branch offices, performance etc. (see Fig. 20).

The atlas team was eventually able to determine the disposable income of each area and sub-area. Since official statistics (usually compiled at the national and provincial levels) could not be used, disposable income had to be determined through direct methods. Information was gathered for each area and sub-area as to the number of commercial banks, savings banks, telephones installed or on request, commercial licences in force, and the total amount of taxes collected on entertainment expenses and stamped commercial paper. A national total of 100,000 was established for each lot of data, which was then broken down by commercial area. Once these basic data were standarised, it was possible to construct the arithmetical mean and determine the final share of each commercial area within the domestic market (see Fig. 20).

Another reference publication on domestic trade is the *Spanish*

*Market Yearbook*, prepared and updated by the atlas team, and published by the Banco Español de Crédito.

## 6. *Sales and advertising costs*

Newspaper advertising rates in Spain depend, as they do elsewhere, on the number of copies printed (which is controlled by the Oficina de Justificación de Difusión para la Prensa — the Newspaper Dissemination Control Office) and the disposable income of readers. The widest-read newspapers are *El País, La Vanguardia, ABC*, and *Diario 16*.

As for the radio, the second oldest medium, several hundred public and private short wave, AM and FM stations operate in Spain. The Sociedad Española de Radiodifusión (SER), Radio Nacional de España and Radio Popular (financed by the Church) are the three leading stations. At the time of writing, Televisión Española still monopolises the television network. The Spanish state network is one of the few that has had to resort to commercial advertising to finance itself. Given the massive size of viewing audiences — up to 25 million when special events or programmes are being televised — and its penetration generally, prime-time spots exact exorbitant prices. While advertising in cinemas is in decline, billboard advertising is growing (and unfortunately cluttering up the landscape).

Apart from the high costs of advertising, pernicious psychological and sociological effects are also being produced with its often excessive expansion: e.g. reflex conditioning and erosion of the learning process for children and young adults.

## 7. *The pricing system*

Spain has basically two indices, the general industrial price index (1974 base year = 100) and the consumer price index (1976 base year = 100). The weighing of the different indices making up the consumer price index indicates the budgetary pattern of a typical Spanish family (see Table 7.1, including price evolution and some international comparisons).

Price control systems, usually an unsuccessful attempt to keep down prices, have been constantly erected and dismantled. At more critical moments these systems have been combined with monetary and loan aid packages. With Decree Law 12/1973 of 30 November

Fig. 20. SHARES OF AGGREGATE INCOME OF SPAIN'S 101 COMMERCIAL AREAS, 1977

This map shows the commercial areas of the Spanish market studied by the *Atlas Comercial de España* team. The share of aggregate income for each commercial area is specified and used to determine disposable income based on a total of 100,000 points: A *per capita* market share index (national average = 1) has also been established for each area.

The map can be compared to those on population and *per capita* income. *Per capita* market shares in Bilbao, Barcelona and Madrid are above average — as, to a less degree, are the Ebro Valley, the Mediterranean coast as far south as Cartagena and the Cantabrian coast as far west as the Galician border. On the other hand, the country's south-eastern, south-western and north-western quadrants register below-average market shares, obviously because of their income/spending ratio.

Information on Spanish commercial areas is periodically updated by the Research Service of the Banco Español de Crédito in the *Spanish Market Yearbook*, which was used to prepare this map, and is useful for detailed regional analyses, market studies etc.

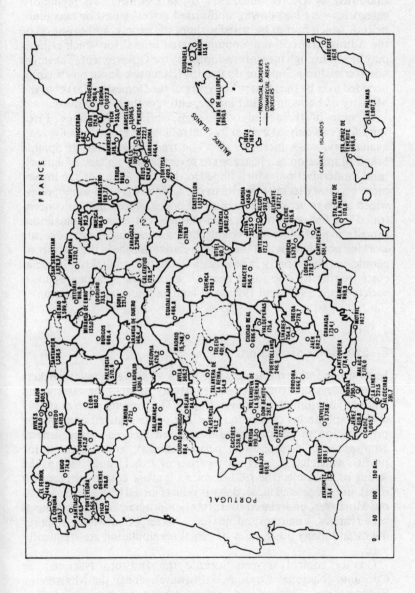

(modified by Decree 2695/1977 of 28 October) two regulatory categories were laid down: 'authorised prices' (fixed or maximum prices), which cannot be raised without the express authorisation of the Administration; and 'communicated prices' for which ceilings may be set through measures adopted by the Government. The interministerial Junta Superior de Precios (Executive Junta on Pricing), presided over by the Deputy Secretary of the Domestic Market of the Ministry of Economy and Finance, enforces these provisions.

In spite of these and other steps, inflation increases. Price spiralling can only be curbed by controlling the money supply, loan availability, wage increases etc. The traditional roots of Spain's brand of inflation can be traced to several causes: a lack of agricultural modernisation, which impeded the channelling of the investment necessary to raise productivity; a high degree of monopolies, which allow many sectors to push up prices, since supply is concentrated in a few economic decision-making centres, where maximum short-term profits are what count; the sharp increase in service sector working populations and the steady relative decline in the number of people working strictly in production; and the gradual rise in social costs, setting off the rapid anarchic expansion of urban Spanish society in the 1960s and 1970s and land and housing speculation.

## 8. *Consumer protection*

In an urban industrial society like Spain — however many pockets of underdevelopment and poverty it may have — the effects and abuses of consumerism cut ever deeper. The concentration of supply and the splintering of demand, the lack of government controls the proliferation of official standards (often ignored in the general atmosphere of irresponsible permissiveness), and the thirst for profits, which has given rise to a variety of lethal frauds, such as the selling of toxic oils (the 1981–2 colza oil affair cost more than 350 lives), unrefrigerated meat, dairy products mixed with grease, and so on. Moreover, undeclared substitutes, improper packaging, banned preservatives, unauthorised mixtures, unrespected weight requirements and many other cases of illegal manipulation are frequently used.

Quality control services include the Instituto Nacional de Consumo (National Consumers Institute), under the Ministry of Economy and Finance and various other consumer and quality control inspection services within the Ministries of Agriculture and Health and Consumer Affairs. Many consumer groups (such as the

## Table 7.1.   PRICE EVOLUTION

### A. *General and partial indices*

|  | Weight % |
| --- | --- |
| Food and beverages | 40.520 |
| Clothing and footwear | 8.165 |
| Housing | 14.005 |
| House services | 7.750 |
| Health services | 3.375 |
| Transport and communications | 9.745 |
| Leisure and education | 6.945 |
| Other expenses | 9.495 |
| *General Index* | 100.000 |

### B. *Increase of index (%)*

|  | Average in year | December– December |  | Average in year | December– December |
| --- | --- | --- | --- | --- | --- |
| 1965 | 13.2 | 9.4 | 1976 | 17.6 | 19.8 |
| 1966 | 6.2 | 5.3 | 1977 | 24.5 | 26.4 |
| 1967 | 6.4 | 6.5 | 1978 | 19.8 | 16.6 |
| 1968 | 4.9 | 2.9 | 1979 | 15.7 | 15.5 |
| 1969 | 2.2 | 3.4 | 1980 | 15.6 | 15.2 |
| 1970 | 5.7 | 6.8 | 1981 | 14.5 | 14.4 |
| 1971 | 8.2 | 9.7 | 1982 | 14.4 | 14.0 |
| 1972 | 8.3 | 7.3 | 1983 | 12.1 | 12.2 |
| 1973 | 11.4 | 14.2 | 1984 | 11.3 | 9.2 |
| 1974 | 15.7 | 17.9 | 1985 | 9.2 | — |
| 1975 | 17.0 | 14.1 |  |  |  |

### C. *International comparisons* (*yearly averages*)

|  | 1961–70 | 1971–80 | 1981 | 1982 | 1983 | 1984 |
| --- | --- | --- | --- | --- | --- | --- |
| West Germany | 2.7 | 5.1 | 6.3 | 5.3 | 3.3 | 1.5 |
| Spain | 6.0 | 15.3 | 14.6 | 14.4 | 12.1 | 11.3 |
| United States | 2.8 | 7.8 | 10.4 | 6.1 | 3.2 | 4.2 |
| France | 4.0 | 9.7 | 13.4 | 11.8 | 9.6 | 7.1 |
| Italy | 3.9 | 13.8 | 17.8 | 16.6 | 14.6 | 9.9 |
| Japan | 5.8 | 9.0 | 4.9 | 2.7 | 1.9 | 2.3 |
| United Kingdom | 4.1 | 13.7 | 11.9 | 8.6 | 4.6 | 4.7 |
| Switzerland | 3.3 | 5.0 | 6.5 | 5.6 | 3.0 | 2.7 |

*Source:* INE and OECD.

OCU and the ACUDE) and associations for, e.g., telephone users and advertisers are being formed. In 1984 the very first consumer protection act was published. Nevertheless, the absence of decisive government action and the prevailing atmosphere of public amorality give cause for concern.

# PART FOUR
# THE FOREIGN SECTOR

## VIII. FOREIGN TRADE

### 1. *General introduction: the balance of payments*

By recording transactions between different domestic sectors, national accounting provides the clearest picture of movements within the domestic economy. The corporation account shows the earnings and expenditure of companies taken as a whole, i.e. of the productive sector. In the family account, income and expenditures are recorded for the consumer sector, comprising the family consumer unit.

Capital formation and savings figures are entered in a separate account called gross capital formation. And transactions between the domestic economy (comprising the three accounts just mentioned) and foreign countries are recorded in a foreign trade operations account. Foreign trade operations can be analysed through national accounting and the balance of payments. The International Monetary Fund defines the balance of payments as a 'systematic record of all economic transactions between residents of one country and the residents of other countries over a given period of time'. And transactions are divided into two groups: the current account and the capital account (see Table 8.1). The current account records transactions that generate or absorb earnings, such as merchandise exports and imports, services (tourism and travel, freight, insurance, investment earnings and government transactions) and transfers. The capital account records movements of capital that influence a country's credit/debit status or its gold reserves. It covers all long-term private and public inward and outward flows of capital. Short-term gold and capital movements are used to balance the account through adjustments to the basic balance.

The Ministry of Commerce has been publishing the annual balance of payments since 1959, in accordance with the model proposed by the International Monetary Fund. The balance shows net profits and losses (capital inflows less currency outflows) under each heading. The basic balance is adjusted for errors and omissions to give us the final balance. And overall surpluses or deficits are brought into balance by either purchasing foreign currency or gold

171

## Table 8.1. SPAIN'S BALANCE OF PAYMENTS
### (US $ million)

| | 1982 | | | 1983 | | |
|---|---|---|---|---|---|---|
| | Receipts | Expenditure | Balance | Receipts | Expenditure | Balance |
| Imports | — | 30,513.0 | 30,513.0 | — | 28,254.8 | 28,254.8 |
| Exports | 21,332.1 | — | 21,332.1 | 20,867.9 | — | 20,867.9 |
| *Trade Balance* | 21,332.1 | 30,513.0 | −9,180.9 | 20,867.9 | 28,254.8 | −7,386.9 |
| Freight, transport and insurance | 2,793.2 | 2,323.6 | 469.6 | 2,765.2 | 2,196.2 | 569.0 |
| Tourism and travel | 7,130.9 | 1,009.2 | 6,212.7 | 6,836.9 | 895.0 | 5,941.9 |
| Investment-generated income | 1,675.8 | 4,094.3 | −2,418.5 | 1,118.8 | 3,467.9 | −2,349.1 |
| Royalties and technical assistance | 143.2 | 711.4 | −568.2 | 127.8 | 622.9 | −495.1 |
| Other services | 1,745.6 | 1,874.7 | −129.1 | 1,926.2 | 1,859.3 | 66.9 |
| *Total services* | 13,488.7 | 10,013.2 | 3,475.5 | 12,774.9 | 9,041.3 | 3,733.6 |
| Transfers | 1,815.1 | 234.2 | 1,580.9 | 1,504.0 | 333.4 | 1,170.6 |
| Total services plus transfers | 15,303.8 | 10,247.4 | 5,056.4 | 14,278.9 | 9,374.7 | 4,904.2 |
| *Current balance* | 36,635.9 | 40,760.4 | −4,124.5 | 35,146.8 | 37,629.5 | −2,482.7 |
| Private long-term capital | 6,028.6 | 5,265.4 | 763.2 | 6,086.4 | 4,014.8 | 2,071.6 |
| Public long-term capital | 1,784.8 | 775.4 | 1,009.4 | 1,531.0 | 569.9 | 961.1 |
| *Long-term capital* | 7,813.4 | 6,040.8 | 1,772.6 | 7,617.4 | 4,584.7 | 3,032.7 |
| Basic balance | 44,449.3 | 46,801.2 | −2,351.9 | 42,764.2 | 42,214.2 | 550.0 |
| Capital movements | 3,154.8 | — | 3,154.8 | 913.4 | — | 913.4 |
| Exchange rate fluctuations | — | — | — | — | 160.7 | −160.7 |
| Errors and omissions | — | 1,594.1 | −1,594.1 | — | 1,709.7 | −1,709.7 |

*Source:* Bank of Spain.

## Table 8.2.

### A. *International Reserves (US $ million)*

|  | Gold | Convertible currency | Total reserves |
|---|---|---|---|
| 1961 | 316.6 | 546.6 | 891.8 |
| 1962 | 446.5 | 560.9 | 1,067.3 |
| 1963 | 573.2 | 519.7 | 1,158.2 |
| 1964 | 615.5 | 791.3 | 1,508.1 |
| 1965 | 809.9 | 458.0 | 1,395.7 |
| 1966 | 784.9 | 254.5 | 1,214.8 |
| 1967 | 784.5 | 264.5 | 1,090.1 |
| 1968 | 784.7 | 310.2 | 1,151.1 |
| 1969 | 784.3 | 48.7 | 886.5 |
| 1970 | 498.1 | 1,143.5 | 1,791.9 |
| 1971 | 498.2 | 2,503.3 | 3,233.5 |
| 1972 | 540.9 | 4,212.2 | 5,006.2 |
| 1973 | 602.3 | 5,884.6 | 6,799.5 |
| 1974 | 602.4 | 5,093.0 | 6,025.3 |
| 1975 | 602.4 | 5,112.8 | 5,950.4 |
| 1976 | 602.4 | 4,178.7 | 4,952.1 |
| 1977 | 609.5 | 5,473.8 | 6,132.4 |
| 1978 | 613.1 | 9,092.6 | 10,015.4 |
| 1979 | 616.7 | 11,884.4 | 12,925.3 |
| 1980 | 616.7 | 11,065.6 | 12,274.5 |
| 1981 | 4,352.6 | 10,234.9 | 15,234.7 |
| 1982 | 3,666.1 | 6,925.4 | 11,529.7 |
| 1983 | 3,826.8 | 6,494.9 | 11,228.3 |
| 1984 (VI) | 3,832.1 | 10,197 | 15,377 |

### B. *Foreign Debt (US $ million)*

|  | Total | Public | Private |
|---|---|---|---|
| 1975 | 8,454 | 3,918 | 4,536 |
| 1976 | 11,241 | 5,211 | 6,030 |
| 1977 | 15,126 | 7,558 | 7,568 |
| 1978 | 17,425 | 7,962 | 9,463 |
| 1979 | 19,497 | 8,546 | 10,951 |
| 1980 | 23,719 | 9,958 | 13,761 |
| 1981 | 27,205 | 11,414 | 15,791 |
| 1982 | 28,772 | 12,841 | 15,931 |
| 1983 | 29,462 | 14,044 | 15,418 |
| 1985 (VIII) | 27,913 | 15,999 | 11,914 |

*Source:* Bank of Spain.

for pesetas in the case of a surplus, or selling foreign currency or gold for pesetas in the case of a deficit (see Table 8.2).

## 2. *The balance of trade*

The autarkic economic possibilities of Spain's economic system were pointed out at different times by Francisco Cambó, Juan Ventosa and Higinio Paris, among others. Cambó is known for having remarked that 'outside factors have little influence on the Spanish economy; the influence of the sun and rain is much more important.' A much less autarkic position was held by Olegario Fernández Baños when, during the world depression of the 1930s, he engendered a debate on whether Spain was self-sufficient enough to escape the effects of the crisis.

Of course, times have radically changed, particularly since 1960. While in 1960 Spanish foreign trade (imports plus exports) represented 16.5% of GDP, by 1984 it had grown to 25% and is still rising. This means that the Spanish economy is now much more involved than formerly in foreign trade. Table 8.3 shows the evolution of the balance of trade since 1960, and the rates of exchange of the peseta to the US dollar and the British pound. Spain is no longer an 'eminently agricultural' country, not even in terms of trade; since 1965 the agricultural balance of trade has shown an increasing number of imports, particularly grain feed (corn) and oilseed. Its oil trade deficit has also shot up with its dependence on crude imports.

The reduction in mineral exports has been due to a decline in raw material reserves. Moreover, minerals imported to satisfy domestic industrial needs (phosphate, rubber, fertiliser, textile fibres, wood etc.) are more than double Spanish consumer goods exports, revealing the introverted nature of the country's industrial development.

Table 8.4 gives the geographical distribution of Spanish foreign trade (both exports and imports) in recent years. For obvious reasons of physical proximity and income levels, Western European countries are Spain's leading trading partners, followed by the United States. Foodstuffs (above all corn and vegetable oils), a wide range of manufactured goods (cloth, clothing, leather goods, furniture etc.) and traditional Spanish exports (olives, olive oil, dried fruit and nuts etc.) are all imported by the United States.

## 3. *The balance of transfers*

According to the IMF, the balance of transfers records receipts and expenditures not made in return for goods or rights, e.g. emigrant

Table 8.3. SPAIN'S FOREIGN TRADE
*(US $ million)*

|      | Imports | Exports | Balance | Ptas for US $1 |
|------|---------|---------|---------|----------------|
| 1959 | —       | —       | —       | 60.00          |
| 1960 | 721     | 725     | 4       | 60.00          |
| 1961 | 1,092   | 709     | − 383   | 60.00          |
| 1962 | 1,569   | 736     | − 833   | 60.00          |
| 1963 | 1,955   | 735     | − 1,230 | 60.00          |
| 1964 | 2,258   | 954     | − 1,304 | 60.00          |
| 1965 | 3,018   | 966     | − 2,052 | 60.00          |
| 1966 | 3,591   | 1,253   | − 2,337 | 60.00          |
| 1967 | 3,167   | 1,418   | − 1,749 | 70.00          |
| 1968 | 3,522   | 1,589   | − 1,943 | 70.00          |
| 1969 | 4,233   | 1,900   | − 2,333 | 70.00          |
| 1970 | 4,747   | 2,388   | − 2,359 | 70.00          |
| 1971 | 4,970   | 2,938   | − 2,032 | 60.30          |
| 1972 | 6,836   | 3,831   | − 3,005 | 64.27          |
| 1973 | 9,681   | 5,218   | − 4,463 | 58.26          |
| 1974 | 15,418  | 7,078   | − 8,340 | 57.69          |
| 1975 | 16,262  | 7,690   | − 8,572 | 57.41          |
| 1976 | 17,468  | 8,719   | − 8,749 | 66.90          |
| 1977 | 17,889  | 10,253  | − 7,635 | 75.96          |
| 1978 | 18,665  | 13,082  | − 5,583 | 76.67          |
| 1979 | 25,410  | 18,188  | − 7,222 | 67.13          |
| 1980 | 34,259  | 20,830  | − 13,424| 71.70          |
| 1981 | 32,179  | 20,411  | − 11,768| 92.31          |
| 1982 | 31,535  | 20,522  | − 11,035| 109.86         |
| 1983 | 29,186  | 19,731  | − 9,435 | 143.52         |
| 1984 | 28,829  | 23,581  | − 5,248 | 160.75         |

*Source:* Bank of Spain.

remittances and charity and inter-governmental donations. Debates have ensued as to whether the balance of transfers should be considered in the current account or the capital account. The IMF believes they are part of the current account, since they do not influence a country's credit/debit status. However, other experts believe that transfers belong under the capital account since they are not current operations and are completely unrelated to normal economic activity.

The most important transfer entries in the Spanish balance of payments are emigrant remittances. It is easy to follow the evolution of net emigrant and transfer balances, since there is a close correlation between chain indices constructed on both time-series. This correlation would be even closer if the real value of emigrant remittances could be accurately determined. Apparently many of

Table 8.4.  SPAIN'S FOREIGN TRADE
(× *1,000 million ptas*)

| IMPORTS | Total | EEC total | USA | Japan | OPEC | Comecon |
|---|---|---|---|---|---|---|
| 1978 | 1,431 | 821 | 190 | 40 | 337 | 37 |
| 1979 | 1,704 | 977 | 212 | 40 | 385 | 43 |
| 1980 | 2,458 | 1,273 | 319 | 60 | 680 | 62 |
| 1981 | 2,970 | 1,518 | 412 | 79 | 901 | 84 |
| 1982 | 3,485 | 1,884 | 478 | 110 | 929 | 107 |
| 1983 | 4,176 | 2,242 | 495 | 140 | 1,048 | 138 |
| 1984 | 4,628 | 1,547 | 519 | 142 | — | 152 |
| | | | | | | |
| EXPORTS | | | | | | |
| 1978 | 1,001 | 664 | 92 | 15 | 126 | 34 |
| 1979 | 1,221 | 801 | 85 | 24 | 135 | 49 |
| 1980 | 1,493 | 960 | 79 | 19 | 192 | 52 |
| 1981 | 1,888 | 1,127 | 130 | 29 | 280 | 89 |
| 1982 | 2,258 | 1,390 | 145 | 28 | 340 | 60 |
| 1983 | 2,839 | 1,843 | 207 | 43 | 397 | 87 |
| 1984 | 3,778 | 1,853 | 361 | 59 | — | — |

*Source:* Bank of Spain.

these remittances (brought in by workers themselves on their frequent visits home) are accounted for as tourism revenue.

Emigrant remittances have clearly enhanced the purchasing power of families left at home. Although hard to quantify, particularly since the beginning of the 1973 crisis, a large percentage of these remittances have been used to purchase homes or start small businesses back home, which are probably the chief goals of most Spanish emigrant workers.

# IX. TOURISM

## 1. *Tourism*

Travel answers a deeply-felt human need, but for technical and economic reasons that need is one which, till recent years, only a few countries and circles of people have been able to satisfy. The development of economic, rapid and comfortable means of transportation and higher standards of living have led to mass tourism in all developed and some semi-developed countries.

Tourism flows can be explained by factors of attraction, which are often infrastructural (climate, especially the number of sunny days per year, coastal beaches, beautiful scenery etc.), structural (a good transportation system, a modern hotel industry, reasonable prices etc.) and cultural (museums, exhibitions, historical monuments, places known to have influenced well-known works of literature, etc.). Tourists spend their money purchasing the goods and services offered by a host-country. Consequently, tourism is a special case of *in situ* exportation for many immobile goods and services such as highways, railways and hotel services etc.

In general, tourism is strictly defined as tourist activities carried out within each country by residents of other countries. But in its generic sense, tourism should include those activities carried out by its own residents as well. Domestic tourism is also an important element in Spanish economic and social life.

## 2. *The development of foreign tourism*

Spain attracts foreign tourists with the sunny climate of the Mediterranean coast, its artistic treasures and monuments, bullfights and the relatively low cost of living. For all these reasons tourist flows have been channelled towards Spain since the 1950s.

Although the development of foreign tourism in Spain only gained momentum from 1951 onwards, it was already considerable before 1936. From 1931 to 1934 an average of 195,000 passport-bearing foreign tourists entered Spain, along with 78,000 passengers who stopped over in Spanish ports *en route* to other countries. The Civil War, the Second World War and the resulting economic and political circumstances caused a long break in the development of tourist activities in Spain. Not till 1949 did the number of incoming foreign tourists surpass pre-war levels. The growth since that time,

### Table 9.1.   TOURISM

| | Foreign Visitors (× 1,000) | Spaniards resident abroad (× 1,000) | Receipts | Expenditure × US $ 1,000 |
|---|---|---|---|---|
| 1970 | 24,105 | 4,682 | 1,680.8 | 113.1 |
| 1971 | 26,758 | 5,391 | 2,054.5 | 136.2 |
| 1972 | 32,506 | 5,997 | 2,486.3 | 190.2 |
| 1973 | 34,559 | 7,377 | 3,091.2 | 270.6 |
| 1974 | 30,343 | 6,419 | 3,187.9 | 325.6 |
| 1975 | 30,122 | 5,970 | 3,404.3 | 385.4 |
| 1976 | 30,014 | 7,433 | 3,083.3 | 404.5 |
| 1977 | 34,259 | 9,757 | 3,973.0 | 532.3 |
| 1978 | 39,971 | 11,363 | 5,488.0 | 566.9 |
| 1979 | 38,902 | 16,875 | 6,483.7 | 921.6 |
| 1980 | 38,027 | 18,083 | 6,968.0 | 1,277.0 |
| 1981 | 40,129 | 14,355 | 6,716.0 | 1,008.0 |
| 1982 | 42,001 | 13,896 | 6.454.0 | 1,009.2 |
| 1983 | 41,263 | 14,245 | 6,836.0 | 895.0 |
| 1984 | 42,931 | 14,619 | 7,717.0 | 835.0 |

*Source:* Bank of Spain.

along with the increase in foreign currency revenues, can be seen in Table 9.1. One trend in tourist flows is that the number of tourists (those bearing passports as well as Spaniards residing abroad) spending more than twenty-four hours in the country is growing.

The seasonal nature of tourism should be mentioned. The largest influx of tourists occurs between June and September, peaking in July and August. And more than 70% of Spain's foreign tourists are French, British and German, making Spain's brand of tourism clearly European.

### 3. *Tourism policy*

State concern for tourism was born under the dictatorship of Primo de Rivera. The upgrading of roads highlighted the absence of adequate lodging on Spain's main highways, and this gave rise to the National Tourism Trust, which built a network of state-run hotels that gained international prestige. After the Civil War the National Tourism Trust, an autonomous agency, became the Office of Tourism. From then until 1950 its activities were limited by the World War and by Spanish foreign policy: the number of state-run hotels did not increase, hotel industry activities were controlled (their prices being officially fixed) and, except in large cities, the hotel industry stagnated, due mainly to poor transportation (particularly by road) and food problems.

Then throughout the 1950s the tourism industry witnessed an explosion. This was undeniably aided by some state measures, such as the smoothing out of administrative difficulties in the granting of visas (formerly restricted for political reasons), a more favourable tourist exchange rate, Spain's accession to international agreements on customs facilities for tourism, and long-term loan concessions through Crédito Hotelero for hotel construction. However, in essence the expansion in tourism occurred spontaneously: European and United States prosperity, low Spanish prices and the saturation of Europe's traditional recreation areas promoted the growing influx of visitors to Spain. In view of the dazzling prospects, private initiative accounted for much of the building activity.

The economic weight of tourism, which became particularly clear in the wake of the Stabilisation Plan, led to a series of changes in the official attitude. Following the recommendation made by the World Bank on this issue, the Office of Tourism (today under the Ministry of Transportation, Tourism and Communication) was established in July 1962 to oversee tourist activities. The Office gave particular attention to four items: pricing systems, hotel credit, advertising and the general planning of tourist areas. Whereas the first two fronts can be handled with relative ease, the last two require a greater effort and a long-term policy going far beyond economic matters.

After many years of price controls, in 1962 the hotel industry price system was relaxed. Maximum and minimum prices were set by companies themselves and announced by the Ministry of Information and Tourism, with penalties for non-compliance.

All experts in the subject agree that touristic advertising is inadequate. The fifty promotional offices of tourism located throughout Europe, the United States and Latin America are commercially ineffective and lack the resources necessary to penetrate the local market effectively. As for the tourist areas themselves, inefficient is the only way to describe them with their numerous problems: a congestion of poor-quality hotels, insufficient green spaces, and absence of overall planning.

# X. FOREIGN CAPITAL INVESTMENTS

## 1. *Traditional foreign investments in Spain*

In Chapter 3 we briefly discussed the role of foreign capital investment in the development of Spanish industry. In the mid-nineteenth century, Spain was what today would be called an underdeveloped country. Scarce domestic capital formation and limited technology did not allow for the development of resources, and foreign capital consequently filled the vacuum.

The reasons for and effects of foreign capital investment in Spain before 1914 were generally similar to those in the developing areas of today. Ragnar Nurkse pointed out that foreigners generally prefer to invest their capital in extractive industries, and the fruit of this work is exported to the large industrial centres of the more advanced countries.

This description fits the first foreign capital investments made in Spain in the nineteenth century. Instead of developing the Spanish economy, which with its deplorable *per capita* income created a weak domestic demand, foreign capitalists fixed their sights on export mining. Foreign investment was simply guided by market demand, and since Spain had no demand for its mineral wealth, these resources were exported to European industrial centres. The general industrialisation of Spain would have created a domestic market, but foreign capitalists saw no immediate incentive to build their foundries and factories there.

Not all foreign investment in Spain was in mining. It also went into railways and some public services. Actually, during the nineteenth and early twentieth centuries, three different types of investment were made by foreign companies. First, there was investment in mining with a view to exportation (Rio Tinto Mines, Orconera Iron Co., Real Cía Asturiana de Minas, SMM Peñarroya, Tharsis Sulphur, the Alquife Mines etc.). Secondly, there was investment through companies legally established in Spain (usually promoted by Spaniards, often in cooperation with foreigners), which placed part of their stocks and bonds abroad. These companies had the largest influence on the development of railways. The French Pereyre financial group (from which the present-day Banco Español de Crédito originated), promoting various companies, is a typical example of this brand of investment. And thirdly there was investment by companies constituted abroad to operate public utilities under a state monopoly concession (electric power) or through local corporations (tramways, water supply etc.). Examples of these investments are 'La Canadiense' in the electric power sector and Lebon y Cía, Aguas de Barcelona, Seville Water Works and Cie de Tramways et Chemins de Fer de Valence in the public utilities sector.

## 2. Investment policy since 1939: from an open door to restrictions and back to open door

Before 1936, foreign investment encountered no difficulties in Spain; foreign capitalists were free to invest, transfer profits and disinvest as they chose. In 1939, however, a new attitude towards foreign investment surfaced with the publication of the Domestic Industry Protection and Defence Act of 24 November, according to which foreign capital could only represent 25% of a company's capital stock, though this could be raised to 45% in certain circumstances. Any higher percentages could only be authorised in special cases. Commercial associations could have up to 10% foreign capital, and mining never more than 49%. In any event, investment authorisation was discretionary, depending on what it would mean for the domestic economy and the balance of payments. This restrictive system, together with the Second World War and its aftermath, resulted in little foreign capital being attracted to Spain till 1952. No official statistics on investment exist for the 1939–60 period, but they would certainly have been meagre.

During the preparation of the Stabilisation Plan of 1957 it was decided that foreign investment should be promoted. The example of other countries, particularly Italy, showed that economic development was aided and the dangers of inflation mitigated when domestic savings were combined with foreign capital. Thus foreign investment was invited back for three purposes: first, to increase the possibilities for capital formation by adding foreign to domestic savings; secondly, to get the balance of payments into balance by using capital account surpluses to offset the traditional income account deficit; and thirdly, to increase productivity, while at the same time making more capital available with foreign capital and technology to fuel economic development.

To this end, legal instruments were created between 1959 and 1985 which envisage the following:

(*a*) Absolute freedom for capital investments representing up to 100% of a company's capital stock — Cabinet approval would be needed in some cases for more than 50%. This act did not usually apply to companies involved in national defence, information and public utilities.

(*b*) By law, investments can be made in pesetas for the equivalent amount of foreign currency brought in; through the importation of machinery and installations; and by means of manufacturing licences and technical assistance.

(*c*) A guarantee on the unhampered transferability of profits in foreign currencies.

(*d*) Disinvestment, permitting invested capital and surplus value to be freely converted and transferred.

### 3. *The penetration of foreign capital in the Spanish economy*

Foreign capital has penetrated Spain directly and through technology. The two are usually combined, since industrial research and financial capacity go hand in hand. Below we have listed by branches of production some of the leading companies partly or completely controlled by foreign capital:

— *Iron mining*. The Cía Andaluza de Minas — in which the Rothschild banks, operating through the French Le Nickel group, have a controlling interest — handles about 35% of domestic production. Altos Hornos de Vizcaya, in which US Steel holds 27% of the stock, represents 15% of domestic production.

— *Lead mining*. Two multinational subsidiaries (Peñarroya, also part of the French Le Nickel group) and the Belgian Real Compañía Asturiana de Minas group (RCAM) represent more than 60% of production.

— *Zinc mining*. The RCAM group controls almost 65% of zinc production and the Peñarroya SMM 25%.

— *Pyrites*. 49% of the shares in the Tharsis company are owned by the Tharsis company of Great Britain. Tharsis produces 45% of domestic pyrites, representing almost 75% of exports. Through its subsidiary Apisa it is connected with the other leading pyrites producer, Unión Explosivos Riotinto.

— *Copper mining*. Riotinto Patiño (with 50% foreign capital) controls 75% of production.

— *Rock salt and potash*. Solvay et Cie, through its subsidiaries and directly, controls 60% of rock salt production and 33% of potash production.

— *Infusorial earth*. Diatomeas, SA, and Minas de Gador, both having controlling foreign interests, have cornered the market in infusorial earth production, which is increasingly needed for detergent and soap manufacturing.

— *Other minerals*. Minas de Baritina (25% owned by the German Kali-Chemie AG) and Minas de Gador (40% owned by Laporte Industries) represent 75% of barytes and bentonite mining efforts.

— *Energy*. Electricité de France has an interest in Hifrensa (the Vandellós thermal nuclear power plant), and Mexicans have invested in Petronor.

— *Aluminium*. All production is controlled by two companies: Endasa (25% owned by the Canadian Alcan) and Aluminium de Galicia, Alugasa, a subsidiary of the Pechiney-Kuhlmann multinational. These two companies form Alúmina Española (with its factory in San Ciprian, Lugo).

— *Metallurgical lead, zinc and copper*. Peñarroya and Asturiana de Cinc of the RCAM group control 70% of lead and zinc mining, while Riotinto Patiño controls 75% of copper refining.

— *Iron and steel*. US Steel has a 27% interest in Altos Hornos de Vizcaya.

— *Passenger cars*. Foreign control in this sector is complete. Five companies Seat, Fasa, Talbot, Citroën and Ford dominate the market. Chrysler, which became the Talbot company in 1978, is controlled by the French SPA Peugeot-Citroën group. In 1979 General Motors decided to invest in Figueruelas (Zaragoza), and at the end of 1983 Volkswagen reached a technological agreement with Seat.

— *Chemical industry*. Solvay, Dow Chemical and the firms cited below as synthetic fibre, pharmaceutical and rubber producers are leaders in their respective sub-sectors. Kodak has sewn up the photography market, and Revlon, Juvena, Estée Lauder, Avon *et al.* work the cosmetic market.

— *Pharmaceuticals*. Most of this industry is in the hands of major European and American firms: Bayer, Schering, Merck, Ciba Geigy, ICI, Lepetit, Abbot, Parke Davis, Pfizer, and others.

— *Industrial and commercial vehicles*. Three multinationals — Daimler-Benz, Massey-Ferguson and Peugeot-Citroën — control 75% of production through their interests in Mevosa, Motor Ibérica and Talbot. International Harvester pulled its interest out of Enasa.

— *Tractors*. The tractor market is equally controlled by John Deere and Nissan (Motor Ibérica).

— *Office machines and data-processing equipment*. IBM, Nixdorf, Olivetti, Fujitsu.

— *Telephone equipment, radio and TV, home appliances*. Standard Electric and Citesa (of the ITT group) completely controlled this market until the 1970s. Now Teletra, Ericson and General Cable, three other multinationals, work in cooperation with Telefónica (having a 20% share in ATT's new investments). Philips, Telefunken and other European, American and Japanese firms are quite active in the market for radios, television receivers and related products. Ibelsa (part of the Italian Zanussi company), AEG and General Electric, among others, have penetrated the home appliance sector.

— *Rubber and tyres*. Three multinationals — Michelin, Firestone and Dunlop-Pirelli — represent 90% of production.

— *Plastics*. Twelve companies, all tied to leading petrochemical multinationals (ICI, Solvay, Monsanto, BASF, Rhone-Pulenc, Gulf *et al.*) have cornered 90% of plastics production.

— *Paint*. Various companies operating with multinational capital (Sherwin Williams, Valentine, Urruzola *et al.*) represent 70% of domestic production. The number one producer, Titán, SA, is 100% national.

— *Detergents and soap*. Unilever, Henkel, Proctor and Gamble, Colgate and Shell supply 60% of domestic production through their subsidiaries. The leading detergent and soap producer, Camp, is also 100% national.

— *Industrial gases*. The French L'Air Liquide and other multi-nationals (Union Carbide, Hoechst, Linde *et al.*) dominate almost 50% of production through four subsidiaries.

— *Artificial and synthetic fibres*. La Seda de Barcelona, SAFA, Cyanenka, Montefibre and Nurel are associated with Azki, Rhone-Pulenc, Montedison and ICI, controlling 80% of production.

— *Glass*. The French Saint-Gobain group has concentrated its production, wielding complete control over certain items (car windows, mineral fibres etc.).

— *Foodstuffs*. Through Gallina Blanca, Purina penetrates the poultry market; Nabisco (Artiach, etc.) — crackers; Kraft — cheeses, butter and sauces; Nestles — dairy products, frozen foods (through Findus) and soup (through Riera-Marsa); Libby's — fruit juices; Unilever — ice cream (Frigo etc.); and Beatrice — meat packing (Campofrio).

— *Service sector*. The Holiday Inn group operates in the hotel industry. Hertz and Avis virtually dominate the car rental business. Foreign insurance companies are many: Assicurazioni Generali, L'Adriatica, Assurances Générales, UAP, La Sudamericana etc. The four foreign banks in Spain between 1936 and 1978 had little market penetration (Crédit Lyonnais, Bank of London and South America, Banca Nazionale del Lavoro and Société Générale). The new banking system has opened the door to US, German, British, French and Japanese banks (see chapter XIII).

## 4. *Spanish investments abroad*

Spanish capital could be freely invested abroad until the exchange rate intervention of the 1930s, which made prior authorisation obligatory. But Spanish assets abroad were almost always those of non-residents, more specifically of '*indianos*' (Spaniards who have migrated to Latin America to seek their fortunes) living in Cuba, Mexico, Argentina, Venezuela and elsewhere. Initially some of this capital was remitted to relatives or simply repatriated, but in 1898, with the loss of Cuba, Puerto Rico and the Philippines, much of this wealth flooded into the country.

After 1939, in a climate of ultra-nationalism, capital exports were rigorously prohibited. To curb capital flight and the withholding abroad of currency generated by exports of goods and services, the Juzgado de Delitos Monetarios (Court on Monetary Offences) was created. Spaniards with foreign asset holdings had to be registered with IEME to control the inflow of these funds. Spanish capitalism made strong efforts to change this situation throughout the 1960s. Banks wanted to get involved in a series of financial markets, and leading industries were eager to obtain a foothold in different energy and raw material sources (oil exploration, iron mines, bauxite, technical engineering and industrial company subsidiaries).

These pressures culminated in Decree 487/1973 of 1 March, liberalising Spanish investments abroad. But the crisis unleashed at the end of that year attacked foreign currency reserves, and thus limited the scope of this decree until 1977. Illegal capital flight increased with the political crisis of the former regime, which began with the assassination of Admiral Carrero Blanco, Franco's right-hand man, by ETA, the Basque separatist organisation, on 20 December 1973, and became irreversible with Franco's death on 20 November 1975. When international reserves rose again in 1978, the need to make specific investments abroad reappeared. Thus Decree 1087/1978 of 14 April was published, defining Spanish investment abroad as that made in foreign countries by Spanish or foreign naturals living in Spain or by Spanish legal entities. Such investment can take the following forms: *direct investment* through an interest in a foreign company or legal entity, by providing setting-up capital or making stock purchases (direct investment also includes business activities abroad through branch offices, agencies or companies); *portfolio investment* through the acquisition of stocks, shares and bonds; and *share account* contracts, land and building purchases, etc.

Foreign investment by Spaniards requires prior administrative approval, specifying the terms and procedure. Depending on the size of the investment, requests are answered by either the Cabinet, the Ministry of Economy and Finance or the Department of Foreign Transactions. Spanish investors are required to transfer convertible currency or profits through the Spanish currency market. When no exchange rates have been set for a given currency, the transfer is made through the Bank of Spain. The same procedure applies to the liquidation or transfer of investments. Spaniards must present an annual report on the development of their investments. The decree on capital exportation is essentially concerned with direct investments, i.e. longstanding investments enabling an 'effective influence' to be exerted on the foreign company in question: either not less than 20% interest in a company's capital stock, or managerial control, or a Spanish technological base.

Royal Decree 2236/1979 of 14 September and Ministerial Order of 15 October the same year modified the legal framework governing investment abroad. Procedures became more flexible and prior authorisation for direct investment became the exception. Added to this framework was the granting of loans (with a five-year minimum repayment period) to companies in which the lender is a majority stockholder. Many portfolio investments were also decontrolled and, regardless of the size of the investment, investment approval and rejection became the sole task of the Foreign Transactions Division of the Ministry of Economy and Finance.

# PART FIVE
# NATIONAL INCOME

## XI. MEASURING NATIONAL INCOME

### 1. *Basic ideas on national product and income*

Gross national product (GNP) is the main indicator of a nation's economic activity. It can be defined as the total value of all final goods and services produced in a nation's economy in a given year (gross domestic product), by subtracting the services provided by foreign factors of production and adding the services provided abroad by national factors of production. GNP is *gross* because it includes investments in replacements (depreciation); and we speak of *final* goods and services because intermediate goods and services are excluded to avoid the same value being computed twice. The chief advantage of GNP is that it is an overall indicator of a nation's economic activity, sidestepping problems such as depreciation assessments. Consequently, for international and time comparisons, it is the most appropriate measurement to use (Figure 21).

Net national product (NNP) is derived from GNP by making an allowance for the depreciation or consumption of capital during the year. NNP only includes net capital investments, excluding replacement investments to maintain previously available capital constant. NNP, as defined above, is the market value of goods and services, and therefore includes indirect taxes. For this reason, it is often called 'NNP at market prices' to distinguish it from 'NNP at factor costs', which does not take into account indirect taxes.

'NNP at factor costs' is called *national income* (NI) — not to be confused with GNP. NI can be defined as the goods and services *received* by the national economic community over a year. National income is considered the most important macro-economic indicator. It indicates how much is spent on consumer goods and in net investment to pay for the factors of production. Two indicators derived from NI, *per capita income* and *income per working individual* (obtained, respectively, by dividing by total population and working population), are the basis of studies on the personal distribution of income and analyses on the overall productivity of the economic system.

Fig. 21. CIRCULATORY DIAGRAM OF THE SPANISH ECONOMY

This diagram, based on national accounting data, presents five sectors that give us an overall view of the macro-economic protagonists in the Spanish economy.

*Domestic economies* are the total of all the units of consumption (families) in the country. The *business* sector is the aggregate of all the units of production (including corporations and other legal entities) constituting the collective producer of goods and services. The *public administration* sector includes the state, local corporations and autonomous agencies, in other words the overall activities of the public sector. The *foreign* sector closes off the circulatory system, encompassing Spain's economic relations with the rest of the world. Lastly, *gross capital formation* is the accumulation of capital with a view to investment, amassing the savings generated by domestic economies, the business sector, the public administration sector and the foreign sector. At the same time, gross capital formation provides funds for the business and foreign sector.

The importance of each sector and its respective economic flows are indicated by the size of the boxes and arrows drawn in the diagram.

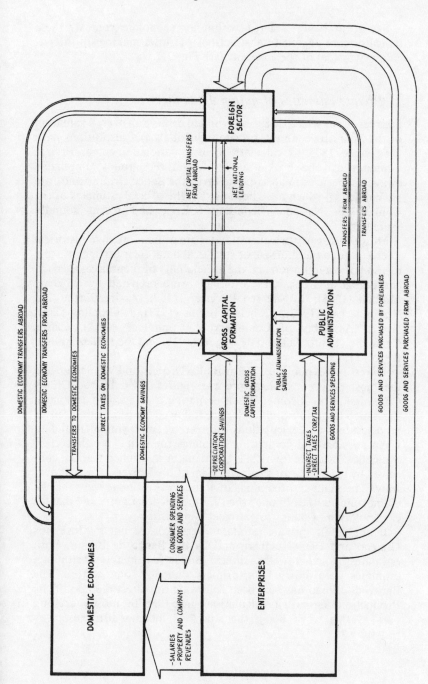

Far from being isolated within an economic context, these indicators are aggregate abstractions of flows making up the circulatory system of the economy (see Fig. 21).

## 2. *Private estimates of national income*

For reasons of scientific curiosity and to achieve an overall valuation of the Spanish economy, private individuals and institutions have tried since 1885 to calculate Spain's national income. Private estimates can be broken down into three groups: unreliable estimates; basic estimates (drawn up by the Banco Urquijo and José A. Vandellós) which have been used in the official estimates of the Council on National Economy (CEN); and recent sounder estimates.

Most of the early private estimates are of no more than historical interest due to the shortage of statistical data, their often confusing method of computation and the unreliability of the sources used. In chronological order, these estimates were prepared by: Michael Mulhall (1885), J. Navarro Reverter (1889), André Barthe and Vizconde Eza (1917), Francisco Bernis (1917), J. Ceballos Teresi (1921), Assembly of Chambers of Commerce (1922), Carlos Caamaño (1930), Antonio de Miguel (1935) and the Ibáñez Annual Report (1943).

The estimates published by the Banco Urquijo and Vandellós were the most accurate official pre-war figures, used by the CEN's Commission on Income. When preparing their income estimates, the Banco Urquijo's Studies Service followed the production census model. Almost all calculations were direct, employing official data when possible and computing estimates for some specific sector. Vandellós' estimate for 1923 is based on the multiplier method, conceived by his instructor Professor Gini of the University of Padova, Italy. The main shortcomings of Vandellós' estimate were that he did not cite how he obtained the 1923 production figures and that his extrapolation of data was extremely simplistic.

In the 1950s, private estimates were worked out by José Ros Gimeno and Paul Hemberg and by the Banco de Bilbao. Both estimates called for the direct calculation method, although estimates were drawn from primary data for some sectors. The Banco de Bilbao has also been following the direct method of the Production Census in its calculations since 1955, the most interesting part of this work being the study of income distribution by provinces.

## 3. *Official national income calculations*

Official concern to determine national income was shown for the first time in 1944; an order from the Office of the President of Government stated that the absence of this figure made it difficult 'to establish a suitable financial, tax and interventionist policy for the different branches of production and to adjust the standard of living through a wage and price policy in harmony with changing conditions'. Following from this ministerial order, a commission, formed within the CEN to study income volumes and distribution, estimated national income from 1945 to 1964.

There were many flaws in the CEN's official calculations. First, the commission only estimated the volume of national income and of income *per capita* and per working individual. These last two indicators are simple to determine. The commission did not take up the second purpose laid down by law, namely to determine personal and spatial income distribution. Figures on income distribution by province and income concentration according to social class would have helped enormously in hammering out an economic development policy for the country's many backward areas and to redistribute income through fiscal, wage and social security policies. Spurred on by the Banco de Bilbao's studies, the CEN finally decided to make an income distribution estimate by province for 1960. Apart from abandoning one of its two main purposes, the commission did not try to establish a solid base for all its calculations; on the contrary, it followed a lengthy indirect method based on the estimates of the Banco Urquijo and Vandellós for 1923. Had the Banco Urquijo directly estimated the value of production in 1923, it would have been much easier for the commission to calculate income for a base year of 1942, for example, so as to make the final results more realistic.

The commission should be criticised for using the same indirect method up to 1959. The CEN did not think of using a more direct method until 1958, when the Ministries of Agriculture, Industry and Public Works were making estimates for their respective industries and the national accounting (CN) team completed a direct estimate for 1954. In addition, the startling contrast between the commission's estimates and those of the national accounting team brought out the weaknesses of the former. From 1958 to 1964 the national accounting team's reputation grew and the CEN at the same time gradually fell into disgrace. For example, the CN's figures were used in the preparations for the Development Plan, giving national accounting a more official status. This strange situation was legally ended by Decree 1291/1965 of 20 May, whereby the INE (National

Statistics Institute) was made responsible for national income estimates. This was the first step towards concentrating statistical authority in the hands of the INE. A few months later, pursuant to Decree 2592/1961 of 11 September, the INE was entrusted to prepare national accounts (formerly done within the Ministry of Finance). Accordingly, it published annual national product and income estimates calculated on paid earnings, the production census and national expenditure.

Changes in *per capita* income from 1955 to 1981 are presented in Table 11.1 in current and 1970 pesetas.

Table 11.1. GROSS DOMESTIC PRODUCT (GDP) AND NATIONAL INCOME

|  | GDP (Million ptas) | National income (Million ptas) | Per capita income | | |
|---|---|---|---|---|---|
|  |  |  | Current ptas | 1970 ptas | $ US |
| 1955 | 422,357 | 413,860 | 14,245 | 35,692 | 393 |
| 1956 | 480,357 | 472,600 | 16,130 | 38,124 | 430 |
| 1957 | 556,990 | 545,806 | 18,472 | 38,718 | 437 |
| 1958 | 637,783 | 622,638 | 20,896 | 40,146 | 445 |
| 1959 | 657,646 | 641,965 | 21,365 | 38,683 | 388 |
| 1960 | 668,846 | 657,532 | 21,700 | 38,387 | 362 |
| 1961 | 765,749 | 758,792 | 24,804 | 42,494 | 413 |
| 1962 | 889,381 | 879,456 | 28,457 | 46,582 | 474 |
| 1963 | 1,031,069 | 1,020,775 | 32,693 | 49,140 | 545 |
| 1964 | 1,154,494 | 1,137,614 | 36,059 | 51,249 | 601 |
| 1965 | 1,138,042 | 1,329,971 | 41,725 | 53,915 | 695 |
| 1966 | 1,556,068 | 1,534,668 | 47,652 | 57,648 | 794 |
| 1967 | 1,735,151 | 1,705,105 | 52,397 | 60,006 | 858 |
| 1968 | 1,932,371 | 1,886,621 | 57,377 | 63,080 | 820 |
| 1969 | 2,169,244 | 2,121,530 | 63,855 | 67,322 | 912 |
| 1970 | 2,424,414 | 2,359,719 | 70,267 | 70,267 | 1,004 |
| 1971 | 2,759,820 | 2,683,780 | 79,053 | 73,252 | 1,176 |
| 1972 | 3,231,322 | 3,173,878 | 92,436 | 79,181 | 1,433 |
| 1973 | 3,894,762 | 3,865,971 | 111,437 | 85,642 | 1,913 |
| 1974 | 4,792,959 | 4,701,053 | 134,197 | 89,304 | 2,326 |
| 1975 | 5,653,211 | 5,495,654 | 155,240 | 88,932 | 2,704 |
| 1976 | 6,843,218 | 6,637,430 | 185,279 | 90,495 | 2,769 |
| 1977 | 8,628,166 | 8,300,134 | 229,666 | 91,315 | 3,024 |
| 1978 | 10,878,798 | 10,214,288 | 279,583 | 91,760 | 3,642 |
| 1979 | 12,818,601 | 12,109,019 | 328,140 | 92,112 | 4,888 |
| 1980 | 14,673,850 | 13,800,156 | 369,858 | 91,785 | 5,158 |
| 1981 | 16,698,773 | 15,661,596 | 415,471 | 90,134 | 4,500 |
| 1982 (prov.) | 19,338,624 | 17,904,651 | 471,448 | 89,996 | 4,219 |
| 1983 (prov.) | 22,010,900 | 20,283,100 | 530,139 | 90,410 | 3,696 |

*Source:* Bank of Bilbao estimates.

## 4. *The informal economy*

Official calculations do not take into account what is called (depending on the country) the informal, submerged or hidden economy. The components of this marginal sector of the economy are:

— the production of goods at home or in clandestine workshops;
— the production of services at home;
— undeclared moonlighting;
— work carried out by individuals receiving unemployment benefits;
— the undeclared activities of small businessmen, commission merchants and self-employed workers;
— illegal foreign employment;
— tips and bonuses;
— tax evasion;
— theft from employers (counted as an expense by the company, but not as income by the employee);
— clandestine gambling;
— prostitution;
— drug dealing.

There have been five main reasons for the growth of Spain's informal economy.

1. Increased economic regulation has encouraged companies to avoid the resulting additional costs by shifting part of their activities into the informal economy. Moreover, heightened fiscal pressure makes it impossible for certain companies, which are slow to adopt new technology, to compete with foreign firms.

2. The labour factor cost (wages and social security payments).

3. The rigidity of the labour market, due to both official regulation and trade unions.

4. A lack of trust in the government and of a stable economic policy. This situation prompts companies to reduce their fixed costs through sub-contracting, which in turn leads to the proliferation of concealed illegal production plants.

5. Another less important factor pointed out by R. Klatzman is male moonlighting, 'to flee from the family afternoons, Saturdays and Sundays'.

It is difficult to calculate what Spain's informal economy might represent in terms of GDP. A. Lafuente estimated that it was 23% in 1978, and J.B. Terceiro put it at 33% in 1981, which is one of the highest percentages in the Western world (Japan, 10%; the United Kingdom, 20%; the United States, 25%; Italy, 40%).

# XII. INCOME DISTRIBUTION

Just as important as national income is its distribution, for distribution indicates the degree of balance and equity in a nation's economic system. It is not enough to know the absolute volume of income, for this value can easily be derived from an economy concentrated in a few sectors. Consequently, we need to know the functional distribution of income to determine its sources. Secondly, it is also important to know how much each region contributes to the formation of the nation's income and its level of economic wellbeing. And thirdly, the social structure of the population can be ascertained through studies on personal distribution.

## 1. *The spatial distribution of national income*

Knowledge of the spatial distribution of income is useful in the planning of a development policy in order to even out income imbalances between different regions. Fig. 22 and Tables 16.3, 16.4 and 16.5 refer to this question. Two conclusions can be drawn from these tables: first, that income is spatially concentrated and, secondly, that *per capita* income by province is very much out of balance (see Fig. 22). The factors behind this picture are complex, but we will try to summarise them.

Natural resources have definitely played a part. Iron deposits, satisfying British and international demand, explain how industrialisation in Vizcaya got its start. The same happened with the coalfields in Asturias, although their market was purely domestic. Location has also been important. The Basque country and Catalonia have undeniably benefited from their coastlines, ports and the proximity of the French frontier, over which European cultural, scientific and technological currents have flowed for a century and a half.

Once the industrialisation process got under way in the iron and steel and textile regions, it was supported by the savings generated by external economies and the consumption potential of these very regions, which attracted new investment. And this investment was fuelled by immigration and the absorption of capital from other regions through the banking system. This was particularly true of the Basque country, a centre of important national banking institutions, where corporation capitalism took root. By contrast, in Catalonia, bereft of its own real banking system, development (with the exception of certain foreign investments) was carried out by family

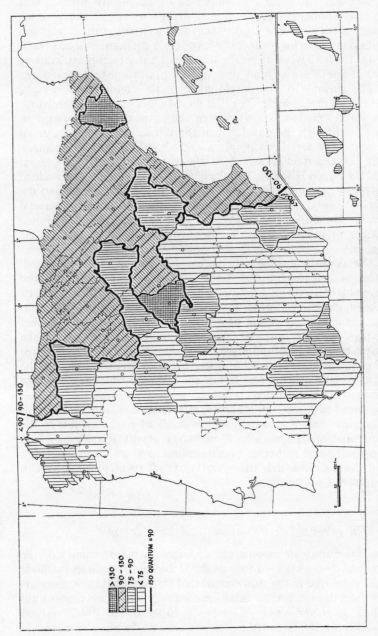

Fig. 22. Provincial per capita income indices (national average, 100).

businesses. The picture is completed by adding the protectionist economic policy enforced at the end of the nineteenth century, which reserved the domestic market for the industries of the North and Catalonia. Leaving aside more favourable climates, business traditions, the hard work of nearby towns etc., these factors explain why two of Spain's three more developed regions came to be that way. The reasons for the development of the country's third more developed region are quite different. Madrid's economic growth is the direct result of it having been chosen as the national capital: slowly, through the unfolding of the service sector, it became an important centre of consumption, and consequently of a wide industrial belt and road system. Also, the creation of the Banco Central and the Banco Hispano-Americano at the turn of the century added financial power to that of the Banco Español de Crédito and the Banco Urquijo, and so strengthened Madrid's position as a financial centre. These four banks, together with smaller banks and branch offices, finance real estate development, industry and services in the region.

The development of other areas has already been discussed. Valencia and the Balearic islands have benefited from fruit and vegetable exports and tourism; Cantabria has made use of its subsoil, climate and geographic location; and the Ebro Valley has become a kind of centre of gravity for population, income and savings. Spain's lower-income areas (minifundiary Galicia, the Duero basin and latifundiary southern Spain), with their high degree of primary-sector activity and low productivity, are basically the result of land distribution. In Galicia it is impossible to consolidate lands to achieve efficient farming. In southern Spain latifundism, combined with absenteeism and spatial income evasion (or the non-productive use of income) and low levels of education due to the concentration of wealth in a few hands, retards development and there will be no gathering of momentum until land is redistributed and the state channels the necessary funds to these areas to turn around age-old backwardness.

## 2. *The personal distribution of national income*

The inaccuracy of income tax declarations makes studies of the personal distribution of income difficult. Hence, indirect methods were employed in the study conducted by the Instituto de Estudios Agrosociales (with 1957 data) for the FAO; and in the report published in *Información Comercial Española* in 1962 entitled 'Estimación de la distribución personal de la renta a través de cuentas familiares' (An estimate of the personal distribution of income based on a family accounts survey). After these first attempts, efforts were launched to compile more reliable data. National accounting data were used to observe changes in the distribution of national income among different groups: wage earners, non-wage earners, farmers, professionals, other individual entrepreneurs, capitalists and corporations. Family budget surveys, however, provided more solid information on the personal distribution of national income.

In 1984 the review *Hacienda Pública Española* put out by the Instituto de Estudios Fiscales, published a paper by Angel and Julio Alcaide Inchausti on the personal distribution of income in Spain in 1980. This research project, like earlier ones in 1967, 1970 and 1974, was based on the INE's family budget surveys. The study adjusted the family budget survey findings to the accounting figures on disposable family income (the survey data on durable goods, luxury and out-of-the-home expenditure were incomplete). It was revealed that *family expenditures greatly exceeded income.*

By distributing disposable family income by deciles i.e. by calculating the percentage of income allocated to 10 out of every 100 families, classified by their increasing order of importance, it was found in 1980 that 10% of the families earning the lowest income absorbed 2.4% of total income, while 10% of the highest income earning families absorbed 29.23%. These figures had been respectively, 1.76 and 39.57% in 1974. Income was therefore most equally redistributed between 1974 and 1980. Sociologists and probably many politicians must be gladdened by this social conquest, but economists are left with the uncertainty surrounding the correlation between the improvement in the personal distribution of income and imbalances produced by the levels of unemployment, which rose from 3.17% in 1974 to 11.79 in 1980 and 18.07 in 1983; by a net domestic savings level equal to 16.1% of GDP in 1974, dropping to 9.4% in 1980 and 7.5 in 1983; and by a public surplus equal to 0.18% of GDP in 1974, turning into a deficit of 2.01 in 1980 and 5.91 in 1983. The interrelationship between the improvement in the personal distribution of income and a larger public deficit is plain to see, for the prime factor behind the growth of the deficit was an increase in 'social programmes' financed by the public sector. The decline in savings can be explained by the greater propensity of lower income persons for consumption. Reduced savings halt private investment, and jobs can only be created through investment.

The circumstances accompanying the foregoing statistics should be borne in mind, namely that the effects of the crisis were only fully absorbed in Spain in 1975, and that the changes that occurred in

1980–4 were not as dramatic as those of 1974–80 because income redistribution, which was heavily promoted by trade unions in 1974–7, was discontinued from 1978 till 1980.

A description of the social situation by means of mere estimates drawn from family budgets does not give an accurate view of the issue. Professor José Cazorla, in an article entitled 'Conflicto y estructura social' (*El País*, 18 Aug. 1984), states that complex, yet comprehensible, collective psychological processes have given rise to a set of expectations and hopes, provoked from outside the lower income sector, that sharpen this sector's awareness of inequality by means of simple comparisons with others. This frustration plays a leading role in advertising and unfulfilled political promises.

Nor has geographical distribution improved in relative terms. The five richest and five poorest regions of the 1950s have not changed in status in the last thirty years. Many rural areas have been given a face-lift with improved public services and the construction of decent housing units, often financed from emigrant savings. But throughout most of the country, the socio-economic structure is the same as it was four decades or more ago. For a time unemployment levels dropped simply because part of the rural population emigrated. However, in some regions, such as Andalucía and Extremadura, situations that had fallen into oblivion have returned. Moreover, in the survey conducted by Murillo and Beltran (the VI FOESSA Report), 84% of those surveyed considered themselves to be 'below the cut-off line separating those on top from those at the bottom'. Not believing that they counted, this percentage saw the state as 'a large machine manipulated by a few'. Spain apparently has a long way to go before people will feel that they have a voice in the decision-making process. It is probably more than a coincidence that, according to the INE's 1980 survey on the working population, 83% of the population aged 14 years and older are poorly educated (57% having completed their primary studies) or completely uneducated (16% having completed no studies whatsoever and 9% being illiterate).

# PART SIX
# THE INSTITUTIONAL FRAMEWORK

## XIII. THE FINANCIAL SYSTEM

The structure of a nation's economy, which consists of production and exchange relationships conducted through the system of production, the channels of distribution and the foreign sector, is enclosed by an institutional framework. Economic institutions facilitate transactions (monetary and credit system), control prices and income distribution (fiscal and social security systems), dictate capital-labour rations (by means of wage regulation and worker representation) and determine professional and educational development.

### 1. *The financial system*

The financial system comprises institutions that channel funds for loans and investment, such as the Banco de España, official credit institutions, private banks and savings banks, all of which are regulated by the 1962 Banking Reform Act and 1971 Official Credit Act. While the greater part of available funds in Spain are absorbed by credit institutions, the stock market draws in a considerable part, directly or indirectly. The different groups of institutions within the financial system vary in terms of absolute and relative importance, the most important group being credit institutions (see Table 13.1).

### 2. *The Banco de España*

The Banking Reform Act of 14 April 1962 expressly states that 'banking reform centres around a Banco de España, which should be nationalised to carry out its mission.' The nationalisation and reorganisation of the Banco de España turned it into an autonomous public agency under the Ministry of Finance.

With this reshaping, it became more of a central institution within the banking system designed to advise and execute monetary, credit and banking policy. The bank advises the government on monetary and credit policy matters, centralises and compiles banking statistics, inspects private banks and savings banks, and ensures that a 'credit rating centre' operates properly. The strictly banking operations of the bank are as follows:

— *Legal tender printing.* The Banco de España exclusively issues legal tender notes up to the maximum circulation limit set by the Cabinet, on the proposal of the Ministry of Economy and Finance.

— *Exchange operations.* The bank can remove or exchange certain series or kinds of notes in circulation.

— *Treasury operations.* The bank gratuitously operates state Treasury services and the financial services of the public debt and Treasury.

— *Public sector credit.* Following the submission of a report by the Council on National Economy, a maximum limit is set by decree to the amount of credits the bank is authorised to grant to public agencies and domestic and nationalised companies for short–term and seasonal operations.

— *Income portfolios.* New regulations froze the bank's corporation securities portfolios, with the provision that portfolios could only be increased or decreased with express Cabinet authorisation, thus upgrading a rather unorthodox activity of central banks.

— *Foreign operations and foreign currency reserves.* Since the Instituto Español de Moneda Extranjera (IEME — the Spanish Exchange Control Board) was dissolved in July 1973, the bank has centralised all foreign economic operations and taken charge of gold and currency reserves.

— *Central bank operations.* The bank carries out all the operations of a central bank with the private banking system, in accordance with the general guidelines dictated by the Ministry of Economy and Finance (loan concessions with public debt pledges, commercial paper rediscounts, the opening of current accounts, personal loan concessions etc.).

— *Operations with the private sector.* The Banco de España may only carry out operations with the private sector when it is in the public interest, provided that case-by-case authorisation is granted by the Cabinet.

— *Open market operations.* Independently of the income portfolios in its possession, the bank may acquire, hold or transfer securities and bills with a view to regulating money markets, according to open market guidelines.

## 3. *Official credit institutions*

Apart from the Banco de España, the official banking system comprises the Banco Hipotecario de España, the Banco Exterior de España, the Banco de Crédito Local, the Banco de Crédito Industrial, the Banco de Crédito Agricola and the Caja Central de Crédito Marítimo y Pesquero. Until their nationalisation in 1962, the official medium- and long-term credit institutions were first coordinated by an official bank commissioner and later by the Instituto de Crédito y Largo Plazo (Medium- and Long-term Credit Institution). And since the 'Official Credit System Act' was enacted in May 1971, coordination has been entrusted to the Instituto de Crédito Official (ICO).

The *Banco Hipotecario de España* (BHC — the Mortgage Bank of Spain), was founded in 1872 to provide building loans for buildings in Spain of up to 50% of the assessed value, and issues bearer mortgage bonds. The *Banco de Crédito Industrial* was set up in 1920 to grant medium- and long-term loans (see p. 89), and, like other official credit institutions operating on ICO allocations, it accepts no deposits. This bank grants loans (which may never exceed 50% of a borrower's capital stock) to establish new industries or enlarge existing ones. The *Banco de Crédito Local*, founded in 1925 to handle the financial requirements of local corporations, intervenes in the repayment of municipal debts, organises the collection of excise taxes on behalf of local corporations, and offers budgetary advice. In return for loans, the bank requires that a corporation's real assets be put up as collateral, normally accepting the allocation of certain public earnings to ensure intervention should that be necessary. The *Servicio Nacional de Crédito Agrícola*, created in 1925 and today called the Banco de Crédito Agrícola, operated with a low-interest-rate fund provided by private banks and savings banks until 1962. The agricultural investment loans made by this bank may not exceed 60% of the value of the guarantee accepted. The *Instituto de Crédito para la Reconstrucción Nacional*, which since 1962 has been the Banco de Crédito para la Construcción, was established in 1939 to finance the reconstruction of property damaged during the Civil War. Most of this bank's funds went into housing construction and shipbuilding. In 1982 the Banco de Crédito para la Construcción was absorbed by the Banco Hipotecario de España.

Till 1962, official credit institutions operated primarily with private capital and were therefore strongly influenced by directors representing commercial banks. Perhaps it was for this reason that they lacked sufficient resources and the flexibility to meet money market requirements; in fact, it was private banks which, by means of pre-financing and short-term credit renewal, satisfied money market demands. The first provision set forth to overcome this situation was the Medium- and Long-term Official Credit Institution Act of 26 December 1958, aimed at closing the institutional medium- and long-term credit gap by increasing the funds available to official credit institutions. To this end the act authorised the government to lay down a legal reserve requirement of 40% on private banks' customer accounts. Had this requirement been met, it would have meant the semi-nationalisation of the banking system. But banks never exceeded 25%. For this very reason, when the Official Credit Bill was enacted in 1971, the 40% legal requirement was replaced by the investment requirement, with 25% being set as the maximum requirement for outside funds.

Official credit institutions depend on the Instituto de Crédito Oficial, which reports to the Ministry of Finance and acts as the channel for the relationship between the government and official credit institutions. With the private sector, the ICO has the power to authorise the issue of bonds and other fixed-income securities and to grant loans for terms of above 18 months on behalf of private banks. In short, the institute has jurisdiction over all private and public medium- and long-term credit. The ICO allocates funds to official credit institutions, drawing its resources from different sources: the issue of bonds and investment securities, treasury advances, loans granted by foreign governments or international agencies, and cabinet-authorised loans from the Banco de España.

## 4. *Private banks*

The private banking system, as we know it today, took shape between 1844 and 1920. Institutions within this system are legally classified as national, regional or local, depending on their number of branch offices, geographic scope and the size of their debts, business and assets.

On 30 December 1984, Spain had 99 national banks and 36 foreign banks. At first glance, the banking system looks fragmented, but this is not so. The bulk of banking activities is concentrated among the 'seven sisters' (Banesto, the Banco Central, the Banco Hispano Americano, the Banco de Bilbao, the Banco de Vizcaya, the Banco de Santander and the Banco Popular). The official *status quo* banking doctrine, maintained until 1963, helped to strengthen the dominant position of the leading national banks (banking *status quo* refers to the situation existing in 1936, after which date new institu-

Table 13.1.　CONCENTRATION OF DEPOSITS IN MAJOR
CREDIT INSTITUTIONS, 30 JUNE 1985

| Banks and savings banks (Cajas) | Million ptas | % |
|---|---|---|
| 1. Banco Central | 1,734,571 | 9.34 |
| 2. Banco Español de Crédito | 1,629,906 | 8.78 |
| 3. Banco Hispano Americano | 1,331,578 | 7.18 |
| 4. Banco de Bilbao | 1,235,866 | 6.66 |
| 5. Caja de Pensiones 'La Caixa' | 994,851 | 5.36 |
| 6. Banco de Vizcaya | 978,860 | 5.28 |
| 7. Banco de Santander | 947,583 | 5.11 |
| 8. Banco Popular Español | 671,009 | 3.62 |
| 9. Caja de Ahorros y Monte de Piedad de Madrid | 629,624 | 3.39 |
| 10. Banco Exterior de España | 579,973 | 3.13 |
| 11. Banco Urquijo-Unión (Industrial) | 420,050 | 2.26 |
| 12. Caja de Barcelona | 388,310 | 2.09 |
| 13. Caja Postal de Ahorros | 365,164 | 1.97 |
| 14. Caja de Ahorros de Valencia | 293,284 | 1.58 |
| 15. Caja de Ahorros y Monte de Piedad de Zaragoza, Aragon y Rioja | 285,904 | 1.52 |
| 16. Banco Pastor | 260,757 | 1.40 |
| 17. Caja de Ahorros de Cataluña-Barcelona | 248,500 | 1.34 |
| 18. Banco de Sabadell | 227,584 | 1.23 |
| 19. Caja de Ahorros de Galicia | 214,745 | 1.16 |
| 20. Caja de Ahorros de Alicante y Murcia | 206,785 | 1.11 |
| First 20 institutions | 16,931,383 | 91.26 |
| 200 other institutions | 1,620,590 | 8.74 |
| *Total banks plus savings banks* | 18,551,973 | 100.00 |

*Source:* Executive Banking Council.

tions could not be added). At the same time, the absorption of small banks by large banks, a process that began in 1918, was stepped up.

At present, four specific features should be singled out:

First, with the crisis among smaller banks, due to the fall in profits resulting from the rise in the cost of money, rates above the legal ones had to be paid, and market rates rose. These difficulties could be seen in the cases of the Banco Condal, Banco Cantábrico, Banco Navarra, Banco del Descuento, Bankunión, Banco Mas Sardá and others. Small banks were hurt too by the growing mistrust of depositors.

Secondly, a short-term solution to the crisis (apart from the founding of the Fondo de Garantía de los Depositos Bancarios

(Bank Deposit Guarantee Fund) in 1977, insuring all depositors up to 1,500,000 pesetas) was the creation of the so-called Corporación Bancaria, SA (Cobasa) in February 1978. This is a non-profit organisation backed by the Banco de España and aimed at putting struggling banks back on sound footing, thus 'making them viable as private banks, regardless of whether they remained independent or merged with or were absorbed by other banks'. Cobasa was criticised by proponents of socialisation, who saw it as a kind of privilege insurance for the financial monopoly, as well as by liberals, who saw the salvaging of inefficient banks as running counter to a market economy. Cobasa was reabsorbed by the Fund in 1980.

Thirdly, in a new wave of banking consolidation, the Banco Central absorbed the Banco Ibérico, of the Fierro financial group, and Banesto (to avoid losing its number one position in the ranking) took over the Banco Coco (soon to become involved in a grave capital flight scandal), and went on later to penetrate the Banco de Madrid; and the Banco de Santander acquired the Banca Jover entirely and part of the Banco Comercial Español. These absorptions were only the beginning of a general trend in which foreign banks, such as Barclays and BNP, were also involved.

And fourthly, private banks (Banco de Bilbao, Banco Exterior, Banco de Santander, Banco Popular, Banco Central *et al.*) increasingly penetrated the foreign sector, and the money market, driven on by the desire to bring capital into the system and fatten up internal resources.

A further factor was that in June 1978 foreign banks obtained the right to enter the Spanish market. Apart from having to comply with all specific Spanish banking regulations (legal requirements, *modus operandi* etc.), the foreign banks were subjected to four specific limitations: 750 million pesetas in initial capital was established for branch offices and 1,500 million for subsidiaries; peseta deposits could not make up more than 40% of a foreign bank's assets; foreign banks could not open more than three offices (most have their main office in Madrid and a branch office in Barcelona); and they were only allowed to have equity securities in their portfolios, except in the case of their own trading subsidiaries. See Table 13.2.

The economic crisis sharpened largely as a result of financial sector operations, specifically those of private banks. High interest rates caused damage to industry by reducing the profits of non-financial enterprises and depressing business prospects.

Table 13.2. DEPOSITS OF FOREIGN BANKS IN SPAIN

| | *Deposits* <br> ($\times 1$ *m. ptas*) | *% of* <br> *total* |
|---|---|---|
| 1. Crédit Lyonnais | 41,302 | 20.5500 |
| 2. Société Générale de Banque en Espagne | 37,673 | 18.7444 |
| 3. Bank of London and South America | 32,894 | 16.3665 |
| 4. Bank of America | 23,335 | 11.6104 |
| 5. Midland Bank | 14,198 | 7.0643 |
| 6. Manufacturers Hanover Trust Co. | 13,402 | 5.6351 |
| 7. Citibank | 4,999 | 2.4873 |
| 8. Commerzank | 4,129 | 2.0544 |
| 9. Bankers Trust Co. | 3,613 | 1.7977 |
| 10. Crédit Commercial de France | 3,161 | 1.5728 |
| 11. Deutsche Bank | 2,485 | 1.2364 |
| 12. First National Bank of Chicago | 2,311 | 1.1498 |
| 13. Banca Nazionale del Lavoro | 2,253 | 1.1210 |
| 14. Algemene Bank Nederland | 2,217 | 1.1031 |
| 15. Banque de Paris et des Pays-Bas | 2,057 | 1.0235 |
| 16. Banco Exterior de los Andes y España | 1,987 | 0.9886 |
| 17. Continental Illinois National Bank | 1,223 | 0.6085 |
| 18. Morgan Guaranty Trust Co. of New York | 1,101 | 0.5478 |
| 19. Chase Manhattan Bank | 1,065 | 0.5299 |
| 20. Dresdner Bank | 928 | 0.4617 |
| 21. Banque d'Indochine et de Suez | 794 | 0.3950 |
| 22. Bank of Tokyo | 753 | 0.3747 |
| 23. Banco do Brasil | 743 | 0.3697 |
| 24. Chemical Bank | 607 | 0.3020 |
| 25. Banque de Bruxelles Lambert | 420 | 0.2090 |
| 26. Banque Nationale de Paris | 218 | 0.1085 |
| 27. National Westminster Bank | 208 | 0.1035 |
| 28. Banco Belga | 199 | 0.0990 |
| 29. Sumitomo Bank | 176 | 0.0876 |
| 30. Banco di Roma | 161 | 0.0801 |
| 31. Banco de la Nación Argentina | 151 | 0.0751 |
| 32. Banco do Estado de Sao Paulo | 92 | 0.0458 |
| 33. First Interstate Bank of California | 41 | 0.0204 |
| 34. Barclays Bank International | 22 | 0.0109 |
| 35. Banca Commerciale Italiana | 5 | 0.0025 |
| 36. Banco Real | — | — |
| *Total* | 200,923 | 100.000 |

*Source: El Pais annual, 1985.*

## 5. *Savings banks*

Savings banks, which are both public (state, provincial or municipal) and private, promote savings by offering higher interest rates than those offered by commercial banks. These banks use their deposits to make loans and state bond investments.

In 1951, savings banks were required to invest a minimum of 60% of their external resources in public funds, three-quarters of which having to be in public debt. After 1957, savings banks had to earmark 10% of their annual growth on deposits for housing construction loans. In 1959, when the state formally stopped issuing government bonds automatically discounted by the central bank, savings banks were forced to invest 65% of their deposits in 'qualified securities' thus guaranteeing the automatic placement of all INI bond issues.

The importance of savings banks can be judged from the fact that at 31 August 1985 deposits totalled 7,109,375 million ptas, equal to 36.6% of all deposits. Moreover, savings banks tend to grow faster than private banks. Spain's 86 confederated but independent savings banks represent 93% of the savings bank total. The remaining 7% belongs to the state-run Caja Postal de Ahorro. The concentration among savings banks is almost as heavy as it is among private banks. The first five control 36% of total deposits, and the first fifteen 55% (this was in December 1983).

State intervention in this sector was carried out through the Instituto de Crédito de la Caja de Ahorros (Savings Bank Credit Institute), reorganised in 1962 as a legal, autonomous, official agency under the Ministry of Finance. The institute carried out upper-management duties (sending instructions to the Minister of Finance, reporting on new companies and mergers etc.) and co-ordinated and checked savings bank records. Following the 1971 Official Credit Act, savings banks fell under the jurisdiction of the Banco de España. Then with the formation of the second government of Adolfo Suárez in July 1977, savings banks underwent a new series of changes. Royal Decree 2,290/1977 of 27 August reshaped savings bank management: the personalist, co-optative structure of their boards of directors was replaced by a general assembly formed by a minimum of 60 and a maximum of 150 representatives, elected by arbiter-depositors (assembly representatives, workers and local governments) chosen by lot.

The royal decree envisaged that savings banks be placed on an equal footing with private banks. In practice, this provision has enabled savings banks to discount paper (prohibited under article 39 of their 1933 by-laws) and to finance foreign trade operations. From that year, financial and commercial criteria, not legal limitations, would govern each savings bank.

Decree 2,291/1977, also published on 27 August, regulated the regionalisation of investments, requiring savings banks to invest at least half their bearer securities, excluding government bonds, and a minimum of three-quarters of their remaining investments, excluding fixed assets and social work investments, in the region or area of their financial activities.

## 6. *Capital markets; the stock market*

The first stock market in Spain was opened in Madrid in 1831, a century after the organisation of the first official European stock market in Paris in 1724. The country's second official stock market was founded in Bilbao in 1890 and the third in Barcelona (where the unofficial Casino Mercantil had been shut down a year before) in 1915. Later stockbrokers' meeting places were established in Valencia, Seville, Zaragoza, San Sebastian and Gijón and in the brokers' associations in the remaining provinces. The stock market of Valencia has been operating since 1981. Tables 13.2 and 13.3 give some information on stock markets.

The many problems which affected the stock market in 1973 gave rise to the creation of a special commission under Ministerial Order of 4 August 1973 (shortly after the general elections in June), presided over by Professor Juan Sardá, which was given six months to determine the necessary reforms to the stock market. After requesting an extension, the commission submitted its report on 12 April 1978, stating that the securities market had declined. Business financing fell from 30% in 1966–8 to 18% in 1976, and to make matters worse, the fixed income securities (government bonds and treasury bills) market, representing a large part of this small percentage, had virtually disappeared, for these securities were

Table 13.3.  SPANISH STOCK EXCHANGE ACTIVITY
COMPARED TO LEADING INTERNATIONAL MARKETS

| | (*Deals in US $ millions*) 1982 | 1983 |
|---|---|---|
| New York | 488,396 | 765,275 |
| Tokyo | 146,917 | 231,440 |
| Geneva | — | 65,897 |
| London | 32,745 | 42,576 |
| Frankfurt | 16,613 | 38,880 |
| Osaka | 18,375 | 35,155 |
| Basel | 19,748 | 31,848 |
| Toronto | 14,323 | 24,499 |
| Paris | 9,561 | 12,537 |
| Madrid | 1,142 | 956 |
| Barcelona | 234 | 343 |

*Source:* International Federation of Stock Exchanges.

Table 13.4.  STOCK EXCHANGE, MADRID INDEX
*(1972 = 100)\**

| | 1978 | 1979 | 1980 | 1981 | 1982 | 1983 | 1984 |
|---|---|---|---|---|---|---|---|
| General | 77.01 | 66.22 | 60.81 | 78.59 | 72.14 | 72.96 | 103.85 |
| Commercial Banks | 107.46 | 104.41 | 101.79 | 152.64 | 145.12 | 133.63 | 158.94 |
| Industrial Banks | 52.83 | 48.77 | 36.95 | 47.92 | 41.60 | 34.27 | 66.29 |
| Electric Power Companies | 64.91 | 56.00 | 58.47 | 62.93 | 55.50 | 49.95 | 66.29 |
| Food, Beverages, Tobacco | 43.59 | 38.25 | 35.17 | 45.23 | 40.63 | 62.44 | 124.97 |
| Building Industries | 95.24 | 72.29 | 59.72 | 75.82 | 71.50 | 79.39 | 100.25 |
| Investment Companies | 69.07 | 52.40 | 51.05 | 71.26 | 72.91 | 80.69 | 153.71 |
| Steel and Metal Industries | 38.41 | 24.90 | 18.63 | 19.97 | 18.67 | 31.59 | 44.78 |
| Public Monopolies | 73.13 | 61.18 | 54.03 | 65.92 | 60.60 | 60.10 | — |
| Chemical and Textile Industries | 69.18 | 44.59 | 33.99 | 39.76 | 30.23 | 38.84 | 80.80 |
| Communication | — | — | — | — | — | — | 84.77 |
| Miscellaneous | 52.67 | 43.83 | 35.48 | 44.50 | 40.43 | 48.49 | 84.66 |

\* As at 31 December except in 1984 (31 August).

*Source:* Bank of Spain.

generally placed through a rationing system by regular banks and savings banks; no secondary market existed. The Sardá report indicated that the market was too narrow, that collective investment institutions were underdeveloped, and that savers preferred other investments. It also made an extensive and detailed list of problems, recommending enlargement of the market through new companies, favouring fixed-income securities, promoting secondary markets, streamlining operations, clarifying information, renewing broker activities, changing taxation, reintroducing a futures market, reshaping equity investment companies and investment clubs, liberalising insurance company investments, and shortening the repayment period on government bonds.

Spanish stock exchanges are also characterised by speculation, particularly when liquidity is high and new investment projects are scarce. At such times, the indices of Spain's four stock exchanges rise, independently of profits and other economic rations.

# XIV. THE TAX SYSTEM

## 1. *The evolution of the Spanish tax system*

The tax system comprises all the means deployed by the state to secure from taxpayers the money it needs to pursue its purposes. Public revenue and spending are forecast periodically in the state budget, which reflects the public finance activities which are vital to a country's economic life. As Gunnar Myrdal states, 'Public finance, like all state activities, forms part of the institutional framework shaping market prices and is, therefore, essential. Financial activities influence the costs of production of all the different branches of a nation's economy; taxes influence capital market supplies and investment flows. Public finance determines the shape of all supply and demand functions and, hence, the evolution of an economy, its direction, advancement, cyclical development, etc. All these conditions would change if public finance were to move in another direction.' Moreover, public expenditure forms part of overall demand, heavily controlling supply and prices. Excessive public pressure on the market fuels inflation, while public expenditure can also offset a drop in demand and keep unemployment levels down.

Spain's present-day tax system dates back to the Budgetary Act of 1845, designed to reform the misshapen tax system that then existed, in which tax privileges were granted to the kingdoms of the crown of Aragon, Navarra, the Basque Provinces and Castile. This reform was carried out under Finance Minister Alejandro Mon, although its foundations had been laid earlier by the findings of a commission appointed in 1843, in which Ramón de Santillán (later to become Finance Minister) played a decisive role. For this reason, the act is known as the 'Mon-Santillán Reform'. The 1845 tax system underwent few changes until the colonial wars of 1898. The state of the economy at that time cried out for a tax revision, and the bill of 27 March 1900, the 'Fernández Villaverde Reform,' was enacted. The revised tax system of 1900 was left intact until 1940.

The Civil War of 1936–9 wrought havoc with the public finance system, and the subsequent need for reconstruction posed new problems. Consequently, the official *Resumen provisional sobre la evolución de la Hacienda desde el 18 de julio de 1936 hasta la fecha* (Provisional summary of the evolution of public finance from 18 July 1936 to the present), published in August 1940, announced a tax reform that began with the enactment of the bill of 16 December

1940, endorsed by José Larraz, the Minister of Finance. However, the reform did not substantially change the system. Although it applied to almost all taxes, its real thrust was limited to enlarging revenue bases and raising tax rates. While in theory the reform meant a sharp rise in fiscal pressure, this rise was not very large in practice, since real revenue bases were unknown. Widespread tax evasion followed.

The Act of 5 January 1939, laying down a special tax on surplus profits generated by the Civil War, added to the atmosphere of fraud, since all profits above 7% were taxed as surplus profits, regardless of the kind of company involved or the effect of inflation. Surplus profit estimates were entrusted to juries which lacked accurate information and were therefore forced to operate on an empirical and sometimes emotional basis beyond the strict limits of the law. The amnesty, moratoriums and retroactive exceptions granted from 1940 to 1957 only increased the incidence of fraud, and administrative behaviour did nothing to dampen it: juries were kind in their estimates, cases were processed slowly, demands for compulsory information and sanctions were soft, confusion was provoked by the multitude of fiscal provisions in force, and so on. As direct tax evasion became uncontrollable, public finance had no choice but to increase indirect taxes. Since budgetary revenue stagnated in real terms, the Government systematically went into debt to cover the deficit with harmful effects for the pricing system (by pushing up inflation) and the peseta exchange rate (by having one unrealistic official rate as well as multiple rates to promote exports during inflationary periods).

An attempt was made to increase direct taxation by establishing a system of agreements between the Administration and different groups of taxpayers (trade unions, professional associations etc.), allowing the further distribution of the overall figure among the individuals of the group. Through this 'distribution' system, taxes were collected on turnover and on professional fees (medical, legal etc.); this system was also used casuistically to determine corporation taxes. The most serious drawback of taxation according to trades was that it meant effecting a transaction between taxpayers and the Administration. In fact, the Administration refused to ascertain real tax bases, delegating tax justice to the different professional/trade groups. Under this mechanism, taxes could raise prices (the inflationary effect) and tax evasion could obtain large additional earnings. The evolution of recent budgetary revenue and expenditure can be seen in Table 14.1.

## 2.  *The 1964 tax reform and the tax system in force up to 1977*

The Spanish tax system that was in force up to 1977 was established largely under the Tax Reform Act of 11 June 1964 — also known as the 'Navarro-Barrera Reform' since it was passed under Mariano Navarro Rubio, the Minister of Finance, and Antonio Barrera de Irimo, his Technical Secretary-General. The 1964 reform was not carried out with the aim of speeding up revenue collections, as had always been the case with past tax reforms. Nevertheless it had to be done, and its two great merits were the personalisation of direct taxation and the management of indirect taxation. Its serious flaws were the establishment of the overall assessment principle introduced in 1967 and excessive indirect taxation.

By 1973, fiscal reform was the main topic of conversation in Spanish economic circles, and the stock market plunged on the eve of publication of the 'White Book', which contained the basis for the future reform. Fiscal reform was inevitable given the extent and complexity of the country's economic growth. Between 1950 and 1970, Spain's dominant rural, agrarian economy had been superseded by an urban, industrial economy. Since taxation did not keep up with these changes, public services desperately required more funds. The very organisation of businesses, stock market expansion and export tax incentive policies called for greater accuracy in tax declarations.

But these needs were put on the back burner, as Franco's regime was unwilling to carry out the reform. Thus, in spite of the efforts of proponents of reform, the promises made in 1973 were left unfullfilled.

## 3.  *The fiscal reform of 1977 and after*

Following the 1977 general elections, Adolfo Suarez's second government (in which Francisco Fernández Ordóñez, a long-time proponent of tax reform, was appointed Finance Minister) included in its legislative programme a Ley de Medidas Urgentes de Reforma Fiscal (MURF — the Emergency Measures for Fiscal Reform Act). Passed on 14 November 1977, the MURF removed the veil concealing bank accounts, standardised fiscal offences, and announced the publication of taxpayer lists. The main thrust of these three mechanisms was to combat fraud.

Before the passing of the MURF, the Moncloa Agreements laid the foundations for a definitive fiscal reform. This can be quickly summarised in five points:

Table 14.1.   PUBLIC ADMINISTRATION RECEIPTS,
EXPENDITURE AND SURPLUS OR DEFICIT ( – )*
AND % OF GDP

| | ( × 1,000 million ptas) | | | $GDP$ | $\dfrac{Balance}{GDP} \times 100$ | $\dfrac{Expenditure}{GDP} \times 100$ |
|------|----------|-------------|---------|--------|--------|--------|
| | *Receipts* | *Expenditure* | *Balance* | | | |
| 1973 | 976 | 929 | 47 | 4,140 | 0.01 | 22.43 |
| 1974 | 1,157 | 1,148 | 9 | 5,102 | 0.00 | 22.50 |
| 1975 | 1,450 | 1,448 | 2 | 6,018 | 0.03 | 24.06 |
| 1976 | 1,803 | 1,825 | – 22 | 7,234 | 0.30 | 25.22 |
| 1977 | 2,389 | 2,446 | – 57 | 9,178 | 0.62 | 26.65 |
| 1978 | 2,994 | 3,190 | – 196 | 11,231 | 1.74 | 28.40 |
| 1979 | 3,651 | 3,868 | – 217 | 13,130 | 1.65 | 29.45 |
| 1980 | 4,778 | 4,782 | – 304 | 15,185 | 2.00 | 31.49 |
| 1981 | 5,234 | 5,757 | – 523 | 17,322 | 3.02 | 33.23 |
| 1982 | 5,926 | 7,040 | – 1,114 | 19,880 | 5.60 | 35.41 |
| 1983 | 7,114 | 8,454 | – 1,340 | 22,778 | 5.88 | 37.11 |
| 1984 | 8,482 | 9,721 | – 1,239 | 25,935 | 4.77 | 37.48 |

(*) Includes all public administration sectors and the social security system.

(*a*)  *Personal income tax*, including property transfer taxes and taxes on earnings. Although this tax had been in existence since 1932, the moderate rates of the progressive schedule had to be increased and rigorously enforced.

(*b*)  *Property tax* was reconciled with the new income tax; taxable sources were better defined.

(*c*)  *Inheritance or donation tax* became simpler, based on a more progressive schedule and coordinated with the property tax.

(*d*)  A revised *Corporation tax* modernised the tax on profits made by corporate bodies and removed all unnecessary exemptions and privileges.

(*e*)  *Indirect taxation*, including the Value Added Tax (VAT), was revised with a view to aligning the Spanish fiscal system with that of EEC member-countries.

The results of the Fernández Ordónez Reform are presented in Table 14.1. The distribution of expenditure appears in Table 14.2.

## 4.  *Public financing at the municipal level*

Municipal treasuries are responsible for the degree and quality of public services and therefore for the wellbeing of a city's inhabitants. In the wake of the first democratic municipal elections since the Civil

Table 14.2.    DISTRIBUTION OF STATE EXPENDITURE
(*millions of ptas and %*)

| | 1984 | % | 1985 | % |
|---|---|---|---|---|
| Royal household | 350 | | 409 | |
| Parliament | 7,179 | 0.1 | 7,708 | 0.1 |
| Official auditing department | 1,439 | | 1,617 | |
| Constitutional Court | 602 | | 631 | |
| Cabinet | 319 | | 332 | |
| Public Debt | 517,380 | 9.5 | 828,849 | 13.6 |
| Official pensions | 328,676 | 6.0 | 341,688 | 5.6 |
| Judiciary Council | 727 | | 832 | |
| *Ministries* | | | | |
| Foreign affairs | 29,750 | 0.5 | 35,617 | 0.5 |
| Justice | 88,942 | 1.6 | 98,933 | 1.6 |
| Defence | 552,834 | 10.2 | 618,731 | 10.1 |
| Economy and finance | 102,971 | 1.9 | 121,614 | 1.9 |
| Interior | 216,759 | 4.0 | 251,300 | 4.1 |
| Public Works and Urban Development | 263,450 | 4.8 | 226,857 | 3.7 |
| Education and science | 523,986 | 9.7 | 493,583 | 8.1 |
| Labour and social security | 1,065,905 | 19.7 | 1,222,628 | 20.0 |
| Industry and energy | 228,328 | 4.2 | 258,398 | 4.2 |
| Agriculture, fisheries and food | 234,355 | 4.3 | 208,722 | 3.4 |
| Presidency of the Government | 23,146 | 0.4 | 26,550 | 0.4 |
| Transport, tourism and communications | 421,188 | 7.8 | 415,473 | 6.8 |
| Culture | 34,606 | 0.6 | 38,144 | 0.6 |
| Territorial administration | 21,943 | 0.4 | 19,984 | 0.3 |
| Health and consumer affairs | 37,933 | 0.7 | 32,131 | 0.5 |
| Miscellaneous expenditure | 80,730 | 1.4 | 85,232 | 1.3 |
| Autonomous Communities | 488,379 | 9.0 | 603,604 | 9.9 |
| Interterritorial Settlement Fund | 127,674 | 2.3 | 152,037 | 2.4 |
| *Total* | 5,399,551 | 100.0 | 6,091,604 | 100.0 |

*Source*: Ministry of Economy and Finance.

War held on 3 April 1979, Spanish municipalities presented the government with a series of needs, part of which were taken up in Royal Decree Law 11/79 of 20 July authorising building and city taxes, reforming local excise taxes, increasing municipalities' share of all indirect taxes from 4 to 7.5% and allocating a percentage of gasoline taxes to municipalities. At the same time, administrative measures were implemented to reform administrations and to prepare city budgets. Royal Decree Law 11/79, however, did not solve the problem of the large debts (some 100,000 million ptas) accumulated by city governments during the 1975–8 transitional period. Royal Decree 1/80 of 1 February ended the long negotiations on this subject by establishing that the government would assume 50% of this debt.

However, the two decree laws and the 1982 Budgetary Act (granting municipalities 10% of all indirect taxes) have proved not to be enough. Articles 140 and 142 of the Constitution of 1978 must be put into effect: municipal political and financial autonomy must become something more than a programmed declaration. Spain is still far from achieving the degree of decentralisation found in Common Market countries, where municipalities represent 25% of all public administration expenditure; in Spain, municipalities barely account for 7%. Hence it stands to reason that if a democracy is measured by how close in effect the people come to the levers of power, the devolution of authority from the centre to the municipalities is a crucial matter for a democratic nation.

# XV. THE SOCIAL FRAMEWORK OF THE ECONOMY

## 1. *Wages and working conditions up to 1977*

In this chapter we will look at wages and collective bargaining, trade union rights, worker participation in company management, social security and educational policy.

Before the Civil War, wages and other working conditions were governed by mixed employer-worker juries, which established 'working bases' or 'wage agreements', in accordance with an Act of 21 November 1931. This system permitted negotiations between employers and unionised workers, with strikes and lockouts being only a last resort.

State wage control was envisaged by Franco in the Fuero de Trabajo (Labour Law) back in 1938, and later consolidated with the 1942 Act on Working Regulations. At this time strikes and lockouts were outlawed and the right to lay off workers and to unionise disappeared. Minimum conditions were laid down for different economic activities, the Ministry of Labour handling all wage-related matters from 1939 to 1958, to the disadvantage of working-class interests. The rigid policy on the fixing of wages established by the Labour Laws of 1942 began to loosen up in the spring of 1956, as strikes in pursuit of higher wages were staged across the country. The Decree of 8 June 1956 gave companies the right to 'freely establish wages above legal minimums without the authorisation of the Ministry of Labour'. This trend towards greater flexibility (together with pressure exerted by the International Labour Organisation — the ILO) led to the passing of the Act of 24 April 1958 on Trade Union Wage Agreements.

On 17 January 1963 a decree was published setting a nationwide minimum wage *(Salario Mínimo Interprofesional Garantizado* — SMIG) for all activities. Although it only applied to less than 5% of the working population, the minimum wage served as a general wage indicator.

## 2. *Labour management*

The return to democracy after the general elections of 15 June 1977 meant the revamping of labour management. With the publications of the Workers' Statute (Act 8/1980 of 10 March), wage agreements were regulated by articles 82–92, which governed everything related to concept and effectiveness, units of negotiation, involvement, content, period of enforcement (one year unless otherwise agreed), capacity to negotiate (company committees at this level and unions representing more than 10% of the workers at provincial or national levels), procedures and so on.

But apart from freedom to negotiate, which was recognised in article 37.1 of the Constitution and reaffirmed in the Workers' Statute, the changed economic and political circumstances that were prevailing in 1977 led to wage ceiling and wage band agreements being reached on different occasions. The first occurred with the Moncloa Agreements in October 1977, in which the government and political parties set a ceiling of 22% (equal to the average consumer price increase for the year) on 1978 wage increases. This was 4 points below expectations, since the Consumer Price Index (CPI) at December 1977 had climbed by 26.4% from the level in December 1976. Businesses, through the Confederación Española de Organizaciones Empresariales (CEOE — Spanish Employers' Association), and the major trade unions Comisiones Obreras (CCOO — influenced by the Communist Party) and Unión General de Trabajadores (UGT — inspired by the Socialist Party), which had not participated directly in the Moncloa negotiations, accepted these wage provisions. In this way the sliding wage-scale system was changed, with increases being pegged to rises in the CPI, taking inflation into account.

The fulfilment of the wage clauses in the Moncloa Agreements was the motive for the 'days of reflection' organised in September 1978 by the Vice-President of the Government for Economic Affairs, Abril Matorell, who called together the CCOO, the UGT and the CEOE, leaving out political parties. These 'three band, negotiations (not 'four-band', as requested by CCOO), together with the government's failure to comply with the other non-wage clauses, prevented any agreement from being reached and created conflicts that lasted a year. In 1979, however, the negotiations turned a corner. The initiative to negotiate 'from above' was taken by the CEOE and the UGT. This was echoed by the CCOO, which felt that the government and political parties should participate in the agreement, so as to include provisions on employment, social security and so on. The *Acuerdo Marco Interconfederal* (AMI — Interconfederal Framework Agreement), signed by the CEOE and the UGT, contemplated a 13–16% wage band for 1980, which could widen downwards to 11–15% in 1981 if the economy worsened and inflation dropped. In 1981, following the traumatic unsuccessful *coup d'état* on 23 February, the *Acuerdo Nacional sobre Empleo* (ANE — National Agreement on Employment) was signed on 9 June by the CCOO, UGT, CEOE and the government, in keeping with the efforts of Leopoldo Calvo Sotelo, then President of the government following Adolfo Suárez's resignation on 28 January 1981. In the ANE a 9–11% wage increase was set for 1982; this band was narrower and lower than the AMI and 2 points below the forecast 1982 inflation rate (13%).

We now turn to the Ley Básica de Empleo (LBE — Basic Employment Act, 51/81 of 8 October), the first article of which defines employment policy as the 'set of decisions designed to strike a short-, medium- and long-term balance between the supply and demand for labour, in both qualitative and quantitative terms, and protect the unemployed'. The LBE made it possible to establish 'national employment programmes' with selective promotional measures at all different levels. But a year after the act was published, unemployment had risen and no national employment programmes had yet been mapped out. Nevertheless, the LBE has made it possible for the Instituto Nacional del Empleo (INEM — National Employment Institute) to claim assistance for unemployed workers receiving unemployment benefits in 'temporary social works'. The LBE has also given loan priority to self-employed workers without work to help them get started. Along these same lines, tax relief has been promised in return for the creation of new jobs.

Unemployment insurance is offered for the following maximum periods, according to the length of time social security payments have been made: for 6–12 months of payments, workers are eligible for 3 months of benefits; 12–18, 6 months; 18–24, 9 months; 24–30, 12 months; 30–36, 15 months; and more than 36 months, 18 months. The size of unemployment benefit is 80% of the basic wage on which social security payments were made during the 6 months preceding the first 180 days of unemployment. Benefits drop to 75% of the basic wage for months 6–12 and to 60% for months 12–18. An insurance ceiling has been set at 220% of the SMIG. Apart from regulating the new unemployment insurance, the LBE created unemployment benefits, representing 75% of the SMIG, for workers with families whose insurance benefits have run out and for Spanish migratory workers registered at employment offices who do not find work within 180 days of their return to Spain.

Employers and employees finance 60% of unemployment insurance and benefits, with the state covering the remaining 40%. The administration of benefits and the operation of employment offices are the responsibility of the INEM, whose tripartite board consists of 13 representatives from the strongest trade unions, 13 from the CEOE and 13 from the Administration.

## 3. *Trade unions*

During the Civil War, Franco abolished the traditional class trade unions — the CNT (anarchist) and the UGT (socialist) — and established vertical unions, the nature of which was accurately defined in declaration 13 of the Fuero del Trabajo of 1938, which stated that the National Trade Union Organisation would be 'inspired by the principles of unity, totality and hierarchy'. The principles of the law were developed in the Union Organisation Act of 6 December 1940, in which the branches of production were listed under their respective vertical unions. The latter were public law organisations requiring the participation of workers, technicians and employers within a given branch of production. Under the Trade Union Act of 17 February 1971, the Minister of Union Relations headed the National Trade Union Organisation. Vertical unions would identify production problems, propose solutions to the Administration, and supply the state with data for statistical purposes. There was also mandatory representation of many public agencies in the National Trade Union Organisation. The unions also put out a number of economic publications.

Pursuant to the 1940 act, twenty-eight vertical unions were organised in Spain, one for each branch of production.* Each union was then subdivided into sectors, sectors into associations, associations into groups, and groups into company sub-groups engaged in specific activities (for example, the 'steel drum' group was with the 'diverse manufacturing' association of the 'metal work and manufacturing' sector of the 'National Metal Union'). These groups made many agreements restricting competition between member manufacturers or merchants.

At the local, provincial and national levels, unions had two associations: a social association, formed by workers, employees and technicians, and an economic association, formed by businessmen. Direct suffrage was the system used for electing union council members; suffrage was direct for work place representatives and indirect for local, provincial and national council members and parliamentary representatives. The method of appointing parliamentary trade union representatives (who took one-third of the seats

---

* In 1977, before their disappearance, these branches were: diverse activities; sanitation activities; water, gas and electric power; foodstuffs; sugar; banking; the stock market and savings; grains; fuel; construction; glass and ceramics; education; entertainment; fruit and vegetables; livestock; hotel industries; chemical industries; wood and cork; the merchant marine; metal; olives; paper and graphic arts; fish; leather; the press, radio, television and advertising; insurance; textiles; transportation and communication; wine, beer and beverages.

in Franco's organic or non-democratic Cortes) was marked by confusion, cooption and the designation of 'natural representatives', namely, union presidents and other officials (often indicated by the Minister of Union Relations). In 1956, the National Trade Union Organisation tried to make some changes, such as calling its divisions 'national' instead of 'vertical' unions, allowing campaigning during union elections, and setting up provincial and national workers' and employer councils. This process culminated in the Act of 17 February 1971, which neither met the social needs of the country nor complied with ILO recommendations: that unions be fully independent of business management and separate from government; that workers have the right to strikes and lockouts; that all union leaders be elected directly; and that workers be given the right to unionise. Of course, these principles could only be recognised once basic democratic principles were recognised.

After Franco's death on 20 November 1975, the free unions coming into the public spotlight set off the largest wave of strikes the country had seen since 1936. All participants demanded the right to unionise. Finally, in the second half of 1976, the Minister of Union Relations met with the CCOO, UGT and the Union Sindical de Obreras (USO — Workers' Union) for this purpose. Later, in 1977, the government under Adolfo Suárez formally dissolved the vertical trade unions, creating the Administración de Instituciones de Servicios Socio-profesionales (AISS — Office for Institutions of Social-Professional Services), handling relations between the government and the trade unions. Next, with the general elections approaching, unions were legalised under Act 19/1977 of 1 April, and trade union elections were held in accordance with Decree-Law 3149/1977 of 6 December. Councils of delegates exist at provincial, and then at national, level: they consist of a single elected delegate from each company with 11–25 workers; 3 delegates from companies with 26–50 workers; and a company committee from companies with more than 50 workers (with 5 members for 51–100 workers, 9 for 101–250, 13 for 251–500, 17 for 501–750 and 21 for 751–1,000).

The large number of employer associations that formed in 1974–7 joined forces in 1977 under the CEOE.

## 4. *Social security*

Social security policies in Spain got their start with the creation of the Instituto Nacional de Previsión (INP — Social Security Office), by an Act of 27 February 1908 which established a voluntary insurance plan. On this were based subsequent compulsory plans, such as the 1919 Worker Retirement Insurance, the 1929 Maternity Insurance and the 1932 Industrial Injury Insurance. An Act of 13 July 1936 envisaged the establishment of the Occupational Disease Insurance, and around the same time the Cortes studied a bill that would introduce (national) health insurance. However, the implementation of these last two plans was postponed by the war.

Later, Declaration III of the Fuero del Trabajo, (1938), laid down by the Nationalists, called for immediate family welfare benefits, and Declaration X of the same text mapped out a complete social security plan, including the following kinds of insurance: 1. *Compulsory*: illness, maternity, old age and disability, family welfare, industrial accidents, occupational illness, *Montepío Nacional del Servicio Doméstico* (Domestic Service Assistance) and *Mutualidad Nacional de Previsión Social Agraria* (Agrarian Social Security Society). 2. *Voluntary*: retirement funds, endowments, mutual benefit educational societies, mutual benefit social security societies (which include civil servants of the Social Security Department), loan repayment insurance, and the *Montepío de la Administración Local* (public assistance for provincial and municipal government officials).

When democracy was restored in 1977, the social security system had a great many flaws: low pensions for the old, an almost complete absence of preventive medicine, huge and unmanageable social security hospitals, with hundreds of patients for medical practitioners; outpatient departments where simple prescriptions took the place of diagnosis, and pervasive bureaucracy at all levels. The defects in the social security systems have forced hundreds of thousands of contributors to join private health plans, making Spain's inadequate social medicine even more expensive. Against this dramatic backdrop, the following aspects of the social security system were covered in the Moncloa Agreements:

— *Social security management*. A bill was hammered out to reshape the whole system into nine smaller, autonomous agencies.

— *Control and supervision of social security management*. Budgets and management reports were to be submitted to Parliament and to the *Tribunal de Cuentas* (official auditing department).

— *Financing*. A graduated contribution system was laid down in accordance with social efficiency and redistribution, based on income levels and real wages.

— *Benefits*. To stop the unnecessary consumption of drugs, the patient's own direct contribution to their cost (at present *ca.* 40%) would be revised in accordance with the cost of benefits.

— *Unemployment insurance.* Direct responsibility for this area was transferred from the Ministry of Health and Welfare to the Ministry of Labour.

— *Agrarian social security.* This was put on an equal footing with the rest of the system.

These reforms were implemented through Royal Decree-Law 36/1978 of 16 November, under which the all-encompassing INP was subdivided into the following agencies:

— The *Instituto Nacional de la Seguridad Social* (INSS — National Social Security Office), to handle social security pensions and the former activities of the *Mutualidades Laborales* (workers' mutual aid societies).

— The *Instituto Nacional de la Salud* (Insalud — National Health Office), to administer health services.

— The *Instituto Nacional de Servicios Sociales* (Inserso — National Social Services Institute), to carry out complementary social security benefit services.

— The *Instituto Nacional de Asistencia Social* (INAS — National Welfare Office) to provide welfare assistance to people who do not possess the legal right to obtain social security benefits.

— The *Instituto Nacional de la Marina* (SIM — National Marine Office), to provide social security for fishing crews and seamen.

— The *Instituto Nacional de Empleo* (INEM — National Employment Institute), created under the Ministry of Labour, comprising the *Servicio de Empleo y Acción Formativa* (SEAF — Employment and Training Service), *Promoción Profesional Obrera* (PPO — Worker Professional Advancement and the *Obra de Formacion Profesional* (Vocational Training Services) of the AISS.

— The so-called *Obra Sindical de Educación y Descanso* (Educational and Recreational Services) of the vertical trade unions was transformed into the *Instituto de Tiempo Libre* (ITL — Free Time Institute).

— The *Instituto Nacional de Higiene y Seguridad en el Trabajo* (National On-The-Job Hygiene and Safety Institute) also reported to the Ministry of Labour. Trade schools, formerly under the Ministry of Labour and financed by the *Mutualidad Laboral*, became responsible to an autonomous agency within the Ministry of Education, the *Instituto Nacional de Enseñazas Integradas* (National Integrated Education Institute).

The involvement of unions, business and the public administration in social security, health and employment programmes was regulated under Royal Decree 3064/1978 of 22 December by the boards of INSS, Insalud, Inserso and INEM, each comprising 13 representatives each from unions, employers and government. The financing of expenditure has been modified in recent years as the state's contribution has increased and rates have changed, as can be seen below:

|  | 1980 | 1981 | 1982 | 1983 | 1984 | 1985 |
|---|---|---|---|---|---|---|
| Contributions | 88.17 | 86.99 | 83.19 | 80.75 | 78.20 | 76.23 |
| State transfers | 8.35 | 10.65 | 15.35 | 17.67 | 20.15 | 21.34 |
| Remainder | 3.48 | 2.36 | 1.46 | 1.58 | 1.65 | 2.43 |
| Total | 100.00 | 100.00 | 100.00 | 100.00 | 100.00 | 100.00 |

Contributions have lately stabilised at 16% for workers and 84% for employers.

## 5. *Education policy*

The sociologist Emile Durkheim defined education as the 'influence of adult generations on those not yet mature enough for social life, with a view to arousing and developing a certain number of physical, intellectual and moral states in a child required by a political society and the particular environment for which he is destined.' In keeping with the foregoing, José Ortega y Gasset said that 'pedogogy is the science of transforming societies', a definition that can be developed: education is the instrument by which, bearing in mind the possibilities and limitations of a given society, it is possible to achieve a better society. In purely economic terms, education enables the formation of a social capital which, together with real capital, can increase productivity, strengthen democracy and improve living conditions. Undoubtedly an economic development policy requires that special attention be given to systems of education and re-education.

Spain's torpid policy on education in the 1960s under Ministers Rubio and Lora, and the university unrest of 1967 and 1968, paved the way for profound changes, of which the main proponents were J.L. Villar Palasí, Minister of Education and Science, and R. Díez Hochleitner, Deputy-Secretary of Education and Science. The way was paved for reform with the writing of a White Paper, giving a technical analysis of the main educational problems. The result of this process was the General Education Act (14/1970), which completely reshaped the educational system, establishing pre-school for children aged 2–5; *Educación General Básica* (EGB — primary schooling) for children aged 6–13; *Bachillerato Unificado Polivalente* (BUP — secondary school curricula), similar to the 'O' level); and *Curso de Orientación Universitaria* (COU — pre-university studies, similar to 'A' level), for the 14–16 age bracket; also vocational training, advanced studies (universities and polytechnics) and adult education. It would be tedious to discuss all the ups and downs of this act, but we can summarise the main developments. First, the budgetary allocations were insufficient, most seriously in the area of EGB (age 6–13) where the means to educate all the children eligible were not available till the 1980s. Secondly, lamentable improvisations took place with regard to COU and provision of textbooks. Thirdly, very little was done in the area of teaching, university autonomy and student organisation until 1977, and serious problems continue to exist in the 1980s. But perhaps the most important issue was the lack of concern shown for the quality of education and of scientific and technological research and the divergence between the needs of society and educational output at all levels.

Since 1978, policies on education have been closely tied to the application of article 27 of the Constitution:

(*a*) All citizens have a right to education. Academic freedom is recognised.

(*b*) Education is to instil democratic and social values.

(*c*) While the state has no official creed, public authorities guarantee the right for children to receive a religious and moral education in keeping with the convictions of their parents.

(*d*) Basic education is compulsory for all children and the choice between public and private schools is free.

(*e*) Public authorities guarantee the right of all citizens to an education by means of a general educational programme, with the participation of all the sectors in question and the creation of teaching institutions.

(*f*) The freedom of individuals and legal entities to create teaching institutions, within the limits of the Constitution, is recognised.

(*g*) Teachers, parents and, if appropriate, students will participate in the supervision and management of all institutions financed by the state, within the limits of the law.

(*h*) Public authorities will inspect and standardise the educational system to guarantee compliance with the law.

(*i*) Public authorities will aid educational institutions which comply with the requirements established by law.

(*j*) The autonomy of the universities, as defined by law, is recognised.

# XXI. ECONOMIC DEVELOPMENT

## 1. *The legacy of Francoism*

The economic changes which took place during the transition to democracy logically got their historical start in the last years of the Franco era. Franco wanted to perpetuate his idea of social order by '*dejandolo todo atado y bien atado*' (a slogan of the régime: 'leaving everything bound up, and well bound up'). But this design was unsuccessful, and Francoism politically ended up in historical failure. Bismarck laid the groundwork for the Germany of today, and Cavour did the same for Italy. De Gaulle saved France from shame and later modernised the Republic. But Franco, like all the other European dictators of this century, will go down in history as, at best, a controversial figure.

Under Franco's authoritarian rule in Spain, an autocratic political system took shape during three clearly marked stages. The first stage saw the passing of the founding provisions, beginning with Decree 29 of September 1936, designating Franco as Head of State, a position reinforced by the Acts of 30 January 1938 and 8 August 1939. The autocratic sub-system entered its second stage in 1942 when, as the Second World War turned against the Axis powers, Franco decided to apply a thin coat of self-styled democratic paint to his régime. To this effect there emerged the Cortes Act of 1942, the *Fuero de los Españoles* (a kind of 'bill of rights'), the Referendum of 1945 and the Law of Succession of 1947. These founding laws, summarised in the 'Principles of the Movement' of 1958, gave a veneer of 'organic democracy' to what continued to be an absolute autocracy. The third stage came about with 'political development', as promised by the technocrats of the régime. At the same time as the Stabilisation Plan (1959–61) stepped up economic growth, it was said that political development would germinate from the publication of the Press and Religious Freedom Act of 1966 and the *Ley Orgánica del Estado* (LOE — Organic Law of the State) of 1962. The liberalising appearances of the laws soon faded, as became evident with the 1969 ministerial changes and the regressive 1971 Trade Union Act. Finally, when the promise of political development was seen to have been broken, and Arias Navarro's 'shift towards greater democracy' (1974) was found to be full of contradictions, Francoism showed that it could not change its fundamental nature, which was based on force and the concentration of power.

Unlike the political system, the economic sub-system underwent important changes during the Franco era, paving the way for social transition. To see how this happened, we should look at the beginnings of the 1939 autarkic system and its rupture in 1959. The autarky that grew out of the Civil War was consistent with the existing autocratic political structure. The basic characteristics of this economic system can be grouped into four categories. First, the aim was self-sufficiency, in response to the post–Civil War collapse of foreign trade. Secondly, many economic freedoms were suppressed by means of interventionist mechanisms defined in the 1939 industrial acts on the protection and promotion of domestic industries. Thirdly, there was direct state intervention in production through the National Institute for Industry. Created as an entity to subsidise private initiative, the INI eventually became a principal source of support for large financial groups. Finally, the system involved control and exploitation of the working class. Programmed declarations (such as the Fuero de Trabajo, based on Mussolini's '*Carta di Lavoro*') quickly showed the true character of the 'new labour order': the dissolution of trade unions and working-class organisations, the existence of a single vertical union, the suppression of the right to strike, imprisonment and exile.

Autarky could not continue indefinitely, and through political and social pressure after 1955, the country moved in a new direction. By 1957 a break from the post-war order began to show, and the Decree-Law on the new economic policy of July 1959 brought forward a number of far-reaching changes: first, the stepping up of foreign relations by liberalising imports, foreign capital investment and other transactions; secondly, the removal of interventionism from the economy by deregulating prices and dissolving many public agencies involved in raw materials distribution; and thirdly, the eradication of some of the main inflationary factors of the autarkic period by prohibiting the issue of discountable government bonds at the Banco de España, holding down wage increases and raising the cost of credit.

Spain's economy moved towards international compatibility with the acceptance of various general standards, such as the IMF fixing of the peseta parity, the adoption of GATT schedules and the agreement to liberalise foreign transactions and payments in accordance with OEEC (today OECD) guidelines. Although the liberalised economic sub-system was not identical to the OECD's (for Spain still outlawed the right to unionise and to strike), the freeing of the forces of production, formerly weighed down by hundreds of restrictions, did change the situation. Import facilities allowed Spanish companies to modernise and raise productivity to a spectacular extent, and the new peseta exchange rate gave fresh life to tourism.

The foreign currency which tourism, emigrant remittances and foreign investments generated caused an expansion of the domestic market, which in turn boosted industrial growth, aided by unheard-of waves of migratory workers and protected by the new 1960 protective customs tariff.

Starting in 1964, three four-year development plans were set in motion, with official growth centres, being set up in less developed areas. Between 1961 and 1963, average annual growth was registered at 6.5%, two points above OECD averages. Accelerated development brought changes in social behaviour and political attitudes, making long-term political change inevitable. This turn of events could be seen in the early 1970s, when the more complex and diversified Spanish economy and society collided head-on with the oligarchic, anachronistic, obsolete political system. This was the situation in Spain at the time of Franco's death.

## 2. *Economic and social problems between 1975 and 1977*

The international crisis that was in full force in 1975 compounded the problem-ridden political situation bequeathed by Franco. When a genuine step was taken towards democracy, Spain found itself in a depression, with widespread stagnation, growing unemployment and inflation, and a rapidly-expanding foreign debt. GNP rose by 0.6% in 1975, barely exceeding 1.5% in 1976. Unemployment was estimated to be between 700,000 and 900,000, and the 22% inflation rate threatened to grow to 30% in 1977. The foreign debt exceeded $12,000 million, and the incidence of capital flight soared. Spain's heavy foreign debt stemmed from the financing of large oil-related deficits through the current account of the balance of payments. Capital flight was the 'response' given by the more powerful classes, fearful of what democracy had in store for them. During the 3½ years from October 1973 to June 1977, eight package deals of economic measures were published, but none of them produced a cure. The crisis proved to be structural and long-term.

On 15 June 1977 the general election promised by Adolfo Suárez (appointed President of the Spanish government by King Juan Carlos in July 1976) was held. Mr Suárez's party, the Unión de Centro Democrático (UCD — Union of the Democratic Centre), received the most votes (though not a majority) and was faced with runaway inflation already hitting the 30% mark, and threatening to reach 40–50% in 1978; 900,000 unemployed, and only 300,000 receiving unemployment benefits, as investment rates plummeted and job creation per unit of value investment dropped off; a foreign

debt of $14,000 million (1.2 billion ptas), which was three times the
gold and foreign currency reserves held by the Bank of Spain;
and — the nation's unprecedented and most serious (but least
talked about) problem — Spanish companies owing millions of
pesetas. These developments affected all the units of production of
goods and services — large- medium- and small-sized businesses,
the public sector with the Ministry of Finance's budgetary deficits,
and the private sector with cash-flow and payment problems. This
crisis was the legacy of so many years of dictatorship in which
competitive industries had not been developed, of irrational policies,
and of a neglected economy suddenly hit by the 1973 oil price
increases.

Barely a month after the general elections, the newly-elected
government announced its official 'programme declaration', which
included an 'economic emergency plan' calling for the immediate
devaluation of the peseta and fiscal reform and designed to situate
wages below prices (freezing wage increases at 17% for 1978 when
prices were expected to rise by 23%), to tighten up the money supply
and to correct the deficit. Shortly after these details were announced,
the need for a national emergency cabinet became a topic of great
parliamentary debate, and the opposition set forth the 'minimum
conditions' that had to be met to support a common economic
programme. These were:

(*a*) to make programmed fiscal measures more progressive;
(*b*) to maintain purchasing power levels and to increase the lower
wages and many pensions;
(*c*) to fight unemployment seriously by enlarging public investment;
(*d*) to give greater attention to the problems besetting small- and
medium-sized companies;
(*e*) to give urgent attention to the difficulties arising in the agricultural, fishing and other sectors; and
(*f*) to introduce a set of economic reforms that would be genuinely
capable of bringing about economic recovery and the restructuring
of the agrarian sector, public enterprises, the social security system,
urban development, workers' rights and intra-company relations.

In August and September 1977 the economy worsened: unemployment and inflation rose, corporations (and even the state) could not
repay their short-term debts, thousands of bills of exchange were
being dishonoured, and countless small- and medium-sized
businesses faced bankruptcy. The first government trade union talks
highlighted the difficulties inherent in the freezing of wages and in
allowing employers to lay-off workers freely.

## 3. *The Moncloa Agreements*

In early October 1977, Adolfo Suárez summoned representatives from each political party represented in the Cortes to participate in an exchange of ideas. Talks centred initially on the 101-page report known as the 'Fuentes Document' (prepared by a team under the Vice-President of the government for economic affairs, Fuentes Quintana). Over the weekend of 8–9 October, the report was thoroughly discussed in the Moncloa Palace and a series of important issues were added. By the Sunday evening, the basis for a future agreement had been written up in a press communiqué modestly entitled a 'working summary'. Talks between government representatives and the political parties continued. The consensus reached on 9 October was worked over by specialised commissions, and after hours of negotiations the agreement was signed on 25 October and approved by the Cortes on 27 October.

The short-term goals of the Moncloa Agreements were to iron out economic difficulties by, first of all, tightening the reins on inflation, which was destructive for both investment and employment. To this end, the agreements allowed for specific increases in 1978 in basic variables, all of which (except for pensions and public investment) were to be lower than those scheduled for 1977. The intention to slow down inflation was particularly clear in the tightening of the money supply, credit, and state and social security expenditures. Next, wages were aligned with prices. These goals are presented below:

### INCREASES IN IMPORTANT VARIABLES

|  | *Average % increase forecast for 1978* |
| --- | --- |
| Social security collections | 13.4 |
| Bank loans | 16 |
| Money supply | 17 |
| Overall social security expenditure | 18 |
| Gross wage bill | 20 |
| GDP in monetary terms | 21.4 |
| Current state expenditure | 21.4 |
| Consumer prices | 22 |
| Net wage bill | 22 |
| Total state spending | 29.2 |
| Pensions | 30 |
| State budgetary investment expenditure | 30 |

|  | %  |  |
|---|---|---|
|  | *1977* | *1978* |
| State social security contributions | 3.5 | 8.2 |
| Taxes (% of GDP) | 11.95 | 13.00 |
| Social security contributions (% GDP) | 10.87 | 10.56 |
| C + D total (% of GDP) | 22.82 | 23.56 |

The short-term steps to be taken by the government, in accordance with the Moncloa Agreements, were summarised as follows:

— *State and social security budgets.* The 1978 state budget was tightened so that consumption increased by no more than 21.4% in 1977, and total spending by no more than 29.2%. A large part of public spending was earmarked for investment that would create jobs.

— *Monetary policy.* The increase in money supply was to be limited to 17%, so as to slow down the rise in prices.

— *Pricing and income policy.* According to this policy, prices were not to rise more than an average of 22% in 1978 as compared to the previous year. Wages were pegged to prices; wage bill increases of up to 22% (allowing for senority and promotions) could be negotiated to keep wages in step with prices.

— *Employment.* New guidelines were envisaged allowing for the temporary hiring of unemployed workers. In addition, to tackle youth unemployment, workers entering the job market for the first time could be temporarily hired for up to two years. In both cases, to promote new forms of employment, the state paid 50% of the social security contributions.

— *The reshaping of the economy.* The short-term policy of rehabilitating the economy included in the Moncloa Agreements focused on re-establishing a basic economic balance. But removing problems made little sense without reshaping the economy. In a climate of democratisation and partly to repay workers for the sacrifices they were being asked to make, the restructuring measures gave society more of a voice in decision-making. Encompassed by these measures were fiscal reform, upgraded public expenditure, educational policy, urban and housing development, a revamping of the social security and financial system, new agrarian and fishing policies, sound energy management and the democratisation of public enterprises.

## 4. *Economic policy, 1978–82*

Wide gaps soon appeared between the formulas agreed on and reality. Most important, the treatment given to the different facets of the Moncloa Agreements varied. Top priority was given to the so-called short-term rehabilitation policy (regarding prices and wages, emergency fiscal measures, budgets and monetary issues), while structural reforms were postponed; indeed the structural changes spelled out in the Moncloa Agreements were never properly carried out. In February 1978, once the government felt more confident, the Agreements were modified and their most progressive aspects abandoned. This marked the end of a genuine economic restructuring policy and a turn towards conservatism.

In 1979, as problems worsened, the opposition sharpened its criticism. Consequently, in September a *Programa Económico del Gobierno* (PEG) was submitted to the Cortes. In terms of job creation, this programme barely came up to expectations, since it repeated the youth employment scheme mapped out in the Moncloa Agreements but never applied. The PEG's treatment of industrial reconversion for crisis-ridden sectors represented nothing new; moreover, in disharmony with the rest of the programme, it moved to liberalise foreign trade completely by adapting the Spanish tariff schedule to that of the EEC. The only guarantee the government could have offered with this decision was that factories would be shut down. It was only logical that this policy should have been cut short by harsh estimates.

As for its remaining aspects, the PEG envisaged the perennial solution of limiting public spending, promising more public investment and announcing enhanced budgetary control and greater productivity within the Administration.

The political ups and downs of the transition period of 1979–80 weakened the government, which came under intense criticism and appeared exhausted. With mounting difficulties, reflected in unemployment and price indicators, and no possibility of holding ordinary debates in the Cortes, the Socialist party tabled a censure motion against the government in May 1980. The ensuing televised debate revealed that the government still lacked the economic policies to handle the crisis effectively. In a delayed reaction to this event, Mr Suárez remodelled his Cabinet later that summer, asking Deputy Prime Minister Fernando Abril Matorell, who had been responsible for the last economic programme (March 1977 to September 1980), to step down. On 11 September 1980, a motion of confidence was presented in the Cortes, but Mr Suárez offered no new economic programme.

Mr Suárez resigned in early February 1981, precipitating a crisis within the government and prompting the UCD to meet in Palma de Mallorca to decide who would take his place. As Leopoldo Calvo Sotelo was being approved for the office of Prime Minister (an event threatened by the attempted *coup d'état* of 23 February 1981), a new economic programme was presented that can be described as follows:

(*a*) Priority was given to the nuclear option to include the new nuclear plants of the 'updated PEN' (National Energy Plan).

(*b*) It was promised that the state would finance a greater share of the social security system.

(*c*) Proposals were made to moderate wages, later taken up in the Acuerdo Nacional de Empleo (ANE — National Employment Agreement).

(*d*) Pledges were made to rehape the most crisis-ridden industrial sectors (iron and steel, shipbuilding and textile).

These rather unrealistic considerations did nothing to improve the economy.

## 5. *The general elections of 1982 and the PSOE economic programme*

With a depression in full swing and both the UCD and the Partido Comunista de España (PCE — Spanish Communist Party) suffering from internal problems, the Partido Socialista Obero Español (PSOE — Spanish Socialist Party), led by Felipe González, won a landslide victory in the October 1982 general election, gaining control of Parliament. The new government's economic policy was entrusted to the new Minister of Economy and Finance, Miguel Boyer. Conservative from the very beginning, Mr Boyer gave priority to the battle against inflation by tightening money supply even more than in the past. He also further moderated wages so that they were set below the forecast inflation rate. These two approaches coincided with a first devaluation of the peseta in December 1982, raising export levels and lowering the current account deficit in the balance of payments.

The Socialists' economic programme increased the number of unemployed by 800,000 between December 1982 and July 1985, and dramatically reduced industrial production through a reconversion policy that cut back on the production capacity of crisis-ridden sectors (iron and steel, shipbuilding, textiles, home appliances, special steels, copper manufacturing, etc.). During the first two

Table 16.1.    DISTRIBUTION OF TOTAL POPULATION BY
PROVINCE, 1970 AND 1981
($\times$ *1,000*)

| | 1970 census | 1981 census | Growth 1970/81 | % of total population | Accumu- lative % |
|---|---|---|---|---|---|
| Madrid | 3,761 | 4,687 | 926 | 12.44 | 12.44 |
| Barcelona | 3,915 | 4,623 | 708 | 12.27 | 24.71 |
| Valencia | 1,770 | 2,066 | 296 | 5.48 | 30.19 |
| Seville | 1,337 | 1,478 | 141 | 3.92 | 34.11 |
| Vizcaya | 1,041 | 1,189 | 148 | 3.16 | 37.27 |
| Alicante | 922 | 1,149 | 227 | 3.05 | 40.32 |
| Oviedo | 1,052 | 1,130 | 78 | 3.00 | 43.32 |
| La Coruña | 1,031 | 1,093 | 62 | 2.90 | 46.22 |
| Málaga | 854 | 1,026 | 172 | 2.72 | 48.94 |
| Cádiz | 879 | 988 | 109 | 2.62 | 51.56 |
| Murcia | 832 | 955 | 123 | 2.54 | 54.10 |
| Pontevedra | 781 | 883 | 102 | 2.34 | 56.44 |
| Zaragoza | 757 | 829 | 72 | 2.20 | 58.64 |
| Granada | 742 | 759 | 17 | 2.01 | 60.65 |
| Córdoba | 731 | 721 | − 10 | 1.92 | 62.57 |
| Las Palmas | 549 | 709 | 160 | 1.88 | 64.45 |
| Guipúzcoa | 626 | 695 | 69 | 1.84 | 66.29 |
| Sta Cruz de Tenerife | 576 | 659 | 83 | 1.75 | 68.04 |
| Balearic islands | 533 | 656 | 123 | 1.74 | 69.78 |
| Badajoz | 702 | 644 | − 58 | 1.71 | 71.49 |
| Jaén | 668 | 640 | − 28 | 1.69 | 73.18 |
| León | 563 | 525 | − 39 | 1.39 | 74.57 |
| Santander | 469 | 513 | 44 | 1.37 | 75.94 |
| Tarragona | 433 | 513 | 80 | 1.36 | 77.30 |
| Navarra | 467 | 509 | 42 | 1.35 | 78.65 |
| Valladolid | 413 | 482 | 69 | 1.28 | 79.93 |
| Ciudad Real | 513 | 475 | 38 | 1.26 | 81.19 |
| Toledo | 478 | 475 | − 3 | 1.26 | 82.45 |
| Gerona | 412 | 467 | 55 | 1.24 | 83.69 |
| Castellón | 387 | 432 | 45 | 1.14 | 84.83 |
| Orense | 441 | 430 | − 11 | 1.14 | 85.97 |
| Cáceres | 468 | 421 | − 47 | 1.12 | 87.09 |
| Huelva | 403 | 419 | 16 | 1.11 | 88.20 |
| Almería | 378 | 411 | 33 | 1.09 | 89.29 |
| Lugo | 423 | 405 | − 18 | 1.08 | 90.37 |
| Salamanca | 380 | 364 | − 16 | 0.97 | 91.34 |
| Burgos | 361 | 364 | 3 | 0.96 | 92.30 |
| Lérida | 347 | 353 | 6 | 0.94 | 93.24 |
| Albacete | 341 | 339 | − 2 | 0.90 | 94.14 |
| Alava | 200 | 258 | 58 | 0.68 | 94.82 |
| Logroño | 235 | 254 | 19 | 0.68 | 95.50 |
| Zamora | 259 | 228 | − 31 | 0.60 | 96.10 |
| Cuenca | 252 | 216 | − 36 | 0.58 | 96.68 |
| Huesca | 222 | 215 | − 7 | 0.57 | 97.25 |
| Palencia | 202 | 188 | − 14 | 0.50 | 37.75 |

Table 16.1   (*continued*)

|  | 1970 census | 1981 census | Growth 1970/81 | % of total population | Accumu-lative % |
|---|---|---|---|---|---|
| Avila | 212 | 184 | − 28 | 0.48 | 98.23 |
| Teruel | 274 | 153 | − 21 | 0.41 | 98.64 |
| Segovia | 162 | 149 | − 13 | 0.40 | 99.04 |
| Guadalajara | 150 | 143 | − 7 | 0.38 | 99.42 |
| Soria | 117 | 101 | − 16 | 0.26 | 99.63 |
| Ceuta | 63 | 65 | 2 | 0.18 | 99.86 |
| Melilla | 61 | 54 | − 7 | 0.14 | 100.00 |
| *Total* | 34,041 | 37,682 | 3,641 | 100.00 | — |

*Source:* INE.

years of the Socialist government (1983–4), monetary formulas prevailed over a few timid attempts at planning. Everything depended on an international economic recovery. Although exports have expanded slightly, unemployment rates have not decreased. Faced with strong union opposition, a proposed agreement to moderate wages early in 1984 proved unattainable. This impasse, together with mounting pressure from organised labour in El Ferrol and Vigo in Galicia, Gijón in Asturias, the Basque country, Sagunto in Valencia and Getafe and the rest of the southern Madrid area, generated deep-seated social unrest. The government rectified its electoral promise to create 800,000 jobs between 1982 and 1986, and finally resigned itself to the unemployment situation.

The PSOE government's central political measures in 1983–5 were:

(*a*) *industrial reconversion*, similar to that promoted by the UCD, with new additions such as job-creating funds, areas of re-industrialisation and joint loans, all of which have done little to abate unemployment;

(*b*) *revision of the Plan Energético Nacional* (PEN — National Energy Plan), authorising a nuclear energy moratorium, and setting up an 'electric power agreement' that would involve the financial rehabilitation of electric power companies, state control of the high-tension network and the complete reshaping of CAMPSA, and the door being opened to private refineries in this public corporation;

(*c*) *introduction of new legal requirements* for private banks and savings banks to provide the state with the financing it needs to cover its growing fiscal deficit (representing 6% of GDP in 1983 and 1984).

Table 16.2. TOTAL WORKING AND NON-WORKING
POPULATION, 31 DECEMBER 1982

| | *Thousands of persons* | *% of population* | *% of working population* |
|---|---|---|---|
| TOTAL POPULATION | 37,833.0 | 100.0 | — |
| WORKING POPULATION | 13,101.1 | 34.6 | 100.0 |
| | | | |
| EMPLOYED | 10,866.3 | 28.7 | 82.9 |
| (1) Non-wage-earners | 3,227.9 | 8.5 | 24.6 |
| (a) Self-employed | 2,358.3 | 6.2 | 18.0 |
| (b) Family aid | 836.3 | 2.2 | 6.4 |
| (c) Others | 33.3 | 0.1 | 0.2 |
| (2) Wage-earners | 7,638.4 | 20.2 | 58.3 |
| (a) Farmers and fishermen | 1,987.2 | 5.2 | 15.2 |
| — Men | 1,456.0 | 3.8 | 11.1 |
| — Women | 531.2 | 1.4 | 4.0 |
| (b) Industry | 2,757.7 | 7.3 | 21.0 |
| — Men | 2,177.8 | 5.8 | 16.6 |
| — Women | 579.9 | 1.5 | 4.4 |
| (c) Building | 914.9 | 2.4 | 6.7 |
| — Men | 897.1 | 2.4 | 6.8 |
| — Women | 17.8 | — | 0.1 |
| (d) Services | 5,206.5 | 13.7 | 39.7 |
| — Men | 2,370.7 | 6.3 | 18.1 |
| — Women | 2,835.8 | 7.5 | 21.6 |
| | | | |
| UNEMPLOYED | 2,234.8 | 5.9 | 17.1 |
| (1) Registered | 2,151.0 | 5.7 | 16.4 |
| (a) Receiving unemployment benefits | 752.8 | 2.0 | 5.7 |
| (b) Not receiving unemployment benefits | 1,398.2 | 3.7 | 10.7 |
| (2) Unregistered | 83.8 | 0.2 | 0.6 |
| | | | |
| Population older than 16 | 27,115.0 | 71.7 | 206.9 |
| NON-WORKING POPULATION | 24,731.9 | 65.4 | 187.8 |
| (1) Of working age | 10,898.9 | 28.8 | 83.2 |
| (a) Students | 2,045.7 | 5.4 | 15.6 |
| (b) Military service | 350.0 | 0.9 | 2.7 |
| (c) Outside the labour market | 8,503.2 | 22.5 | 64.9 |
| (d) Housewives | 7,423.4 | 19.6 | 56.7 |
| (e) Men (retired, disabled etc.) | 1,079.8 | 2.8 | 8.2 |
| (2) Children and old people | 13,833.0 | 36.6 | 105.6 |
| (a) Children (up to 16 years) | 10,718.0 | 28.3 | 81.8 |
| (b) Old people (70 and older) | 3,115.0 | 8.3 | 23.8 |

*Source:* INE.

Table 16.3.   PER CAPITA INCOME

|  | Population (thousands), 1 July | Per capita income at market prices | | Per capita income (US $) |
|---|---|---|---|---|
|  |  | (Current ptas) | (1970 ptas) |  |
| 1955 | 29,054 | 14,245 | 35,692 | 393 |
| 1956 | 29,299 | 16,130 | 38,124 | 430 |
| 1957 | 29,547 | 18,472 | 38,718 | 437 |
| 1958 | 29,797 | 20,896 | 40,146 | 445 |
| 1959 | 30,048 | 21,365 | 38,683 | 388 |
| 1960 | 30,301 | 21,700 | 38,387 | 362 |
| 1961 | 30,592 | 24,804 | 42,494 | 413 |
| 1962 | 30,905 | 28,457 | 46,582 | 474 |
| 1963 | 31,223 | 32,693 | 49,140 | 545 |
| 1964 | 31,549 | 36,059 | 51,249 | 601 |
| 1965 | — | — | — | — |
| 1966 | 32,206 | 47,652 | 57,648 | 794 |
| 1967 | 32,542 | 52,397 | 60,006 | 858 |
| 1968 | 32,881 | 57,377 | 63,080 | 820 |
| 1969 | 33,224 | 63,855 | 67,322 | 912 |
| 1970 | 33,582 | 70,267 | 70,267 | 1,004 |
| 1971 | 33,949 | 79,053 | 73,252 | 1,176 |
| 1972 | 34,336 | 92,436 | 79,181 | 1,433 |
| 1973 | 34,692 | 111,437 | 85,642 | 1,913 |
| 1974 | 35,031 | 134,197 | 89,304 | 2,326 |
| 1975 | 35,031 | 155,240 | 88,932 | 2,704 |
| 1976 | 35,824 | 185,279 | 90,495 | 2,769 |
| 1977 | 36,140 | 229,666 | 91,315 | 3,024 |
| 1978 | 36,534 | 279,583 | 91,760 | 3,642 |
| 1979 | 36,902 | 328,082 | 92,111 | 4,887 |
| 1980 | 37,312 | 368,069 | 91,335 | 5,133 |
| 1981 | 37,712 | 412,492 | 90,113 | 4,468 |
| 1982 | 38,013 | 475,524* | 90,833* | 4,323* |
| 1983 | 38,279 | 536,316* | 92,105* | 3,830* |

\* = provisional. *Source:* Banco de Bilbao.

(*d*) *heightened fiscal pressure*, raising both direct and indirect taxes with a view to financing an ever-growing bureaucracy and inefficient public enterprises and services (Iberia, Seat, Hunosa, Renfe, postal services and the·social security system);

(*e*) *the expropriation of Rumasa*, carried out on 23 February 1983 with little forethought and at great expense (500,000 million pesetas, financed by the national debt), only to be subsequently sold back to the private sector;

(*f*) *zero growth in purchasing power* for the working class, since the lowering of inflation has been the government's primary objective, even at the cost of a growth in unemployment;

Table 16.4.   SURFACE AREA POPULATION DENSITY AND
PRODUCTION PER KM², 1973 AND 1981

| Autonomous Communities | Surface area km² | Population density | | GDP per km² (× 1,000 ptas) at 1973 prices | | Annual growth (%) |
| --- | --- | --- | --- | --- | --- | --- |
| | | 1973 | 1981 | 1973 | 1981 | 1973/81 |
| Andalucía | 87,268 | 69.1 | 74.0 | 5,638 | 6,773 | 2.26 |
| Aragón | 47,669 | 24.2 | 25.1 | 2,782 | 3,230 | 1.88 |
| Asturias | 10,565 | 101.4 | 107.1 | 12,175 | 13,462 | 1.26 |
| Balearic islands | 5,014 | 112.0 | 131.3 | 18,757 | 19,692 | 0.61 |
| Canary islands | 7,273 | 165.7 | 196.5 | 16,930 | 21,252 | 2.88 |
| Cantabria | 5,289 | 90.3 | 97.2 | 10,762 | 12,078 | 1.45 |
| Castille-La Mancha | 79,226 | 21.2 | 20.8 | 1,856 | 2,030 | 1.13 |
| Castille and Leon | 94,147 | 27.6 | 27.4 | 2,573 | 2,911 | 1.56 |
| Catalonia | 31,930 | 167.5 | 187.0 | 24,484 | 28,866 | 2.08 |
| Extremadura | 41,602 | 26.9 | 25.6 | 1,789 | 1,997 | 1.39 |
| Galicia | 29,434 | 91.7 | 95.6 | 7,209 | 9,588 | 3.63 |
| Madrid | 7,995 | 501.6 | 588.2 | 71,357 | 90,319 | 2.99 |
| Murcia | 11,317 | 75.3 | 84.7 | 7,085 | 9,011 | 3.05 |
| Navarra | 10,421 | 45.5 | 48.9 | 5,668 | 6,776 | 2.26 |
| Basque country | 7,261 | 269.5 | 295.5 | 40,941 | 41,342 | 0.12 |
| Rioja (La) | 5,034 | 47.1 | 50.6 | 5,466 | 6,999 | 3.13 |
| Valencia | 23,305 | 138.0 | 156.9 | 16,101 | 20,035 | 2.77 |
| *Spain, total* | 504,750 | 68.7 | 74.7 | 7,716 | 9,160 | 2.17 |

*Source:* Banco de Bilbao.

(g) A *wage moderation obsession* manifested through budgetary decisions and concerted employer/trade union policies;

(h) An emphasis on *monetary policy*, systematically rejecting any move towards overall planning and worker participation in public enterprise management.

## 6.  *The evolution of macro-economic indicators*

The following tables summarise Spain's most recent demographic and economic changes, and provide some structural data and information on income distribution at provincial and regional levels.

Table 16.1 presents figures on population by provinces in the census years 1970 and 1981. The rapid growth of Madrid and Barcelona and the depopulation of 20 provinces (indicated by a minus-sign) can be seen. The rate of provincial depopulation from 1970 to 1981 was much less than it had been in previous decades.

Table 16.5.   REGIONAL PER CAPITA INCOME,
1973 AND 1981

| Autonomous Communities | 1973 ptas | 1981 ptas | Comparative index (National average = 100) | | Annual growth (%) 1973–81 at constant price |
|---|---|---|---|---|---|
| | | | 1973 | 1981 | |
| Andalucía | 73,874 | 286,967 | 71.7 | 72.2 | 1.07 |
| Aragón | 102,905 | 399,817 | 99.8 | 100.6 | 1.07 |
| Asturias | 95,661 | 384,228 | 92.8 | 96.7 | 1.50 |
| Balearic islands | 137,024 | 508,653 | 132.9 | 128.0 | 0.50 |
| Canary islands | 88,722 | 346,846 | 86.1 | 87.3 | 1.15 |
| Cantabria | 105,630 | 425,487 | 102.5 | 107.1 | 1.53 |
| Castille-La Mancha | 76,766 | 281,367 | 74.5 | 70.8 | 0.34 |
| Castille and Leon | 83,211 | 321,619 | 80.7 | 80.9 | 1.01 |
| Catalonia | 134,492 | 502,368 | 130.5 | 126.4 | 0.58 |
| Extremadura | 61,029 | 245,076 | 59.2 | 61.6 | 1.49 |
| Galicia | 73,548 | 314,005 | 7.14 | 79.0 | 2.27 |
| Madrid | 143,412 | 571,929 | 139.1 | 143.9 | 1.41 |
| Murcia | 81,474 | 304,571 | 79.0 | 76.6 | 0.59 |
| Navarra | 115,043 | 418,711 | 111.6 | 105.4 | 0.25 |
| Basque country | 142,931 | 448,615 | 138.7 | 112.9 | − 1.59 |
| Rioja (La) | 107,629 | 413,495 | 104.4 | 104.1 | 0.93 |
| Valencia | 105,484 | 399,780 | 102.3 | 100.6 | 0.76 |
| *Spain, total* | 103,075 | 397,365 | 100.0 | 100.0 | 0.98 |

*Source:* Banco de Bilbao.

Table 16.2 records a working and non-working population balance drawn from the latest available data. The working population is broken down by wage-earners and non-wage-earners, sectors, sex etc. This table shows Spain's low percentage of working population compared to other European countries (34% compared to 40–52%) as well as high unemployment levels (20% in July 1984 — 2.7 million Spaniards according to INI estimates).

Table 16.3 presents the evolution of Spain's total population since 1955 and of *per capita* income in both current and constant pesetas (translated into dollars). The effects of the 1970s crisis can be seen in constant pesetas as of 1974. The dollar conversions reflect fluctuations in the exchange rate.

Table 16.4 gives 1973 and 1981 data on the *Autonomous Communities*, such as surface area, population density and Gross Domestic Product (GDP) per square km. Differences in population are great and in GDP even greater. While in 1971 Madrid (the most populous region) had 28.2 times the population of Castille-La Mancha (the least populous), Madrid's GDP/km.[2] was 44.5 times

Table 16.6.   GROSS DOMESTIC PRODUCT COMPARISONS, 1973–1981

| Autonomous communities | Total (millions of ptas) | % | A Agriculture and Fisheries | | B Industry | | C Building | | D Services | |
|---|---|---|---|---|---|---|---|---|---|---|
| | | | 1973 | 1981 | 1973 | 1981 | 1973 | 1981 | 1973 | 1981 |
| Andalucía | 2,102,420 | 12.59 | 19.7 | 12.5 | 22.8 | 19.7 | 8.2 | 8.1 | 49.3 | 59.7 |
| Aragón | 552,792 | 3.31 | 16.8 | 6.7 | 32.6 | 29.5 | 6.1 | 7.6 | 44.5 | 56.2 |
| Asturias | 498,417 | 2.98 | 7.7 | 5.3 | 50.0 | 40.5 | 5.3 | 5.2 | 37.0 | 49.0 |
| Balearic islands | 381,147 | 2.28 | 7.2 | 3.2 | 13.1 | 12.2 | 8.9 | 8.1 | 70.8 | 76.5 |
| Canary islands | 585,908 | 3.51 | 11.3 | 7.0 | 14.3 | 10.6 | 13.0 | 9.9 | 61.4 | 72.5 |
| Cantabria | 225,208 | 1.35 | 11.4 | 8.0 | 41.1 | 32.4 | 4.9 | 5.9 | 42.6 | 53.7 |
| Castille-La Mancha | 555,499 | 3.33 | 31.1 | 16.3 | 22.7 | 23.1 | 8.1 | 10.9 | 38.1 | 49.7 |
| Castille and Leon | 969,483 | 5.80 | 21.7 | 9.6 | 26.9 | 28.2 | 6.2 | 7.8 | 45.2 | 54.4 |
| Catalonia | 3,327,963 | 19.93 | 5.6 | 2.7 | 42.0 | 35.4 | 6.4 | 5.0 | 46.0 | 56.9 |
| Extremadura | 291,617 | 1.75 | 29.3 | 17.1 | 17.5 | 15.0 | 8.0 | 10.2 | 45.2 | 57.7 |
| Galicia | 994,510 | 5.96 | 19.7 | 12.8 | 25.5 | 22.7 | 8.2 | 9.0 | 46.6 | 55.5 |
| Madrid | 2,756,320 | 16.51 | 1.0 | 0.4 | 26.6 | 21.1 | 6.9 | 5.2 | 65.5 | 73.3 |
| Murcia | 361,806 | 2.17 | 14.6 | 9.8 | 28.6 | 26.9 | 7.8 | 8.6 | 49.0 | 54.7 |
| Navarra | 244,236 | 1.46 | 16.7 | 8.6 | 36.3 | 38.0 | 5.5 | 6.1 | 41.5 | 47.3 |
| Basque country | 1,050,829 | 6.29 | 4.7 | 3.5 | 49.7 | 44.1 | 5.2 | 3.5 | 40.4 | 48.9 |
| Rioja (La) | 121,078 | 0.73 | 23.3 | 13.6 | 26.9 | 29.5 | 6.6 | 6.9 | 43.2 | 50.0 |
| Valencia | 1,679,540 | 10.05 | 11.4 | 6.2 | 32.5 | 29.4 | 7.6 | 6.4 | 48.5 | 58.0 |
| Spain, total | 16,698,773 | 100.00 | 11.6 | 6.4 | 31.9 | 27.4 | 7.1 | 6.6 | 49.4 | 59.6 |

*GDP structure in % (A + B + C + D = 100)*

*Source:* Banco de Bilbao.

## Table 16.7. CONSUMPTION STRUCTURE

| Areas | Annual average consumption in constant 1958 ptas | | | | Weight (%) food consumption within total consumption | | | |
|---|---|---|---|---|---|---|---|---|
| | 1958 | 1964–5 | 1973–4 | 1980–1 | 1958 | 1964–5 | 1973–4 | 1980–1 |
| Urban | 11,100 | 16,553 | 31,321 | 32,208 | 54.9 | 45.8 | 34.2 | 27.7 |
| Rural | 9,128 | 10,786 | 21,965 | 24,951 | 59.0 | 54.7 | 42.8 | 34.7 |

| Consumption (%) structure | | | | Diet structure (% of value ptas) | | | |
|---|---|---|---|---|---|---|---|
| Groups of goods and services | 1964–5 | 1973–4 | 1980–1 | Kinds of food | 1964–5 | 1973–4 | 1980–1 |
| Foods and beverages consumed at home | 48.72 | 38.04 | 30.73 | Bread, pastry, cereals, potatoes, vegetables | 28.2 | 19.9 | 19.4 |
| Clothing, footware | 14.89 | 7.70 | 8.52 | Fruit, meat, poultry, fish | 36.5 | 44.6 | 47.9 |
| Houses, heating, electricity | 11.02 | 14.53 | 17.84 | Eggs | 6.2 | 4.0 | 2.9 |
| Domestic services | 5.59 | 8.13 | 7.51 | Milk, cheese, butter | 8.5 | 10.2 | 11.8 |
| Health, medical services | 2.48 | 2.64 | 2.36 | Oils, fats | 9.3 | 6.6 | 4.9 |
| Transport, communications | 3.71 | 9.36 | 13.73 | Sugar, sweets, coffee, wines, beverages | 10.6 | 11.8 | 11.9 |
| Other expenses | 9.28 | 12.49 | 12.63 | Other | 0.7 | 2.9 | 1.2 |

*Source:* INE.

that of Castille-La Mancha. The last column records average annual accumulated growth from 1973 to 1981. Galicia, La Rioja and Murcia are in the lead, expanding at more than 3% annually; the Basque country, on the other hand, registers zero growth rate, due to its political problems.

Table 16.5 shows *spatial income distribution* in 1973 and 1981. *Per capita* income for the Community of Madrid is 43.9% above the national average, while that for Extremadura is 38.3% percent below — respectively the national maximum and minimum. The last column on average annual *per capita* growth underlines the effects of the crisis, which have been particularly harsh in the Basque country.

Table 16.6 gives structural variations in GDP between 1971 and 1983 as a result of changes in *four basic sectors* (agriculture and fisheries, industry, construction and services), in the autonomous communities and in Spain as a whole. A number of conclusions can be drawn from this table: that agriculture's share of GDP fell from 11.6 to 6.4%; that the country is undergoing a process of comparative de-industrialisation; that the construction sector is in a period of regression; and that services are going through a period of comparative expansion. The percentages in column 3 indicate the relative importance of each of Spain's seventeen regions.

Lastly, Table 16.7 gives available data on *consumption*, taken from a 1983 research publication based on the National Statistic Institute's 1980/1 family budget survey. In general, *per capita* consumption is stagnating, even though a certain degree of growth is registered in rural areas. The percentage of family budgets earmarked for food purchases is falling. The lower part of the table offers some interesting figures on changes in goods and services consumption and in the composition of family diets.

# XVII. THE CONSTITUTION AND THE AUTONOMOUS COMMUNITIES

## 1. *The economic content of the Constitution*

This chapter presents an economic discussion of the 1978 Constitution viewed as a set of general principles, as a set of instruments designed to economically develop and manage the nation, as a public finance planning system, and as a framework for industrial relations.

The general economic principles of the 1978 Constitution can be summarised as follows:

(*a*) recognition of the capitalist system, based on the right to own and inherit private property (art. 33);

(*b*) freedom of enterprise and a market economy (art. 38); and

(*c*) moderation of the capitalist/market framework by means of redistribution and participatory standards (art. 40, 128 and 129).

The right to own and inherit private property is recognised in art. 33. This declaration, typical of the constitutions of all countries where capitalist principles prevail, states that property and inheritance may not be contemplated as absolutes as they were under Roman law and the Napoleonic Code. On the contrary, the social function of property is determined in each case by a law that expressly defines the limits of ownership so as, for example, to protect natural resources such as woods, water, landscape and rich cultivable land. At the same time, guarantees are established to prevent unjustified expropriation. Of course, this general statement is made against the background of environmental aggression, imbalances in the distribution of wealth and public interventionism.

Article 38 recognises the freedom of enterprise and a market economy. The many interpretations of the market economy all agree that it implies the possibility to create enterprises and the right of consumers to procure what they wish from the sources they choose. Nevertheless, a market economy should respect the environment (art. 45), prohibit building site speculation (art. 51), allow for the public sector to be actively present in the economy (art. 128), and allow for planning (art. 131).

The moderation of the capitalist framework is carried out in the following ways:

(*a*) A policy of income redistribution and full employment (art. 40), must be combined with economic stability (an obviously difficult

proposition) so that these goals are attained without fuelling inflation, and so that social imbalances are evened out.

(*b*) Article 129 states that the ways in which interested parties will
participate in the social security system and in other public agencies
will be laid down by law, this being the only way to put an end to
social security problems. This article is aimed at breaking the
bureaucracy's hold on public agencies by making agencies
constantly and directly responsible to consumers and users. Worker
participation in company management, taken up in section 2 of
article 129, is a requirement of developed societies, in which
increases in productivity can only be attained through joint
management.

(*c*) Article 128 states that the whole of the nation's wealth is sub-
ordinate to general interests, a declaration based on the 1931
Constitution. This article recognises public initiative in economic
activities, which theoretically means abandoning the theory of sub-
sidiarity, which reserves all economic activity for private initiative.
The public sector would only step in if private initiative were to find
itself unable to respond. The second section of article 129 contains a
declaration that is oriented towards socialisation: 'Public authorities
will effectively promote the various forms of company participation
and, through appropriate legislation, advance cooperative enterprises. Means facilitating the access of workers to own the means of
production will be established.'

## 2. *Economic development and planning*

The Constitution's treatment of economic development and
planning is in keeping with the following principles:

(*a*) The state will plan general economic activity according to article
131, the second part of which describes the planning procedure to be
followed, based on Autonomous Community estimates and on the
advice and cooperation of trade unions and professional, business
and economic organisations (the last-named including consumer,
ecological, neighbourhood and other associations concerned, e.g.,
with consumer affairs, the environment, urban development and
housing). This same section of article 131 announces the creation of
what could be called a planning or economic and social council,
which has yet to be established.

(*b*) Article 47, dealing with the right to housing and land use, defines
the basic social right to decent housing, and establishes the uncon-
stitutionality of land speculation and the principle that unearned

increments should be returned to the community. But '*del dicho al hecho hay mucho trecho*' (there's many a slip twixt the cup and the lip).

(*c*) Article 130, on economic development, expresses concern for depressed sectors (agriculture, livestock, fisheries and crafts), which need some kind of official support to prevent their earnings from straggling behind the rest of the economy. This article also touches on the special treatment of mountain zones. More than 20% of Spain's surface area is 1,000m. above sea level, and 40% is between 500 and 1,000m. Consequently, as modern production techniques were introduced, people tended to move from the mountains to the valleys and plains, leaving entire districts depopulated and creating overcrowding in the cities. Mountain economy areas must be helped through measures such as reforestation, livestock management and the development of tourism.

(*d*) According to article 51, public authorities guarantee to protect consumers and users. This new addition to the Constitution is in response to complaints against, for example, low-quality production, adulterated ingredients and inefficient services. Consumer organisations must be advanced to tackle these many problems and producers must be required to prove that what they claim is true.

(*e*) Article 45 recognises the right to enjoy a suitable environment; both renewable and non-renewable natural resources must be given great attention. To this end, the Comisión Interministerial del Medio Ambiente (CIMA — Interdepartmental Environmental Commission) must be given executive powers, and ecological associations broader representation in the CIMA and in other similar regional agencies.

## 3. *Public finance and industrial relations*

All constitutions make reference to public finance, and the Spanish Constitution is no exception. A number of important provisions are made: the principle that contributions to public spending are compulsory (art. 31); the authority to establish taxes (art. 133); the guidelines for preparation of the Budget (art. 134); the conditions established for government bond issues (art. 135); and the basis for fiscal control management through the Tribunal de Cuentas, an official auditing court (art. 136).

Regarding Budget preparations, article 134 describes the process with specific deadlines and mechanisms to control public expenditure. The government is responsible for the preparation of the draft

Budget, amendments to which may of course be presented to the Cortes. Budgets must take into account the entire public sector, including the social security system, and set exemption and allowance levels to prevent improvisions from cutting into tax collection.

Under article 135, public debt is limited by law. The state must fully respect the issuance act, and include all the funds necessary to cover interest rates and repay the principal.

Article 136 lays down the foundations for the future management of the Tribunal de Cuentas, whose organic law was enacted in 1982. Under the 1978 Constitution, this department gains strength as the accounting arm of the Cortes.

The regulation of employer-employee relationships and the definition of the general social security and employment structures are established under article 35 on the duty and right to work; article 28 on the right to unionise; article 37 on general guidelines for collective bargaining; article 41 on the social security system; article 50 on the pension system; and article 42 on emigrant rights.

## 4. *Self-government*

Heading VIII of the Constitution (articles 137–158) sets forth a new notion of autonomous bodies, as 'territorially organised into municipalities, provinces and Autonomous Communities', which, aimed at achieving an economic balance based on the principle of "solidarity" (art. 137), should under no circumstance imply any form of economic or social privilege." These political bodies should be interrelated so that, while regional self-government is allowed for, "solidarity" prevents greater imbalances from arising. Article 139 states that no measures whatsoever may be taken that may 'directly or indirectly impair freedom of movement and settlement" within the Spanish market; such measures would break up the Spanish common market.

Following the constitutional provisions of Heading VIII, seventeen Autonomous Communities took shape in 1979–82 (see Fig. 23 and Tables 16.4, 16.5 and 16.6, above). The Constitution sets forth that Autonomous Communities will assume certain areas of responsibility in accordance with their statutes. Although such areas should be the same for each Community, the degree of self-government will vary according to the Community's own statute. These areas are detailed in article 148:

— Territorial, urban development and housing planning.
— Public works of interest to an Autonomous Community under construction within its territory.

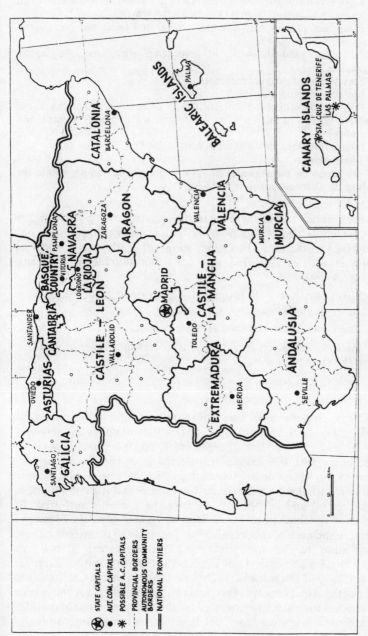

Fig. 23. The Spanish Autonomous Communities.

— Railways and highways which begin and end within the boundaries of an Autonomous Community, and their respective traffic.
— Ports and airports used for recreational and other non-commercial purposes.
— Agriculture and livestock, in accordance with general economic programmes.
— Forests and forestry management.
— Environmental protection activities.
— Projects concerning construction, the use of water resources, canals and irrigation systems of interest to an Autonomous Community; mineral and hot springs.
— Inland fisheries, shellfish farms, hunting and river fishing.
— Trade shows.
— The economic development of Autonomous Communities within the goals set in national economic policies.
— Crafts.

An even clearer idea of these areas of responsibility is given in article 149, which defines the scope of activities over which the state has exclusive jurisdiction. The Constitution sets forth strictly financial limits in articles 156, 157 and 158. Autonomous Community resources comprise:

(*a*) Taxes partly or fully assigned by the state; state tax surcharges and other contributions to state revenue.

(*b*) Their own taxes and special contributions.

(*c*) Interterritorial settlement fund transfers and other allocations from the state budget.

(*d*) Yields from community assets and private law income.

(*e*) Returns on credit operations.

Under no circumstances may Autonomous Communities tax assets outside their territory or hamper the free flow of goods and services.

Assigned taxes and surcharges are fixed under each statute in accordance with the services transferred from the central government to an Autonomous Community. In the case of the Basque country, with the exception of customs duties and fiscal monopolies (tobacco, oil and telephones), all taxes have been transferred. In exchange for these transfers, a fiscal agreement is reached between the state and each of the three Basque provinces to contribute annual fixed sums to the state treasury. This agreement is made in accordance with article 41 of the Basque Country Statute (Organic Law 3/1979 of 18 December). The taxes transferred to Catalonia are net worth taxes, property taxes, inheritance and gift taxes and luxury taxes when such taxes are collected on goods at their point of destination. Similar transfers have been made in the remaining statutes.

In the Ley Orgánica de Financiación de la Comunidades Autónomas (LOFCA — Organic Law on the Financing of Autonomous Communities), article 11.2 of Organic Law 8/1980 of 22 September specifies those taxes that may not under any circumstances be transferred by the state: personal income tax, corporation taxes, production or sales taxes unless stated otherwise, foreign trade taxes, and taxes currently collected by fiscal monopolies. The Fondo de Compensación Interterritorial (FCI — Interterritorial Settlement Fund), mentioned under article 158, was developed by the LOFCA in article 16 of the same. Under this law, the FCI will be assigned each year a minimum of 30% of the public investment funds approved in the state's general Budget. The fund invests in less developed areas, and resources are distributed according to the following criteria: *per capita* income, the rate of emigration in the previous ten years, the percentage of unemployment among the working population, and the surface area of the region concerned, among others.

# XVIII. SPAIN AND THE EUROPEAN COMMUNITIES

## 1. *Introduction*

Ever since the European Economic Community (EEC) was founded with the signing of the Treaty of Rome in March 1957, Spain has followed the European integration process with definite interest. In 1962 Spain formally asked to join the EEC, Euratom and the European Coal and Steel Community (ECSC), but for political reasons — the absence of democracy under Franco — only a preferential agreement was reached in 1970.

Although the 1970 agreement was open to criticism on many grounds, its implementation in fact allowed all Spain's export elasticities to come into play. As can be seen in Table 18.1, Spanish exports to the EEC (six countries in 1970–2, nine countries after 1973 and ten countries after 1981) grew more rapidly than imports. By 1983 exports were well ahead of imports, and in 1984 Spain had a surplus of almost 20%. In the period 1974–84, overall trade (imports plus exports) between Spain and the EEC swelled from 2.3 to 3.4 trillion pesetas, a real increase of 47.82%. There was also a spectacular 114.2% rise in the volume of Spanish exports. It should also be noted that in 1984 almost half of Spain's exports were earmarked for the community, whereas 33.43% of imports came from EEC countries. Spain's energy-related purchases abroad represented 37% of total imports, and if we subtract these from our calculations (as almost no energy-related products are imported from the EEC), the community would account for 53.06% of Spain's imports, which points to a high degree of interpenetration. Table 18.1 also presents the gradual increase in the degree of coverage provided to imports by exports, rising from 55% in 1970 to almost 120% in 1984.

Table 18.2 has also been prepared with figures on Spain's trading record with the EEC for three different periods: for the 6-member, 9-member and 10-member community. It shows the relative importance of these activities and a trade balance for each member-country.

To sum up, the 1970 agreement clearly favoured Spanish-community trading, putting export elasticities to full use. Apart from the impact of the agreement, the profound crisis registered in Spain's domestic demand prompted companies to seek out foreign

Table 18.1  SPAIN'S TRADING RECORD WITH THE EEC, 1970–1984
(*millions of ptas*)

| | Imports | | | Exports | | | | Exchange in 1984 constant ptas ($10^9$) | | | | Coverage index |
| | *A* Total | *B* EEC | % B/A | *A* Total | *B* EEC | % B/A | (*) | Imports (M) | Index 1970= 100 | Exports (X) | Index 1970= 100 | $\left(\frac{X}{M} \times 100\right)$ |
|---|---|---|---|---|---|---|---|---|---|---|---|---|
| 1970 | 332,000 | 109,347 | 32.94 | 167,087 | 60,342 | 36.11 | 6.778 | 739 | 100 | 407 | 100 | 55.07 |
| 1971 | 347,415 | 113,596 | 32.70 | 205,645 | 76,381 | 37.14 | 6.256 | 713 | 96 | 475 | 117 | 66.61 |
| 1972 | 437,566 | 146,141 | 33.40 | 245,215 | 89,987 | 35.47 | 5.781 | 844 | 114 | 520 | 128 | 61.61 |
| 1973 | 561,543 | 240,994 | 42.92 | 302,670 | 144,819 | 47.85 | 5.191 | 1,251 | 168 | 753 | 185 | 60.19 |
| 1974 | 888,688 | 319,563 | 35.96 | 407,972 | 193,485 | 47.43 | 4.483 | 1,435 | 194 | 865 | 213 | 64.07 |
| 1975 | 931,986 | 323,431 | 34.70 | 491,091 | 196,886 | 40.09 | 3.835 | 1,239 | 168 | 755 | 186 | 60.93 |
| 1976 | 1,169,412 | 387,481 | 33.13 | 583,222 | 270,570 | 46.39 | 3.260 | 1,261 | 171 | 883 | 217 | 70.02 |
| 1977 | 1,350,352 | 464,176 | 34.15 | 775,150 | 358,753 | 46.28 | 2.619 | 1,215 | 164 | 940 | 231 | 77.36 |
| 1978 | 1,431,033 | 495,743 | 34.64 | 1,001,383 | 463,622 | 46.30 | 2.187 | 1,085 | 147 | 1,015 | 249 | 93.54 |
| 1979 | 1,704,022 | 612,192 | 35.93 | 1,221,441 | 586,002 | 47.98 | 1.890 | 1,157 | 157 | 1,107 | 272 | 95.67 |
| 1980 | 2,450,653 | 752,382 | 30.70 | 1,493,187 | 731,368 | 48.98 | 1.636 | 1,230 | 166 | 1,196 | 294 | 97.23 |
| 1981 | 2,975,966 | 864,197 | 29.04 | 1,889,716 | 812,482 | 42.99 | 1.427 | 1,233 | 167 | 1,159 | 285 | 93.99 |
| 1982 | 3,474,813 | 1,088,083 | 31.31 | 2,233,934 | 1,022,785 | 45.78 | 1.248 | 1,358 | 184 | 1,277 | 314 | 94.03 |
| 1983 | 4,177,034 | 1,348,619 | 32.29 | 2,846,749 | 1,366,439 | 48.00 | 1.113 | 1,501 | 203 | 1,520 | 373 | 101.26 |
| 1984 | 4,628,991 | 1,547,536 | 33.43 | 3,778,071 | 1,853,300 | 49.05 | 1.000 | 1,547 | 209 | 1,853 | 455 | 119.78 |

*Source:* These figures were computed by the Spanish Customs Bureau, based on peseta values taken from the Banco de Bilbao, 1984 (*Economic Report*, p. 392).
(*) Value in given year of 1 peseta in 1984.

Table 18.2.   SPAIN'S TRADING RECORD WITH THE
6-MEMBER, 9-MEMBER AND 10-MEMBER EEC

| 6-member EEC (1970) | Imports | | Exports | |
|---|---|---|---|---|
| | Millions of ptas | % | Millions of ptas | % |
| West Germany | 41,930 | 38.35 | 19,716 | 32.67 |
| Belgium-Luxembourg | 7,724 | 7.07 | 3,596 | 5.95 |
| France | 33,154 | 30.32 | 17,281 | 28.64 |
| Netherlands | 9,240 | 8.45 | 8,759 | 14.52 |
| Italy | 17,298 | 15.81 | 10,984 | 18.22 |
| Total | 109,346 | 100 | 60,336 | 100 |

| 9-member EEC (1973) | Imports | | Exports | |
|---|---|---|---|---|
| | Millions of ptas | % | Millions of ptas | % |
| West Germany | 76,565 | 31.79 | 35,586 | 24.58 |
| Belgium-Luxembourg | 13,439 | 5.57 | 7,927 | 5.47 |
| Denmark | 3,912 | 1.62 | 2,810 | 1.94 |
| France | 57,660 | 23.93 | 38,711 | 26.74 |
| Netherlands | 18,158 | 7.53 | 18,468 | 12.76 |
| Ireland | 1,748 | 0.72 | 904 | 0.62 |
| Italy | 33,832 | 14.03 | 16,088 | 11.10 |
| United Kingdom | 35,679 | 14.81 | 24,235 | 16.79 |
| Total | 240,993 | 100 | 144,729 | 100 |

| 10-member EEC (1984) | Imports | | Exports | |
|---|---|---|---|---|
| | Millions of ptas | % | Millions of ptas | % |
| West Germany | 458,737 | 29.64 | 361,796 | 19.52 |
| Belgium-Luxembourg | 67,596 | 4.37 | 96,171 | 5.19 |
| Denmark | 22,721 | 1.47 | 24,637 | 1.33 |
| France | 398,049 | 25.72 | 566,574 | 30.57 |
| Greece | 9,900 | 0.64 | 22,294 | 1.20 |
| Netherlands | 92,959 | 6.01 | 198,304 | 10.70 |
| Ireland | 21,169 | 1.37 | 14,841 | 0.80 |
| Italy | 195,322 | 12.62 | 225,641 | 12.18 |
| United Kingdom | 281,083 | 18.16 | 343,042 | 18.51 |
| Total | 1,547,536 | 100 | 1,853,300 | 100 |

*Source:* EUROSTAT report.

markets, which became increasingly important to the development
of their activities in comparison to others that were harder hit by the
depression.

## 2. *The Treaty of June 1985: Spain becomes a member of the EEC*

In the following pages we discuss the agreement signed on 12 June 1985, whereby Spain joined the European Community. New negotiations between Spain and the EEC began symbolically on 28 July 1977. Having surmounted the political difficulties raised during the regime of Franco, the young Spanish democracy requested membership of the community, and it seemed as if Spain's accession would come about quickly, in 1983 or even 1982. However, economic difficulties which arose during the negotiations proved to greater than could ever have been expected. This development was noted in the opinion (*avis*) which the European Commission submitted to the community's Council of Ministers in October 1978, and which served as a basis for lengthy deliberation among member-states.

Negotiations were officially opened on 5 February 1979, and later a procedure for negotiations between Spain and the 9-member (after Greece's accession in 1981, 10-member) community was more or less established. When it came down to membership, the European Commission's only role was that of coordinator, for the member-states were the ones that did all the real talking.

Problems related to agriculture, fishing and the movement of workers proved the most troublesome, and in 1980 the situation became even more complicated when, near the end of his term of office, Giscard d'Estaing, President of France, did not hesitate to paralyse the negotiations with Spain. Consequently, almost a year was lost until Mitterrand's Socialist victory in May 1981 led to a slow, partial reactivation of the earlier process, over which France, responding to pressure from the extreme right and the French Communist Party, showed great hesitation. But apart from French and non-French mistrust, the fact of the matter is that for Spain's membership to be viable — in the case of Portugal, the much smaller size of its economy posed no special problems — the community had to revise its agricultural policy in the complex areas of fruit and vegetables, wine and vegetable fats. The fishing sector also required long negotiations, which did not come about till March 1983, to lay the foundations for 'Blue Europe'. Months and years passed. As for other matters, the most difficult problems came from the growing cost of the Feoga (European Fund for Agriculture) entry in the community budgets. Pricing policy also called for a change of direction. The issue of financing had to be resolved once and for all, not only for the sake of the EEC's general aims, but also to grapple with extending the market to include the countries of the Iberian peninsula.

The entire community found itself enmeshed in a crisis-ridden debate registering a lack of unity and of willingness to make concessions. Only in June 1983, when the European Council met in Stuttgart to lay the foundations for future community financing, could it be said that light was visible at the end of the tunnel. At this memorable session, new budget contributions were tied to Spain and Portugal's membership. This decision marked the overcoming of one of the main obstacles blocking the last leg of the interminable negotiations, in the midst of public scepticism and weariness. After Stuttgart the negotiations, with their inevitable ups and downs, acquired a certain impetus, with 1 January 1986 becoming the likely date for the accession of Spain and Portugal. In Spain the political party in power, the PSOE, saw this date as a key to its electoral strategy for the 1986 general elections, and began to present Spanish membership of the community as its most significant political achievement. This attitude made it possible to smooth out differences — to Spain's disadvantage — and finally, on 12 June 1985, the Accession Treaty was solemnly signed in Lisbon in the morning and in Madrid in the afternoon.

Now we will turn to the Accession Treaty and its components, covering the general framework, the free movement of goods, agriculture, fishing, movements of the factors of production, taxation, and budgetary and monetary matters, without overlooking measures to harmonise other areas within a common policy.

## 3. *General framework*

The following section covers everything related to Spain's presence in community institutions, as well as some comments on the two least discussed European Communities: Euratom (European Atomic Energy Community) and ECSC (European Coal and Steel Community), both of which emerge on the initial sectoral road to European integration.

3.1. *Institutions.* Spain will have medium-level representation in the institutional bodies of the European Economic Community — namely two Spanish commissioners in the Commission, the same as France, West Germany, Italy and Britain (the more important states), 60 seats in the European Parliament (81 are granted to the more important states), eight votes in the Council of Ministers (ten for the more important states), where the simple majority is 54 out of 76 votes, one judge in the Court of Justice (like all the other members), 21 representatives on the Economic and

Social Council (24 for the more important states) and one of the six vice-presidential posts at the European Investment Bank.

3.2. *Euratom.* Spain will simultaneously join the EEC, the ECSC and Euratom. As a member of Euratom from 1 January 1986, Spain will comply with the community standards (regarding safety controls) on atomic energy, have access to community benefits and aid, and exchange information with other member-states. In addition, Spain will not be required to sign the Nuclear Non-Proliferation Treaty — this was an obstacle during the negotiations, partly because of the Spanish Navy's desire to have nuclear submarines. This posture has been widely criticised by all in Spain who support Spanish neutrality and withdrawal from NATO.

3.3. *ECSC.* Spain will have three years from the date of its accession to complete the recoversion of its iron and steel industry with state aid, provided that the Commission is empowered to approve measures to supplement those of the Spanish government in the second year. Spain's production capacity for hot laminated steel products will be guaranteed at 18 million tons at the end of the first three years, which is well above the country's 1984 production level of 13.5 million. During the same period, the community quota on Spanish exports shipped to other member-states will be 827,000 tons annually.

Within the same time-frame, Ireland, Italy and Denmark will have the right to restrict their scrap metal exports to Spain, where they are in great demand.

## 4. *Free movement of goods*

This heading covers matters related to the free circulation of all kinds of products, by means of the dismantling of tariffs and a move towards the EEC's common external tariff. Moreover Spain will be required to take on the wide range of EEC foreign commercial relations. In other words, Spain must accede to the many treaties signed by the community, involving a complexity of relations with most countries of the world. In this section we will also see what this new relationship will mean for Spain and for specific areas of the country, namely the Canary islands, Ceuta and Melilla; for years these have enjoyed special trade regulations, which they hope to safeguard as much as possible after 1 January 1986.

Because of their importance, both agriculture and fishing, which should properly be included here, will each be dealt with separately.

4.1. *Customs union.* Industrial tariffs will be gradually removed during a 7-year transitional period, by means of the following eight reductions to be effected on 1 January each year (after 1986) as follows:

|      | Reduction (%) | Accumulated (%) | Residual (%) |
|------|---------------|-----------------|--------------|
| 1986 | 10.0          | 10.0            | 90.0         |
| 1987 | 12.5          | 22.5            | 77.5         |
| 1988 | 15.0          | 37.5            | 62.5         |
| 1989 | 15.0          | 52.5            | 47.5         |
| 1990 | 12.5          | 65.0            | 35.0         |
| 1991 | 12.5          | 77.5            | 22.5         |
| 1992 | 12.5          | 90.0            | 10.0         |
| 1993 | 10.0          | 100.0           | 0.0          |

Contrary to the initial designs of the EEC countries, there will be no sudden fall or accelerated dismantling of the highest Spanish tariffs levied against certain products. Only community automobiles, which will remain subject to annual quotas, will have a special 17.4% tariff during the first 3 years; the figures for automobile quotas (32,000 vehicles in 1986, 36,000 in 1987, 40,000 in 1988) will represent barely 5% of Spain's production in 1987.

Spain will immediately adopt EEC external common tariffs when the difference between Spanish and community rates is less than 15%. Spanish tariffs on the remaining items will be brought gradually into line according with the schedule given above up to the seventh year. The relaxation of trade controls will not be immediate. Both sides have set quotas on various categories of textile products, primarily those using cotton. Moreover, there will be a 2-year transitional period to adapt Spanish regulations to the entrepôt system (drawbacks, tax relief, temporary imports etc.).

4.2. *Foreign relations.* The liberalisation of Spain's trading activities with non-member states will also not be immediate. A list of specific products from GATT countries, Eastern Europe and Japan will undergo quantitative restrictions for six years. Quotas on imports have also been set for products from Mediterranean countries, overseas territories and countries with preferential agreements. Spain will benefit from quotas on textile products from Eastern European countries.

With its EEC membership, Spain will enter into the special agreements which the community has signed with members of the European Free Trade Association (EFTA — comprising Austria, Finland, Iceland, Norway, Sweden and Switzerland), the Maghreb (Morocco, Algeria and Tunisia), the Machrek (Egypt, Syria, Lebanon and Jordan), the People's Republic of China, Yugoslavia, Rumania, Israel and so on. At the same time, Spain will enter into the community's agreement with the ACP countries (Africa, the Caribbean and the Pacific), which are linked to the Common Market by the Third Lomé Convention.

*4.3. The Canary islands and Ceuta and Melilla.*   Goods will move freely between the enlarged community and Ceuta and Melilla. Neither the common external tariff, Value Added Tax (VAT), nor the Common Agricultural Policy (CAP) will be applied in these two Spanish cities on the North African coast. On the other hand, neither the customs union nor VAT (which will be calculated into Spain's contribution to the community) will come into effect in the Canary islands. While the CAP and the common fishing policies will not be applied in the islands, structural aid and, in the case of fishing, resource policies will be applied. Import protection aimed at developing local industry in the Canary islands, provided it is not discriminatory, may be continued.

Canary island agricultural products will be brought into community territory freely within the framework of limitations (defined by the islands' average export levels for 1983, 1984 and 1985), which in future may be modified according to specific criteria. The islands' banana exports will continue to be reserved for the Spanish domestic market, and a quota has been set for processed tobacco free of EEC duties based on traditional export trends (the average figure for the best three of the last five years), thus allowing the continuation of traditional Canary exports, which till 1985 were channelled almost exclusively to the Spanish mainland.

An element of flexibility is introduced into the special treatment given the Canary islands, for the Council of Ministers may, at the request of the Spanish government, approve modifications to these regulations without having to modify the membership treaty.

## 5. *Agriculture*

Two large sectors are distinguished as Spain enters the Agricultural Common Market: the classical transition and the specific transition. The former comprises the gradual application of Common Agricultural Policy (CAP) regulations. Over seven years, Spanish prices will slowly come into alignment with community prices, as tariff barriers are removed. At the same time, the so-called compensatory amounts, which will logically disappear at the end of this transitional period, are set to offset price differences at any given moment.

The thrust of Spanish-EEC agricultural exchange is subject to the so-called specific transitional regulations, which apply to fresh fruit and vegetables, wine and oil, as we will see below. There are also special rules governing what are called continental products.

5.1. *Fresh fruit and vegetables.*   A 10-year period is envisaged for removing tariff barriers on fresh fruit and vegetables. The first of the eleven (10%) reductions will be implemented two months after Spain's accession and the remainder on 1 January each year: 10% at the end of the first, second and third years; 25% at the end of the fourth year; 15% at the end of the fifth year; and 4% at the end of the remaining five years. The largest reductions are scheduled for Years 4 and 5, so that after the fourth year, Spanish fruit and vegetables will be at the level currently held by Morocco, the community's third most favoured country in terms of tariff arrangements.

The so-called Complementary Intervention Mechanism (CIM) will be in operation throughout the second phase (Years 5–10), so as to coordinate a series of actions and monitor trading. With a view to offsetting Spain's integration, the Common Market will set in motion the Integrated Mediterranean Programmes, providing aid to French, Italian and Greek farmers to enhance their capacity to compete against Spain. Israel and the entire Maghreb, for their part, have requested import privileges for their agricultural exports, in an attempt to keep up with Spain.

5.2. *Wine.*   Following the agreement reached in Dublin in 1984, the maximum quota on Spanish table wine at a guaranteed price will be 27.5 million hectolitres, which means that all wine over and above 85% of this quota will be turned into alcohol and so removed from the market. Thus the level at which, every year, distillation will become compulsory will be 23,375,000 hectolitres, a cut-off point which would normally be considered highly disadvantageous for Spanish vineyards.

The appellation 'sherry' will continue to be recognised by the community. Nevertheless, by means of a calculated ambiguity, the names *British sherry* and *Irish sherry*, marketed in the United Kingdom and Ireland, will not be dropped. The Spanish government may negotiate this matter with the governments of both countries at a future date.

**5.3.** *Olive oil.* The difference between Spanish and community intervention prices for olive oil will grow closer by 5% each year, although aid provided under the present community regulations on vegetable fats (scheduled for revision) will not apply to Spain until the new and most likely less protectionist regulations have been drafted. This is the clearest case of Spain signing a blank cheque.

Spain's present controls on the marketing of seeds, fats and oil seeds will remain intact during the first five years. Colza and sunflower oil production levels will be subject to limitations similar to those that were in force before membership. Producers who exceed these levels will be penalised.

**5.4.** *Continental products.* Maximum quotas on community imports for the first 4 years have been agreed upon for continental products — an area admitted to be a particularly sensitive one for Spain. The following base amounts were set for the first year (1986):

|  | Tonnes |
|---|---|
| Fresh milk | 160,000 |
| Butter | 1,000 |
| Beef and veal | 20,000 |
| Cheese | 14,000 |
| Soft breadmaking wheat | 175,000 |

In addition, a production quota for Spain has been established for sugar (1 million tonnes) and isoglucose (83,000 tonnes); at the same time, a 370,000 tonne quota has been set for exports of tomato concentrate.

## 6. *Fishing*

Spain will be integrated into the common fishing policy and will respect the balances struck in this area. Consequently the country's licensing system will be done away with. During the established 10-year transitional period, Spain will have a right to fish the equivalent of 30% of the community's total allowable catch (TAC) for hake, with a maximum supplement of 4,500 tonnes. Thus the initial annual amount will be set at 18,000 tonnes, to be revised after 3 years, in accordance with changes in hake supplies in specified areas. Quotas have also been set for dory, angler fish, crayfish, pollack, cod and Mediterranean sardines.

During the transitional period, only 150 of the 300 Spanish vessels allowed to fish in community waters may do so at the same time. From 31 December 1995, the date scheduled for reshaping the common fishing policy, Spanish vessels may have access to the famous 'Irish box' (the Bantry Bay district, in the south of Ireland).

Special measures will be taken for sardine and anchovy fisheries outside the 12-mile limit off the French coast; these species are a sensitive subject for both sides. The present conditions governing the 12-miles of French national waters up to the southern point of the Île de Ré (on the same parallel as the port of La Rochelle) will not be changed.

While no restructuring of the Spanish fleet has been agreed upon, if the capacity of the present member-states does not grow, it is expected to be renewed at the rate of 2:1; in other words, when an old vessel is removed from the fleet, it may only be replaced by a new one representing up to 50% of its tonnage. The community aid of 28.5 million ECUs (some 3,500 million pesetas) granted before Spain's accession to restructure the Spanish fishing fleet will be continued.

In the remaining areas, Spain will lose its sovereignty to negotiate fishing agreements, as community agreements will supercede current ones. A 6-year transitional period has been established for the closing down of the joint companies which Spain has set up with other community countries.

## 7. *Free movement of the factors of production*

The European Communities constitute a project that goes beyond the Customs Union, and is on the way to becoming a genuine economic union. This transformation calls for the free movement of the factors of production: capital, labour and the different forms of association between the two (various services). In the section on capital, we will discuss matters dealt with in the Membership Treaty regarding the mobilisation of various kinds of investment; then we will look at how the free movement of workers will come about; and lastly we will give some attention to transportation and other services, particularly financial services (banking and insurance).

7.1. *Capital movements.* The community regulations (total liberalisation) applied with effect from 1 January 1986 are as follows:

*Current payments*: from the date of accession.
*Invisible transactions*: from the date of accession.
*Portfolio investments*: with the exception of securities that have already been freed of restrictions, the acquisition of foreign securities marketable on the stock market will be liberalised within 3 years.

*Financial investments*: the direct investments of Spanish residents in the stock of companies of the present member-states will be liberalised within 3 years.

*Property investments*: investments in member-states made by Spanish residents will be liberalised within 5 years.

**7.2. *Free movement of workers.*** In 1984 there were approximately 240,000 Spanish workers, with 366,000 dependent family members, living in the ten EEC member-states. Of these 25,000 are unemployed, and as of 1 January 1986 they have the right to receive the same treatment as is given to community workers with regard to working conditions, taxation, housing, transportation and education rights and benefits. Spaniards established in EEC countries with family members still residing in Spain will receive family benefits from their country of employment after 3 years.

As for the free movement of workers, a transitional period of 7 years (10 years in the case of Luxembourg), with a revision clause after 5 years, has been established. This penalising clause should be attributed to fear originating from Spain's high level of unemployment. During Years 1–3 the family members of Spanish workers will not have access to employment; during Years 4 and 5 they will have access after eighteen months, and from the sixth year no time requirements will be in force.

**7.3. *Transportation.*** A 1-year period is established for the application of community regulations governing public services. From Day 1, tachographs will be mandatory equipment on all vehicles with new licence plates carrying passengers and goods, and on vehicles carrying dangerous materials or crossing national borders. In the case of vehicles carrying passengers and goods within Spain, 3 and 4-year periods, respectively, have been envisaged for installing this control and safety mechanism.

**7.4. *Right to settlement.*** While direct investments will be liberalised from the start, in the area of banking a transitional period of 7 years is established for authorising banks of the other EEC countries to settle freely in Spain, during which time the limitations on the creation of branches and subsidiaries, the accumulation/calling in of liabilities etc. will remain unchanged. Nevertheless, in the case of authorised banks of the member-countries, one branch office may be opened in Year 5, two in Year 6 and two more in Year 7.

Turning to insurance and coinsurance, a 6-year period is established to eliminate the percentage of the contract which may be reserved for insurers operating in Spain. This percentage will be cut back to 75% in Year 4, 40% in Year 5, 20% in Year 6 and nil in Year 7.

Except for *'practiciens de l'art dentaire'* (this speciality did not come into existence in Spain till 1985), who will be granted a 5-year adaptation period, all the regulations applied to professionals will be adopted from the start.

## 8. *Taxation and budgetary and monetary matters*

An important part of the shaping of the economic union of the European Communities, reflected in the treaty for Spain's membership, lies in taxation and in budgetary and monetary matters. The subject of taxation is basically limited to harmonising indirect taxation, beginning with the introduction of the VAT. Budgetary matters involve setting criteria for Spain's future contributions to the community budget. Lastly, the monetary segment establishes some estimates for Spain's participation in the European Monetary System.

8.1. *Taxation.* From 1 January 1986, Spain introduced Value Added Tax (VAT), which can be broken down into three types: an average tax of 12%; a higher tax of 33% on so-called luxury items; and a reduced tax of 6% on basic necessities. An 'equivalence tax', which facilitates tax collection, will be introduced for retailers whose level of annual invoicing stays within certain limits.

A 4-year period is established to equalise Spain's tobacco taxes, which at present treat varieties of tobacco differently, with Virginia-type being taxed more heavily than black tobacco. The 1985 Common Market taxes all varieties of tobacco equally.

8.2. *Budgetary contribution.* The criterion establishing that during a basic transitional period of 7 years Spain's net contribution to the community budget will be zero has, in principle, been accepted. To this end, the contribution Spain will pay into the community coffers under the application of the VAT will be reimbursed for 6 years. These reimbursement percentages (of the theoretical amount to be transferred) are as follows:

| Year | % |
|------|-----|
| 1 | 87 |
| 2 | 70 |
| 3 | 55 |
| 4 | 40 |
| 5 | 25 |
| 6 | 5 |

At the end of this transitional period, Spain will be a net receiver of community funds, undoubtedly due to its status as a country whose average income is below that registered for the 10-member community.

Spain's contribution to the EDF (European Development Fund) has been set at 499.6 million ECUs (some 60,000 million pesetas). The EDF funds projects in less developed ACP countries under the Third Lomé Convention. At the same time, Spain's contribution provides for the possibility of formulating a plan for cooperation with Latin America. A contribution to the European Investment Bank of 1,100 million ECUs has been agreed.

**8.3.** *Monetary matters.* Spain may become a member of the European Monetary System when it so wishes by including the peseta in the ECU during the first readjustment of the currency 'basket'. As soon as it joins, it may Participate in the community's medium-term financial support mechanisms, within the bounds of a 1,295 million limit. As for short-term financial support mechanisms, Spain may borrow up to 725 million ECUs and lend a maximum of 1,450 million.

## 9. *Regional policy*

As a member of the EEC, Spain will apply the full set of community regulations on regional policy and will have the right to benefit from the aid provided through the European Regional Development Fund (Feder). Before Spain's accession, the community made the necessary changes to the rules governing the fund, primarily insofar as they relate to determining the Spanish contribution. Spain has not established specific areas for the application of Feder funds, and therefore all parts of the national territory may be eligible to receive this kind of community aid.

## 10. *Various legal matters*

Under this heading we look at some important remaining matters, such as patent rights — a decisive subject in all industrially advanced societies — and the harmonisation of some specific legislation.

**10.1.** *Patents.* Spain's present patenting system will be replaced by the EEC system, calling for the patenting of products in accordance with the Munich Convention. Spain must subscribe to the latter by October 1986 at the latest. On 7 October 1992, after a lapse of 6 years, the Spanish system must be adapted to that set forth in the Luxembourg Convention, by establishing the 'inversion of the burden of proof' whereby the accused and not the accuser must prove he is innocent of patent infringement. Under the present Spanish system it is the accuser's responsibility to substantiate his charge. While the inversion of the burden of proof may not be invoked for existing patents until they have expired, this procedure may be invoked immediately for new patents.

10.2. *Harmonisation of legislation.* The exceptions to the community directives that entered into force on 1 January 1986 are as follows:

*Lead in gasoline.* 0.4 gr./lit. became the limit for 'regular' from 1 January 1986. 'Super' and 'extra' will maintain their current limits (0.60 gr./lit. and 0.65 gr./lit. respectively) till 1 January 1987.

*Cocoa and chocolate for human consumption.* The present composition of these items will not change in the first 2 years. The appropriate direction will be studied later with a view to including Spanish denominations where appropriate.

*Partly or completely dehydrated milk.* The expression '*leche concentrada*' will not be changed. '*Lait concentré*' will be translated as '*leche evaporada*' and '*lait concentré sucré*' as '*leche condensada*'. The Spanish authorities have agreed to put multilingual labels on these products.

## 11. *Final considerations*

In our discussion of the Membership Treaty, we have looked at the specific mechanisms which will bring about the conditions governing Spain's participation in the Common Market. This process, however, will not end with the Customs Union or the Common Agricultural Policy. As we saw earlier, the EEC is moving towards the shaping of a genuine economic union. This is the objective of the efforts aimed at ultimately unifying the three communities and at formulating a single European union treaty (which already exists in draft). All of this points to a design for a common future of undeniable political importance.

It is a mistake to view Spain's involvement in the European Communities solely in economic terms, in the same way that the effects of integration cannot be quantified in an unrefined, mechanistic way. The fallacies skilfully elaborated by an assortment of individuals must be got rid of. While Spain's integration will undoubtedly (in this writer's opinion) fuel inflation, prophets of doom are condemned to oblivion when they assert that Spanish exports will be unable to withstand the impact of the VAT. And those too who complain bitterly that Spain's agricultural potential will be stunted are guilty of taking a static and unscientific stand, even though attempts to move in this direction can be found in the most obscure passages of the treaty. The view that the treaty will lead to the shutdown of many companies, owing to inequalities in the dismantling of tariffs, appear to lack perspective. However, there is an element of truth in claims that many such provisions do not take account of Spain's relative lack of development.

We could, of course, make similar observations regarding fishing matters, restrictions on Canary islands agricultural exports, the long postponement of the free movement of workers and so on, but our discussion will take a more promising turn instead. The treaty was negotiated by a scheduled date, concluded on 29 March 1985 still with a number of loose ends, and then signed on 12 June, with some passages left blank (particularly those related to vegetable oil and fruit and vegetables). Such a treaty is not exactly a model of perfection, but merely to lament these shortcomings is to narrow one's horizons and ignore past experience in the area of elasticities and renegotiation. Elasticities always have an important role, for they form part of the eternal game of challenge and response. Fears about the possible economic consequences of dismantling tariffs and removing quotas to pave the way for free trade should move Spaniards to reflect on past experiences of a similar kind and to realise that out of these fears new ideas often arise.

There is plentiful historical evidence that with courage a challenge can be met. One need only look back to 1959, when Spanish trade was liberalised and the Stabilisation Plan set in motion, leading to Spain's membership of OECD, the IMF, the World Bank and GATT. Another example is the 1970 preferential agreement between Spain and the EEC. These two instances undeniably fuelled modernisation through efforts to increase Spain's capacity to compete. The overall challenge facing Spain in becoming a member of the Common Market will be a third such experience, with enormous historic significance. Naturally it will not be a bed of roses. Difficult situations will accompany the depreciation of the peseta (a lubricant for the dismantling of tariffs); businessmen will seek new customers in trans-Pyrenean Europe with renewed vigour; unions will accept integration; and it is to be hoped that the executive, judiciary and legislature branches, faced with the need for immediate self-reform, will pare down the bureaucracy and do away with inefficiency. This new experience will put an end to outdated nationalism and open the door to possibilities for political, social and economic advance.

Turning to the subject of renewed negotiations, a treaty like that which Spain and representatives of the community's member-states signed on 12 June 1985 is not the end of the process. The blank passages left in the treaty speak for themselves. To put it simply, parts of this document are still waiting to be written, and parts that have been written need to be renegotiated, as has occurred in the past within the framework of the European Communities. De Gaulle renegotiated the entire mechanism for decision-making based on a qualified majority. Mrs Thatcher, by pushing through her 'community check', made it possible for the United Kingdom to use its positive balance to make its EEC contribution through the budget. West Germany was able to annul the agreement allowing Turkish workers to move freely. Italy has always manoeuvred itself in such a way that agricultural regulations, particularly those concerning wine, oil and fruit and vegetables, work in its favour. Greece knew how to use its veto threat to further Integrated Mediterranean Programmes. Similarly, Ireland brought the entire institutional apparatus to the brink of paralysis in order to achieve its objectives in the area of milk product prices.

We could add to this list, but the point of the matter is that Spain's integration into the EEC, embracing a transitional period of 7–10 years depending on the case, will be a dynamic process marked by structural elasticity and institutional adjustments in the wording of the treaty, where room has been left for improvement at a steady pace.

In short, the Spain that we have studied in this book is facing momentous economic, social and political changes; and will be substantially modernised as the result of its political decision to join the European Communities. Despite the difficulties arising in many areas, the vast majority of Spaniards will know how to accept this decision as something not only inevitable, but also necessary for a more dynamic and hopeful future.

# SELECT BIBLIOGRAPHY

The following is a very brief bibliography on the Spanish economy. Those interested in something more extensive may consult the many footnotes listed in the bibliography of my book *Estructura Económica de España*, which is only available in Spanish (Alianza Editorial, 16th edn, Madrid, 1985).

*Anuario El País (El País* Yearbook), edited by Ramón Tamames and Jose Manuel Revuelta. Published by PRISA, publishers of the daily newspaper *El País*.

Banco de Bilbao, *Renta Nacional de España y su distribución provincial*. (The Spanish National Income and its provincial distribution), published every 2–3 years since 1955.

Banco de España, *Boletín Estadístico*. A monthly statistical publication, providing considerable information, particularly in the field of monetary matters.

*Informe sobre la Economía Española*. The Annual Report of the Bank of Spain. Its comments on economic policy have great influence.

Banco Internacional de Reconstrucción y Fomento, *Informe del BIRF. El desarrollo económico de España*. One of the most celebrated reports on the Spanish economy. Generally known as the *World Bank Report of 1962*, it was used as a tool in subsequent official planning.

*Boletin de Estudios Economicos (BEE)*. A private economic review, published by the Commercial University of Deusto, a Jesuit institution.

*Boletin Mensual de Estadistica*. The monthly bulletin of the INE, the National Institute of Statistics, covers many areas of the Spanish economy and other state and social activities.

Carrion, P., *Los latifundios en España. Su importancia, origen, consecuencias y solución*. A very well-known book on the problems, origins, consequences and possible solutions of *latifundia*. Published in 1932 during the Agrarian Reform of the Second Republic, it has been republished several times (in 1972 by Ediciones Ariel).

Gamir, L. *et al., Política Económica Española*. Alianza Editorial, Madrid 1972 and after. A collection of systematic surveys on economic policy, written by senior academics and well-known sectoral experts.

Garcia de Blas, A., and Ruesga Benito, S., *Economía irregular en el mercado de trabajo: algunas líneas de investigación*. An article on Spain's underground economy, prepared by two leading economists in this area and published in the review *Información Comercial Española*, no. 587, July 1982.

*Informacion Comercial Española (ICE)* (Spanish Commercial Information). This important monthly economic review has been published since 1930, originally by the Ministry of Commerce and today by the Ministry of Economics and Finance, which now encompasses the state's Secretariat of Commerce.

Instituto de Estudios Fiscales, *Hacienda Pública Española*. A monthly review, published by the Institute of Fiscal Studies, including articles by foreign and Spanish authors.

Instituto Geográfico Nacional, *Atlas Nacional de España*. A very ambitious unfinished project, combining text with a wide range of maps.

Instituto Nacional de Estadística (INE), *Anuario Estadístico*. The official statistical yearbook of Spain. Given its bureaucratic structure, it lacks sensitivity in the area of new problems, and is subject to very long delays in the publication of annual figures and census.

——, *Principales actividades de la vida española en la primera mitad del siglo XIX*, Madrid, 1952. This special issue of the INE's Statistical Yearbook summarises the first half of the twentieth century.

—— *Primer Censo Agrario de España*, 1962. The first Agrarian Census was made in 1962, and the second in 1972. The third one, for 1982, was published in 1985.

—— *Contabilidad Nacional de España*. The National Accounts of Spain are published, with some delay, by de INE.

Jovellanos, M.G. de, *Informe sobre la Ley Agraria*. This report on agrarian law is undoubtedly the best-known work written by the Spanish *illustré* Jovellanos.

Klein, Julius, *The Mesta. A study on Spanish economic history*. Cambridge, 1920. Spanish translation by *Revista de Occidente*, Madrid, 1936.

Macias Picavea, R., *El Problema Nacional,* Librería de Victoriano Suárez, Madrid, 1899. One of the most representative books of the Spanish *regeneracionista* movement of the late nineteenth century.

Mallada, L.S., *Los males de la patria y la futura revolución de España*, Madrid, 1980. Another *regeneracionista* survey, on the 'Evils of the Fatherland and the Future Revolution in Spain'.

Martin Echeverria, L., *España, el país, los habitantes*, Atlanta, Mexico, 1940. An excellent introduction to Spain's human geography.

*Moneda y Credito* (Money and Credit). A quarterly publication, at present enjoying special prestige because of its articles on Spanish economic history. Edited by Prof. Gonzalo Anes.

OECD (Paris), *Reports on the Spanish Economy*, published annually in French and English since 1959.

*Papeles de Economia Española*. Published quarterly by the Savings Bank Foundation, and edited by Prof. E. Fuentes Quintana. It has a monographic approach towards Spain's most relevant economic topics.

Perpiña Grau, R., *De estructura economica y de economía hispana*. Rialp, Madrid, 1952 (Ariel, Barcelona, 1972). This classic work on the Spanish economy develops a very interesting hypothesis for its time.

Pugés, M., *Cómo triunfó el proteccionismo en España. La formación de la política arancelaria español*, Editorial Juventud, Barcelona, 1931. Another classic, this book deals with the Spanish controversy on protectionism versus free trade. Pugés explains how protectionists finally succeeded in attaining a very protective customs policy.

Roldan, S., Muñoz, J., and Serrano, A., *Qué es el capitalismo español?* La Gaya Ciencia, Barcelona, 1977. A short but enlightening essay on Spanish capitalism.

Tamames, R., *Estructura Económica de España*. 1st edn, Sociedad de Estudios y Publicaciones, Madrid, 1960; 16th edn, Alianza Editorial, Madrid, 1985. The mainspring of the present work, *Estructura Económica de España* provides a large amount of bibliographical information.

Teran, M. de, *Geografía de España y Portugal*. Barcelona, 1952. A good geographical analysis of the two Iberian countries.

Velarde Fuertes, J., *Sobre la decadencia económica de España*, Editorial Tecnos, Madrid, 1967. Perhaps the most representative work on Spanish economic decadence, written by one of the outstanding Spanish university professors of applied economics.

Vicens Vivies, J., and Nadal Oller, J., *Historia Económica de España*, Editorial Teide, Barcelona, 1959. The best available synthesis of Spanish economic history.

# INDEX